THE OFFICIAL **itv**SPORT GUIDE

# GRAND PRIX 2007 »

This edition published in 2007 by
Carlton Books Limited
20 Mortimer Street
London W1T 3JW

10 9 8 7 6 5 4 3 2 1

A CIP catalogue record for this book is available
from the British Library.

The publisher has taken reasonable steps to
check the accuracy of the facts contained herein
at the time of going to press, but can take no
responsibility for any errors.

ISBN: 978-1-84442-088-9

Editor: Martin Corteel
Project Art Editor: Darren Jordan
Designer: Ben Ruocco
Picture Research: Paul Langan
Production: Lisa French

Printed in Great Britain

ABOVE: Victory in the British GP was one of Fernando Alonso's eight 2006 wins. How many
will he manage for McLaren in 2007?
PREVIOUS PAGE: A helpful reminder: drivers have so much to think about, a few hints are
always welcome ...

THE OFFICIAL itv SPORT GUIDE

# GRAND PRIX 2007»

**BRUCE JONES**

**CARLTON**
BOOKS

# CONTENTS

**LEFT:** Tyres are always vital but there will be no tyre war as Bridgestone has assumed a monopoly
**OVERLEAF:** Fernando Alonso celebrates his second Formula One title with a few neighbours in Oviedo ...

# ANALYSIS OF THE 2007 SEASON

Formula One appears to change with every passing season, and no change will be bigger this year than the absence of seven-time World Champion Michael Schumacher. And while Fernando Alonso has shown his hand as world champion, can anyone hit a run of form to stop him making it three titles in a row?

When a major shake-up takes place in Formula One, fans have to become quickly accustomed to faces in places where they aren't used to seeing them. For example, seeing Kimi Raikkonen in a red set of overalls will seem wrong, but he's a Ferrari driver now, and it will be Alonso wearing white after moving across from Renault. One of the most important changes, though, will be the driver occupying the second McLaren. It will be last year's GP2 champion, Lewis Hamilton, who has as good a pedigree from the

junior categories as anyone who has broken into Formula One. And being black he's opening up the sport to a far wider audience.

There are no teams making their debut as Super Aguri Racing did in 2006, or teams dressed in new colours which is what happened to Scuderia Toro Rosso after it took over Minardi. What we have now, though, is the maturing of the teams at the tail, with Spyker having taken over what was Midland, and Super Aguri barely having had five minutes of preparation, suggesting that the

midfield is going to become even more crowded and the action even wilder.

There are no new venues, just a rejigging of the order with Australia regaining its place as the venue for the opening round, and Imola being bypassed until its facilities are brought up to standard. But the best circuit of all, Spa-Francorchamps, is back and the drivers can't wait. Conversely, they've lost the chance to show their skills at Suzuka as the Japanese GP is being moved to the revamped, but much less challenging, Fuji Speedway.

This year also marks the first year of an alternating pattern between the Nurburgring and Hockenheim to host the German GP, with the Nurburgring being given the nod and Hockenheim having to wait until 2008.

The sharing of chassis was a hot topic last year, and the discontent continued into winter as rivals stated that it was in breach of the Concorde Agreement which states that all teams must design and manufacture their own cars. The concern had focused on one team using a chassis which had been used by another team the previous year, as Scuderia Toro Rosso did last year when they used a lightly modified version of Red Bull's 2005 RB1. Now the concern is that Scuderia Toro Rosso are using Red Bull's 2007 chassis, meaning that there will be four of the chassis designed by Adrian Newey. Yes, they will be using different engines, with a Renault in the back of the Red Bulls and a Ferrari V8 powering the Toro Rossos, but the rivals aren't happy and the lawyers have been looking into intellectual property.

What's not in doubt is that there won't be a tyre war because all 22 cars will be running on Bridgestones.

A major concern of the sport's governing body in recent years has been cutting costs, and one way of doing this has been limiting the amount of testing to prevent the well-heeled teams developing an even greater advantage. So, testing has been capped at 30,000km and 300 sets of tyres. The teams have agreed on 16 three-day tests (with six pre-season and two post-season); 12 shake-downs and 12 "aero runs".

Testing on the Fridays at each of the grands prix has also been altered to two 90-minute sessions, but only for two cars per team, albeit shared and with a chance to give their third drivers a run. Another change is to the rule stating that an engine must last for two grands prix meetings; now it covers just the Saturday and Sunday, so an engine failure on a grand prix Friday won't lead to a 10-place grid demotion.

The qualifying format is not due to change, meaning that there is no way of knowing just which 10 drivers will be going out at the Melbourne opener to gun for pole, and that's a great position for Formula One to be in, making it healthier and stronger than it has been for years.

# RENAULT

It looked so easy for Renault in 2005, but then Ferrari got serious and the English-based, French-financed team had to get serious. That's when they showed their strength in depth and their quality in every facet required to be champions, which they duly became again.

Fisichella will be giving his all to move out from Alonso's shadow

Ready for action again and looking to make it three in a row, gunning for both the drivers' and constructors' championships, Renault is missing two ingredients which may clip its wings in 2007 and offer its leading rivals a chance of toppling it.

First is Fernando Alonso, world champion for the past two seasons, who elected even before the start of last year's championship to move to McLaren in place of Kimi Raikkonen. He may yet regret his decision if McLaren doesn't raise its game, but he's committed to the move and in his place comes Heikki Kovalainen, a driver who is considered hot stuff but has yet to start a grand prix. He knows the Renault team well, though, having covered thousands of miles testing for them last year. But a proven star of Alonso's calibre he is not. Kovalainen's place leading the Renault test team has been taken by one-time BAR racer Ricardo Zonta who has transferred from Toyota's test line-up. He will be supported by GP2 runner-up Nelson Piquet Jr, who has already let team leader Fisichella know that he hopes to replace him in the race line-up for 2008. That's one way of making friends.

One of the features of the season ahead will be how Fisichella and Kovalainen gel as team-mates, as rivals. Fisichella

## HISTORIC MOMENT

Although Renault won the first ever grand prix, way back in 1906, it wasn't until 1977 when Jean-Pierre Jabouille rolled out on to the grid for the 1977 British GP that the French manufacturer made its modern-day grand prix debut. He started in 21st place on the 26-car grid at Silverstone, having qualified some 1.62s behind James Hunt's pole-sitting McLaren. The afternoon's outcome was less than ideal, too, as Jabouille retired just after quarter-distance, but what made this race momentous, other than it being Renault's debut, was the fact that the Renault RS01 was powered by the first turbocharged engine used in F1. An arbitrary ruling stated that turbocharged engines must have a capacity of no more than 1500cc, half that of the normally-aspirated engines used by its rivals. Producing a competitive 510bhp, the engine was no great shakes to start with as it was blighted by turbo lag but development led to a huge increase in power output and just a few years later, all the top teams had turbo charged engines and, by then, Renault was no longer languishing at the back but competing for victories.

starts as number one but may be destabilised if he starts to be outpaced by Kovalainen. The second element that has been removed is the tyre war featuring Michelin, supplier of rubber to Renault and others, and thus the creation of a tyre monopoly for Bridgestone. This is a shame because the Michelin v Bridgestone tyre war was exciting. There is one element that Renault can do without this time around, though, and that is the furore which surrounded its mass damper system which it had through the first half of 2006. The mass damper system appeared to give it an advantage, even though other teams also tried their own versions. The FIA's decision to outlaw it seemed clumsy in its reasoning, but that was of little compensation to the team as it had to try and make up for the loss of a 0.3s per lap advantage.

One element that Renault is pleased to keep, though, is executive director of engineering Pat Symonds, the man who oversees engineering

and tactical matters in the same way that Ross Brawn has done for years at Ferrari. For 2007, though, Pat will be less hands-on with Alan Fermane taking on some of his jobs at the races in his role as chief race engineer.

Renault is also pleased to have the champion team's right to have the pit garage either nearest the pit entrance or pit exit, making the entry into, or the exit from, a pit stop much easier. The team's charismatic managing director Flavio Briatore will be staying on after overcoming a health scare when he had to have a cancerous tumour removed from a kidney last summer. Indeed, he has signed a contract to keep him at the helm until the end of the 2008 campaign. Better still, this means that any rumours of Renault boss Carlos Ghosn wanting to wind up the team once it had become world champions have receded. Indeed, Renault's Formula One team, under chairman Alain Dassas, is set to be around until the end of the FIA's next Concorde Agreement in 2012.

Renault has impressed over the past few years by winning races and especially world titles, despite spending considerably less than its rivals in Formula One's upper echelons. There might be some changes on that front now because Renault has announced a three-year deal with the ING finance house to be its title sponsor in place of the Mild Seven tobacco brand with whom they have worked for years.

Finally, Renault engines will be fielded by another team for 2007, Red Bull Racing, and all eyes will be on whether Renault can gain from this, and not just financially. Indeed, Red Bull's Adrian Newey is expected to deliver a competitive chassis, so ...

## FOR THE RECORD

| Country of origin: | England |
|---|---|
| Team base: | Enstone, England |
| Telephone: | (44) 01608 678000 |
| Website: | www.renaultf1.com |
| Active in Formula One: | From 1977–85 and from 2002 |
| Grands Prix contested: | 211* |
| Wins: | 33 |
| Pole positions: | 49 |
| Fastest laps: | 27 |

* NOTE THAT THESE FIGURES DO NOT INCLUDE THE 238 RACES THE TEAM RAN AS BENETTON

## 2006 DRIVERS & RESULTS

| Driver | Nationality | Races | Wins | Pts | Pos |
|---|---|---|---|---|---|
| Fernando Alonso | Spanish | 18 | 7 | 134 | 1st |
| Giancarlo Fisichella | Italian | 18 | 1 | 72 | 4th |

## THE TEAM

| | |
|---|---|
| Chairman: | Alain Dassas |
| Managing director: | Flavio Briatore |
| Deputy managing director: | Andre Laine |
| Technical director (chassis): | Bob Bell |
| Technical director (engine): | Rob White |
| Engineering director: | Pat Symonds |
| Engine director: | Denis Chevrier |
| Chief designer: | Tim Densham |
| Team manager: | Steve Nielsen |
| Test drivers: | Nelson Piquet Jr & Ricardo Zonta |
| Chassis: | Renault R27 |
| Engine: | Renault V8 |
| Tyres: | Bridgestone |

Jean-Pierre Jabouille ploughed a lonely furrow in 1977

# GIANCARLO FISICHELLA

**This is it, the big time, the chance of a lifetime: Giancarlo is the number-one driver for the team that has scooped both championship titles for the past two years. It's now or never if this happy Italian wants to become World Champion. And he knows it.**

Imagine being a grand prix winner and still being overlooked. Yet, that is what Giancarlo Fisichella has had to live with since he returned for a second spell with the team that had been Benetton, becoming Renault in 2005, with Fernando Alonso holding all the aces.

The team, and particularly the executive director of engineering, Pat Symonds, appreciated his input but it was largely seen as a supporting role. Indeed, a win in 2005 and last year paled into insignificance against the seven collected in each of those years by the Spaniard.

Ever the optimist, and delighted to be with a team that offered a chance to show his skills to the full after spells with Jordan and Sauber, Giancarlo even felt confident last January that the team might get behind him rather than Alonso, once it was known that Alonso was departing for McLaren for 2007. His pre-season testing form was good, and pole position and victory in the second round at Sepang became a good launch pad. Sadly, even

Giancarlo knows that he must win on a consistent basis in 2007, or else

podium visits were scarce after that as Alonso clocked up win after win. Still, he renewed his contract in June, signing for a further year, but this didn't result in greater things although third places in

the Chinese and Japanese GPs helped the team reclaim the constructors' title.

To ensure his future at Renault, Giancarlo must keep ahead of new team-mate Heikki Kovalainen and produce a string of wins to challenge for the drivers' title. Test driver Nelson Piquet Jr has already let it be known that he wants his ride for 2008.

## TRACK NOTES

| | |
|---|---|
| **Nationality:** | ITALIAN |
| **Born:** | 14 JANUARY 1973, ROME, ITALY |
| **Website:** | WWW.GIANCARLOFISICHELLA.IT |
| **Teams:** | MINARDI 1996, |
| | JORDAN 1997 & 2002-03, BENETTON |
| | 1998-2001, SAUBER 2004, RENAULT 2005-07 |

| CAREER RECORD | |
|---|---|
| **First Grand Prix:** | 1996 AUSTRALIAN GP |
| **Grand Prix starts:** | 179 |
| **Grand Prix wins:** | 3 |
| | 2003 Brazilian GP, 2005 Australian GP, |
| | 2006 Malaysian GP |
| **Poles:** | 3 |
| **Fastest laps:** | 2 |
| **Points:** | 246 |
| **Honours:** | 1994 ITALIAN FORMULA THREE |
| | CHAMPION & MONACO FORMULA THREE |
| | WINNER, 1991 EUROPEAN KART |
| | RUNNER-UP, 1990 WORLD KART RUNNER-UP, |
| | 1989 EUROPEAN KART RUNNER-UP |

## HIS GREATEST WIN

Runner-up in the world karting championship of 1990, Giancarlo was soon winning races in Italian Formula Three. He took the title in 1994, also winning the Formula Three invitation race at Monaco, but then he ran out of money to progress to Formula One's feeder category – Formula 3000 – and it took input from Alfa Romeo to get him in touring cars and bolster his career. A year later, Minardi took him to Formula One but it was only when Giancarlo joined Jordan in 1997 that he had the chance to impress. And how! He was knocked out of second place in Argentina by his own team-mate Ralf Schumacher. He was second in Germany until an oil cooler failed with five laps left. And finally, at Spa that year, he came second behind Michael Schumacher in a race when many fumbled in the wet-dry conditions.

# HEIKKI KOVALAINEN

**Kimi Raikkonen and Heikki Kovalainen are both fast Finns, but one is smiley and entertaining. (Clue: it's not Kimi.) Facing each other from rival teams ought to provide the young pretender with the ideal opportunity to rank himself against his compatriot.**

With Kimi Raikkonen settling in at Ferrari, and perhaps fighting an internal battle with second-year Ferrari racer Felipe Massa, and Heikki stepping up from the test team for reigning world champions Renault, there'll be plenty of rivalry between the two. Kimi has the advantage of years of experience and a winning pedigree, while Heikki already knows the inner workings of the Renault team. He also covered more kilometres in testing last year than any other driver in Formula One, covering a shade over 10,000 miles in his quest to help develop the Renault R26, also giving him intimate knowledge of the forerunner to this year's R27. In addition, you can be sure that the media will take to Heikki as he's a bright and breezy character who is ever ready with a smile, which Kimi isn't.

So, here's the question: can he race? Yes, although he was edged out in the final round shoot-out for GP2 honours by Nico Rosberg at the end of 2005. Winning the

**Heikki knows that he must hit the ground running as he steps up from the test team**

Formula Nissan World Series title the year before was a sign of his abilities, because anyone winning a one-make single-

seater formula title must have a certain something. But one single event marked Heikki out as a driver worth watching, and that was also in 2004. It was the Race of Champions, a multi-formula knock-out event held in an indoor arena in Paris with the best racing and rally drivers competing in karts, buggies and sports cars. And the winner was Heikki, knocking even Michael Schumacher off his perch. First, though, there's the small matter of how he compares with team-mate Giancarlo Fisichella.

## TRACK NOTES

| | |
|---|---|
| **Nationality:** | FINNISH |
| **Born:** 19 OCTOBER 1981, SUOMUSSALMI, FINLAND | |
| **Website:** | WWW.HEIKKIKOVALAINEN.NET |
| **Teams:** | RENAULT 2007 |

**CAREER RECORD**

| | |
|---|---|
| **First Grand Prix:** | 2007 AUSTRALIAN GP |
| **Grand Prix starts:** | 0 |
| **Wins:** | 0 |
| **Pole positions:** | 0 |
| **Fastest laps:** | 0 |
| **Points:** | 0 |
| **Honours:** | 2005 GP2 RUNNER-UP, 2004 FORMULA NISSAN WORLD SERIES CHAMPION, 2004 CHAMPION OF CHAMPIONS AT RACE OF CHAMPIONS, 2000 NORDIC KARTING CHAMPION |

## HIS GREATEST WIN

After two years of car racing, Heikki had risen to single-seater category Formula Nissan, competing in its World Series in 2003. And during this season he moved out of the shadow of his much-favoured Gabord Competition team-mate Franck Montagny to take his first win mid-season. This came at the Lausitzring in Germany. Heikki had started the first of the two races there from pole position, but had to trail home behind Montagny. Then, in the second race, again starting from pole, it all came right and he got that all-important first win. Montagny went on to win the title at a canter, but this upswing of form meant that Heikki was able to end the campaign as runner-up, and use this experience to stay on for a second season and romp to that title ahead of Tiago Monteiro, earning the attention of Renault for whom he became a Formula One test driver for 2006 on the way to landing his race seat alongside Giancarlo Fisichella for this year.

# FERRARI

With Michael Schumacher having retired, and technical gurus Ross Brawn and Paolo Martinelli having moved on, will Ferrari ever be the same again? That is what the tifosi are asking. But with huge strength in depth at Maranello, expect more wins.

Ferrari will be facing up to life after Michael Schumacher

No driver has ever stamped his mark on a team as Michael Schumacher did in his 11 seasons with Ferrari. The team obeyed his every wish and was rewarded by every moment of his brilliance. But now he's gone, and there's no Michael Schumacher-Kimi Raikkonen dream team as had been predicted in many quarters last year, even with talk of Marlboro being prepared to put up $70m to make it happen. When Michael's retirement was announced at last September's Italian GP he wasn't, judging by his body language at the press conference, 100 per cent sure that he really could put racing behind him. It's thought that Ferrari's hierarchy had to be tough with him because they didn't want to miss out on the chance to snap up Raikkonen. No sentimentality there.

After the final race last season, team principal Jean Todt became chief executive officer of Ferrari SpA, with Amedeo Felisa being promoted to take some of his workload. Stefano Domenicali was restored to the post of sporting director, taking on some of outgoing technical director Ross Brawn's duties. Brawn is taking a one-year sabbatical to recharge his batteries before returning, perhaps in Todt's old role. However, nothing is to be decided until Brawn meets Todt and Ferrari chairman Luca di Montezemolo this summer.

## HISTORIC MOMENT

Ferrari wasn't created simply for the first World Championship in 1950, having been racing on the grand prix scene since 1946 after Enzo Ferrari decided to stop running the works Alfa Romeos and run his own instead. After missing the 1950 opener at Silverstone, Alberto Ascari marked the team's World Championship debut at Monaco by racing to second place. He lined up seventh on the 21-car grid, one place behind team-mate Luigi Villoresi and two ahead of Raymond Sommer, and advanced steadily up the order when no one could get close to the pace of Alfa Romeo's pole-starting Juan Manuel Fangio. The key to his success was avoiding a first-corner pile-up which eliminated the Alfa Romeos of the front-row starters Giuseppe Farina and Luigi Fagioli, and Jose Froilan Gonzalez's Maserati. Fangio used this moment to make his break and was a lap clear by the finish. Ferrari's first win would have to wait until the middle of 1951, but the start of their ascent had begun and they're the only team from that first year still with us.

Meanwhile, Mario Almondo has become the team's technical director, with Aldo Costa reporting to him from the chassis division and Gilles Simon from the engine division. Simon has taken the place of Paolo Martinelli who has been moved to the parent company FIAT, most likely meaning that former chief engineer Luca Baldisserri will effectively run the team at the circuits. Nicolas Tombazis has returned from McLaren as chief designer to work alongside long-standing designer Rory Byrne. So there has been a considerable rejigging of Ferrari's hierarchy, but they are certainly not short of people of calibre.

Don't forget, though, that Ferrari is famous for its strength in depth. Not only that, Michael - the seven-time world champion - was an excellent motivator

firing up every Ferrari employee from top to bottom. Judging by his character and past record, Raikkonen is going to have to lift his game considerably to match this.

There are signs that Felipe Massa (with two wins last year) is liked and admired by the team, but he is young and it remains to be seen whether he can help them technically as well as emotionally. What he did show last year, though, was the pace to keep Michael on his toes, and he was seen as a key element in Michael's title bid as he took points off title rival Fernando Alonso in the latter part of the year. Maybe he will be able to play a similar supporting roll to Raikkonen in the season ahead, or perhaps his two wins might make him want to go for glory himself. Having Todt's

son Nicolas as his manager certainly ensures that he won't be forgotten ...

Exciting as a head-to-head competition would be, it would force Ferrari to consider a different way of running their drivers because they traditionally want one to support the other. It's safe to say, then, that pre-season testing speed will be paramount to working out which

driver gets their fullest support, but Raikkonen won't expect to be anything less than the team leader. He will also be excited about getting a car which doesn't fail under him, as happened too often with his McLaren in 2006. But didn't Michael have two failures in the last two grands prix? Rest assured, Ferrari won't be planning to trip up like that again.

## FOR THE RECORD

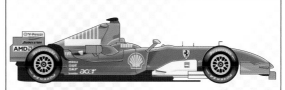

| Country of origin: | Italy |
| --- | --- |
| Team base: | Maranello, Italy |
| Telephone: | (39) 0536 949111 |
| Website: | www.ferrariworld.com |
| Active in Formula One: | From 1950 |
| Grands Prix contested: | 741 |
| Wins: | 192 |
| Pole positions: | 186 |
| Fastest laps: | 191 |

## 2006 DRIVERS & RESULTS

| Driver | Nationality | Races | Wins | Pts | Pos |
| --- | --- | --- | --- | --- | --- |
| Felipe Massa | Brazilian | 18 | 2 | 80 | 3rd |
| Michael Schumacher | German | 18 | 7 | 121 | 2nd |

## THE TEAM

| | |
| --- | --- |
| Chief executive officer: | Jean Todt |
| Sporting director: | Stefano Domenicali |
| Technical director: | Mario Almondo |
| Chassis director: | Aldo Costa |
| Engine director: | Gilles Simon |
| Chief designer: | Nicolas Tombazis |
| Chief engineer: | Luca Baldisserri |
| Team manager: | Nigel Stepney |
| Test drivers: | Luca Badoer & Marc Gene |
| Chassis: | Ferrari 248B |
| Engine: | Ferrari V8 |
| Tyres: | Bridgestone |

Having missed the first World Championship GP, Ferrari raced next time out at Monaco, with Alberto Ascari (here leading "B Bira") placing second

# FELIPE MASSA

**Felipe has a taste for winning, and anyone who heard him explain that his runaway victory in last year's finale in Brazil was one of the easiest of his life will shudder at the prospect of what he might manage in 2007.**

To those who don't follow Formula One too closely, it might seem that Felipe Massa is simply moving from being in Michael Schumacher's shadow at Ferrari to another shadow cast by the incoming Raikkonen. They could be right, and will be if Raikkonen gets to grips with the latest Ferrari chassis and the workings of Scuderia Ferrari. However, this 25-year-old Brazilian is popular within the team and is awash with confidence, stating that he won't be looking to play a supporting role.

This tallied with his smile through much of the second half of last season, a calm confidence that suggested that he'd be all right for 2007, even though people were talking of Raikkonen joining Michael Schumacher in the Ferrari line-up and pushing Felipe to one side. The news that Michael would be retiring didn't break until after the Italian GP, but by then Felipe's continually improving on-track form made it look ever less likely that he would be shown the door, his early-season mishaps perhaps consigned to the past.

The shades may hide his eyes, but everyone can guess Felipe's inner thoughts for 2007

That he was already a race winner, in Turkey, showed that he was more than a simple support player. He benefited there from qualifying in pole position, but think how few Ferrari number twos have out-qualified Schumacher over the years. Not many. Two further poles in the final two races, and that season-ending win at Interlagos demonstrate that Felipe might have a hope of being seen as Ferrari's equal No. 1.

Felipe and Kimi ought to have a slight tyre advantage in the season ahead as the rival front-running teams become accustomed to Bridgestone tyres after swapping over from Michelin. It's up to Ferrari chargers to make the most of this.

## TRACK NOTES

| | |
|---|---|
| **Nationality:** | BRAZILIAN |
| **Born:** | 25 APRIL 1981, SAO PAULO, BRAZIL |
| **Website:** | WWW.FELIPEMASSA.COM |
| **Teams:** | SAUBER 2002 & 2004-05, |
| | FERRARI 2006-07 |

**CAREER RECORD**

| | |
|---|---|
| **First Grand Prix:** | 2001 AUSTRALIAN GP |
| **Grand Prix starts:** | 71 |
| **Grand Prix wins:** | 2 |
| | 2006 Turkish GP, Brazilian GP |
| **Poles:** | 3 |
| **Fastest laps:** | 2 |
| **Points:** | 107 |
| **Honours:** | 2001 EUROPEAN FORMULA |
| | 3000 CHAMPION, 2000 EUROPEAN & ITALIAN |
| | FORMULA RENAULT CHAMPION, 1999 BRAZILIAN |
| | FORMULA CHEVROLET CHAMPION |

## HIS GREATEST WIN

As Felipe's rise to Formula One was so fast, taking just four years as he rocketed from karts to the big time, it's not surprising that his greatest win was last year's Turkish GP. Indeed, it was rare enough as few of Michael Schumacher's Ferrari team-mates are expected to win, but the key was that he qualified on pole and was leading from Michael when the safety car was deployed after Vitantonio Liuzzi's spun Toro Rosso blocked the track on lap 14. Instantly, the field dived for the pits, and this was the key: Michael followed Felipe in to the pit lane and had to wait behind him for his car to be serviced. Advantage to the Ferrari number two, particularly as Fernando Alonso was able to jump Michael because of this, and Felipe drove beautifully to claim what might be the first of many wins.

# KIMI RAIKKONEN

**Team changes can make even the most passionate fan look twice, and it's going to take some time to get used to Kimi racing for Ferrari. Yet, after a troubled 2006 with McLaren, it might seem strange to have him racing at the front.**

For the past half dozen years Formula One's commentators have been asking, who'll be the next Michael Schumacher? When Kimi broke on to the scene with Sauber in 2001 after contesting just 23 car races – and all below Formula Three level – since moving up from karts, he was seen as the one. Particularly after he finished in sixth place on his debut in Melbourne. Kimi's form in subsequent races was enough to convince McLaren to sign him, and we'd better get used to seeing him in red because he's likely to spend a lot of time on the podium, just as Michael did.

Kimi may not crack jokes very often; he smiles even less and whispers when interviewed, seemingly in fear of the microphone, but all his eloquence is in his driving. That he had to spend last season struggling to propel his McLaren to where he wanted it to go was galling for a driver who had raced to seven wins the year before. But, to Kimi's credit, he gleaned the maximum from the MP4-21, even if that

**Kimi wants a world title, desperately, thus his move to fill Schumacher's seat**

meant three poles and a pair of seconds.

One thing that Kimi will have to watch out for is that everyone at Ferrari, from the top to the most junior team member,

was charmed by Michael, and the more personable Felipe Massa is already winning hearts and minds. Certainly, if Kimi delivers on track, all will go well, but if the car isn't up to it and he doesn't, then cracks could appear in their relationship.

## TRACK NOTES

| | |
|---|---|
| **Nationality:** | FINNISH |
| **Born:** | 17 OCTOBER 1979, ESPOO, FINLAND |
| **Website:** | WWW.RACECAR.NET/KIMI |
| **Teams:** | SAUBER 2001, McLAREN 2002-06, FERRARI 2007 |

**CAREER RECORD**

| | |
|---|---|
| **First Grand Prix:** | 2001 AUSTRALIAN GP |
| **Grand Prix starts:** | 105 |
| **Grand Prix wins:** | 9 |
| | 2003 Malaysian GP, 2004 Belgian GP, 2005 Spanish GP, Monaco GP, Canadian GP, Hungarian GP, Turkish GP, Belgian GP, Japanese GP |
| **Poles:** | 11 |
| **Fastest laps:** | 19 |
| **Points:** | 336 |
| **Honours:** | 2005 AND 2003 FORMULA ONE RUNNER-UP, 2000 BRITISH FORMULA RENAULT CHAMPION, 1999 BRITISH FORMULA RENAULT WINTER SERIES CHAMPION, 1998 EUROPEAN SUPER A KART RUNNER-UP, FINNISH KART CHAMPION AND NORDIC KART CHAMPION |

## HIS GREATEST WIN

Not only was the 2005 Japanese GP Kimi's greatest win to date, it was also one of the greatest races of all time. Kimi started back in 17th place on the 22-car grid after his McLaren had an engine change on the Friday. With Michael Schumacher and Fernando Alonso also starting well back, from 14th and 16th, after rain hit the second half of qualifying, the midfield runners had unusual company. But not for long as this trio swept through them, and Schumacher even led before his first pit stop. Alonso overtook him on the track twice, but Raikkonen's second stint took the Finn to the front, passing Schumacher, unusually around the outside at Turn 1. He fell behind the second Renault of Giancarlo Fisichella when he made his second stop late on, but gave chase and dived past him for the lead on the final lap after a breathtaking drive again around the outside at Turn 1.

# McLAREN

**Reigning champion Fernando Alonso has joined McLaren wanting a third straight title, and they don't intend to disappoint. Top teams can drop from the peak for a year or two, but their expertise and financial clout ensure that they will be back.**

**Raikkonen has gone, but will world champion Alonso fare any better?**

After five years Kimi Raikkonen seemed like a fixture at McLaren, but he is no longer part of the squad and will be racing for Ferrari this year. Likewise, if you think of Fernando Alonso, you think yellow and blue Renault. Yet, this year, he'll be out in a McLaren, anxious to prove that he can win in a car which isn't a Renault and that he didn't make a duff move when, at the end of 2005, he negotiated to join the men from Woking, something that looked to be the case in 2006 when even Raikkonen couldn't produce a win.

Alonso is a special talent, and team principal Ron Dennis will be relishing the prospect of seeing how he fits in, no doubt convinced that he will do better than the much-vaunted Juan Pablo Montoya did in his 18 months in this most formal of teams. There's a change in the second seat, too, with Dennis promoting Lewis Hamilton, a driver he has supported since karting. This emphasises how the senior teams have taken over from the tailenders in promoting young talent, with Williams having done so with Nico Rosberg last year and then BMW with Robert Kubica last autumn. It breaks with McLaren's time-honoured approach of exclusively focusing on the top stars – think Alain Prost and Ayrton Senna in the late 1980s – and it's more than likely to yield

## HISTORIC MOMENT

**Sir Jack Brabham may have been the only driver to win a World Championship crown in a car bearing his own name, but the legacy laid down by fellow Antipodean Bruce McLaren was all the greater. A team-mate of Brabham's in their Cooper days, Kiwi McLaren first fielded a car under his own name in the 1966 season-opener at Monaco. He qualified 10th out of the 16 cars entered, but his white M2B didn't last the distance as Ferrari's John Surtees and then BRM's Jackie Stewart dominated proceedings, retiring after nine laps when its American Ford V8 sprung an oil leak. It wasn't much of a start, but Bruce was soon finishing in the points, by coming sixth in the British GP then fifth in the United States GP, and the McLaren story grew from there. Emerson Fittipaldi took McLaren's first drivers' world title in 1974 along with its first constructors' crown. James Hunt gave the team its second drivers' championship two years later. McLaren's greatest days were to come long after his death in 1970 when Ayrton Senna and Alain Prost dominated in the late 1980s.**

dividends, such is Hamilton's remarkable talent. Let's hope this faith in youth doesn't backfire on them as it did when Jody Scheckter scattered the field and forced a restart at the British GP in 1973.

The technical side is also different, with Adrian Newey having moved on to Red Bull Racing, followed by chief aerodynamicist Peter Prodromou, with Nicolas Tombazis rejoining Ferrari as chief designer. Despite these transfers, the drivers needn't be too fearful, as Formula One is too elaborate and complex for one man to make a comprehensive difference. McLaren has huge strength in depth in its design and engineering departments, with the likes of Neal Oatley, Paddy Lowe, Mike Coughlan, Simon Lacey and Steve Hallam.

If last year's MP4-21 chassis wasn't quite the pick of the pack, it was probably better than last year's Mercedes V8, an engine which had problems

at the start of its life, displaying a lack of power and reliability, delaying the testing programme last January. But, by mid-season, Mercedes had turned it into the highest-revving V8 of all, by which point Raikkonen was starting to qualify in pole position. There was a problem in getting heat into the tyres, but McLaren will be hoping that they get this right in the season ahead. And hoping, too, that its drivers and engineers can get used quickly to the Bridgestone tyres which all 11 teams will be using, although the five teams that raced on the Japanese company's tyres in 2006 might well start with something of an advantage, even though this year's spec tyres are going to be different.

Despite lost opportunities in Monaco and China, no wins came for the first time since 1996 as the car proved more of a qualifier than a racer when it couldn't match the Renaults and Ferraris, and Raikkonen had

to make do with seconds and thirds, with Montoya and his replacement, Pedro de la Rosa, also visiting the podium.

Money has always seemed in abundance at McLaren, but with rumours of massive debts from the construction of the phenomenal McLaren Technical Centre, Alonso's arrival has been welcomed because it has helped fill their coffers

with the sponsorship from Spanish insurance group Mutua Madrilena and Banco Santander.

If the team does meet its aims and again become Formula One's pace-setter then, and only then, will Dennis start considering handing over power. To leave with McLaren not among the winners would be unthinkable for this ultra-competitive perfectionist.

## FOR THE RECORD

| Country of origin: | England |
| --- | --- |
| Team base: | Woking, England |
| Telephone: | (44) 01483 728211 |
| Website: | www.mclaren.com |
| Active in Formula One: | From 1966 |
| Grands Prix contested: | 614 |
| Wins: | 148 |
| Pole positions: | 125 |
| Fastest laps: | 129 |

## 2006 DRIVERS & RESULTS

| Driver | Nationality | Races | Wins | Pts | Pos |
| --- | --- | --- | --- | --- | --- |
| Pedro de la Rosa | Spanish | 8 | - | 19 | 11th |
| Juan Pablo Montoya | Colombian | 10 | - | 26 | 8th |
| Kimi Raikkonen | Finnish | 18 | - | 65 | 5th |

## THE TEAM

| Team principal: | Ron Dennis |
| --- | --- |
| CEO Formula One: | Martin Whitmarsh |
| Design & development director: | Neal Oatley |
| Engineering director: | Paddy Lowe |
| Chief designer: | Mike Coughlan |
| Chief aerodynamicist: | Simon Lacey |
| Team manager: | Dave Ryan |
| Test drivers: | Pedro de la Rosa & Gary Paffett |
| Chassis: | MP4-22 |
| Engine: | Mercedes V8 |
| Tyres: | Bridgestone |

Bruce McLaren brought his own marque to Formula One at Monaco in 1966

# FERNANDO ALONSO

**He's super fast, ultra cool, and was a two-time world champion by the age of 25. Now he has changed teams to try and do it all over again. The big question is whether McLaren will be able to provide Fernando with the machinery to do just that.**

One of the first things that strikes you about Fernando Alonso is that he is calm. He doesn't fit the stereotype of a Spaniard. Good grief, people compare him with the coolest of the cool, "The Professor", Alain Prost, because he wins with the minimum fuss. However, we saw last year when the championship battle fired up that his blood can boil if he feels that he is being crossed or not receiving the fullest support.

At the start of last year, Formula One ringmaster Bernie Ecclestone said that Fernando was too young to defend his world title. Perhaps that provided Fernando with extra impetus to finish the job. The question is what will happen to that flash of passion now that he has joined the men from Woking. He won't have Michael Schumacher to fight against any more, but the driver he's replacing at McLaren, Kimi Raikkonen, isn't exactly going to be a slouch in a red car.

McLaren may seem very different to Renault, but that's down to their corporate image. Underneath, the attitude is very

The team has changed, but Fernando's desire to dominate will be even stronger than ever

similar. In fact, McLaren's desire will be the greater after a year off the boil. However, Fernando's chief concern is that McLaren can provide him with the sort of car that can help make him champion again. Don't

forget, though, that McLaren no longer has the services of Adrian Newey. Mind you, the ace designer produced a fast car last year but not a winning one, so perhaps that won't be a factor.

## TRACK NOTES

| Nationality: | SPANISH |
| --- | --- |
| Born: | 29 JULY 1981, OVIEDO, SPAIN |
| Website: | WWW.FERNANDOALONSO.COM |
| Teams: | MINARDI 2001, RENAULT 2003-06, McLAREN 2007 |

**CAREER RECORD**

| First Grand Prix: | 2001 AUSTRALIAN GP |
| --- | --- |
| Grand Prix starts: | 88 |
| Grand Prix wins: | 15 |
| | 2003 Hungarian GP, 2005 Malaysian GP, Bahrain GP, San Marino GP, European GP, French GP, German GP, Chinese GP, 2006 Bahrain GP, Australian GP, Spanish GP, Monaco GP, British GP, Canadian GP, Japanese GP |
| Poles: | 14 |
| Fastest laps: | 8 |
| Points: | 471 |
| Honours: | 2006 & 2005 FORMULA ONE WORLD CHAMPION, 1999 FORMULA NISSAN CHAMPION, 1997 ITALIAN & SPANISH KART CHAMPION, 1996 WORLD & SPANISH KART CHAMPION, 1995 & 1994 SPANISH JUNIOR KART CHAMPION |

## HIS GREATEST WIN

This will become an increasingly hard choice, but for now the 2005 Japanese GP stands out as the apogee of a career that had an astral projection after he won the world karting title in 1996. He started in cars in 1999, winning the Formula Nissan series and then laid down his marker by blitzing the Formula 3000 race at Spa in 2000. This landed him his Formula One break with Minardi in 2001, then Renault brought him on, first as a test driver in 2002 and then giving him a race seat a year later. Two-thirds of the season on, he rewarded them with victory in Hungary, becoming Formula One's youngest winner at 22 years and 26 days. Having previously finished second in Spain, he led from pole and lost the lead only when he made the first of three pit stops, crossing the line 17s ahead of Kimi Raikkonen's McLaren.

# LEWIS HAMILTON

**After a gilded career in karts, grooming from McLaren and then an exemplary ascent through junior single-seaters, Lewis has just become the first black Formula One driver. It's huge news, but his driving is what really excites.**

There are very few 11-year-olds (at the cadet carting stage) who would have the balls to ask McLaren supremo Ron Dennis to help them race in Formula One. Yet, this is just what Lewis did at an awards evening in 1996 and he hasn't looked back since. Armed with support from McLaren and Mercedes, he climbed steadily through the ranks with last year's run to the GP2 title the greatest of his feats, exciting even the most wizened members of the press pack. It wasn't just his speed but the way that he could overtake. It was mesmeric. Lewis is the most exciting talent to hit motor racing's big time since Fernando Alonso did so in 2001. (And if Lewis wants guidance, he can always ask his new team-mate, Fernando.)

There was much discussion that Lewis ought to have been given a run-out in the last few grands prix of last season, but Pedro de la Rosa was kept on in the second McLaren. Lewis displayed impressive maturity by saying that he wouldn't have been ready for it. Since then, though, he

He's fast, he's smooth, he's aggressive and he's here to stay at racing's top table

has had a winter of testing, so watch out.

For all the adulation that was directed towards Lewis as he raced to the GP2 title, and all the support that he received when people suggested that he rather than de

la Rosa should have taken over after Juan Pablo Montoya quit, there was a degree of backtracking last November when it was announced that Lewis had indeed claimed the second seat for 2007. It's hard to understand this reticence, as he has the speed and knows the team intimately, which ought to more than overcome his lack of Formula One experience.

## TRACK NOTES

| | |
|---|---|
| **Nationality:** | BRITISH |
| **Born:** | 7 JANUARY 1985, STEVENAGE, ENGLAND |
| **Website:** | WWW.LEWISHAMILTON.COM |
| **Teams:** | McLAREN 2007 |

**CAREER RECORD**

| | |
|---|---|
| **First Grand Prix:** | 2007 AUSTRALIAN GP |
| **Grand Prix starts:** | 0 |
| **Wins:** | 0 |
| **Pole positions:** | 0 |
| **Fastest laps:** | 0 |
| **Points:** | 0 |
| **Honours:** | 2006 GP2 CHAMPION, 2005 EUROPEAN FORMULA THREE CHAMPION, 2003 BRITISH FORMULA RENAULT CHAMPION, 2000 EUROPEAN FORMULA A KARTING CHAMPION, 1999 ITALIAN INTERCONTINENTAL A KARTING CHAMPION, 1996 McLAREN MERCEDES CHAMPION OF THE FUTURE, 1995 BRITISH CADET KARTING CHAMPION |

## HIS GREATEST WIN

There's no doubt that ART Grand Prix is the team to race for in Formula One's feeder formula, GP2. The chassis may be identical, but ASM's success the year before in guiding Nico Rosberg to the title showed that the French team was the pick of the pack. Hamilton made the most of their prowess to claim his five wins en route to the title in 2006, but it was his drive to second place in the second of the pair of races at Istanbul Park that showed his ability to overtake like no other. Having started seventh, he spun and fell to 16th. To most people, passing rivals in identical cars is extremely difficult, but Lewis picked off every driver ahead of him until he reached second place, with his supreme ability on the brakes being the key to his overtaking. He then chased down Andreas Zuber, slashing his advantage to just 3s by the flag, racing in a class of his own.

# HONDA RACING

**If the confidence which was oozing from the pores of Honda Racing at the final race of 2006 can be carried over into this season, then the team will be expecting to win grands prix and even gun for the championship. And why not?**

**Jenson Button will be looking for more wins for Honda in 2007**

Ladies and gentlemen, the monkey is off their back. Yes, Honda Racing can now go about its work without the pressure mounting when the wins just wouldn't come. They have Jenson Button to thank for this, and they will reward him and team-mate Rubens Barrichello by operating with that great sporting ingredient, confidence. They will also hope that the axiom "success breeds success" holds true.

Consider the case: Honda Racing, a re-branded incarnation of BAR, set the pace through the winter testing ahead of the 2006 World Championship. It didn't seem to matter at which circuit they tested, their RA106 was the fastest. Hopes soared that they would soon have their first victory, but boy, had they been deceived. Perhaps they'd been testing with a lighter fuel load than their rivals. Perhaps their car handled better on cool tracks. Whatever, when the racing kicked off last March, they were never close to a win.

To make matters worse, the team and technical director Geoff Willis parted company in June after he was demoted when Shuhei Nakamoto was brought in from Honda Racing Development and appointed above him as the team's senior technical director. There was a certain amount of turmoil as the appointment had been made by

## HISTORIC MOMENT

**Ronnie Bucknum was never a driver expected to set F1 alight. In fact, he was little known when Honda brought him in to guide them into F1, which is precisely why they introduced him, little being expected of this American sports car racer and of their first car, the RA271. Their debut came midway through the 1964 World Championship at the German GP when BRM Ferrari and Lotus were ruling the roost. Bucknum qualified the white car with the red rising sun on its nose in 22nd place out of 24 starters on the tricky 14-mile Nurburgring, but failed to last the distance, spinning out of 11th place in a trouble-strewn race when the car's steering failed. However, the Honda show was on the road and he was fifth next time out, at Monza. Amazingly, the Japanese manufacturer was a winner by the Mexican GP just over a year later, emphasising the progress made by the personnel and by Goodyear tyres for whom this was their maiden win. Their battle in those early days was not only to develop their car but also to adjust to vast cultural differences.**

the parent company and not the team, and team CEO Nick Fry had to walk a political tightrope for a while. Others just kept their heads down. This echoed what had happened at the other Japanese manufacturer-funded team, Toyota, with Mike Gascoyne also chosing to walk.

Honda had to fight hard to find more power and downforce, and it speaks volumes for their application that they got there by the 13th round, on a berserk day at the Hungaroring when Jenson delivered. Yes, a couple of retirements helped him to the front, but a win is a win.

It was what followed next that makes people believe that more wins will follow in the season ahead, with both drivers gathering points at will from that race on. Best of all, Jenson's run to third in Brazil sent Honda into the close-season on a high. Yes, Felipe Massa was dominant for Ferrari that day, but most of this was down to Bridgestone tyres being exceptional that day and, remember, there will be no

tyre advantage this year, with everyone on Bridgestones.

Honda now seems more settled than ever, with continuity of driver line-up something which none of the three teams who finished ahead of them in 2006 can claim. Button is certainly hungry for more success as he starts his fifth campaign for the squad, and Rubens Barrichello is anxious to prove that his winning days aren't behind him. His race engineer, Jock Clear, said early last year that Rubens had that "x-factor" which ought to help Honda become a winning team. Perhaps now that Rubens is accustomed to the team, that will prove to be the case.

One person who will be missed is Anthony Davidson who performed so strongly as the lead test driver in recent seasons. He is off to race for Honda-engined Super Aguri Racing, with his place being taken by former Red Bull Racing man Christian Klien.

A factor to consider is how quickly the team can get to

grips with running its cars on Bridgestone tyres. Yes, all 11 teams will be using them, but Honda is one of six teams which was on Michelin rubber last year.

On a more positive note, Fry believes that the team's new wind tunnel will help craft the RA107, and it's known that Honda were aggressive in the

development of their V8 before engine specs were frozen after the final race of 2006.

By way of a parting word, worldwide Honda boss Takeo Fukui, who happened fortuitously to be in Hungary when they won, said that he won't be satisfied until Honda are world champions. That should keep the purse strings open.

## FOR THE RECORD

| | |
|---|---|
| Country of origin: | England |
| Team base: | Brackley, England |
| Telephone: | (44) 01280 844000 |
| Website: | www.hondaracingf1.com |
| Active in Formula One: | From 1999 (as BAR until 2005) |
| Grands Prix contested: | 136 |
| Wins: | 1 |
| Pole positions: | 3 |
| Fastest laps: | 0 |

## 2006 DRIVERS & RESULTS

| Driver | Nationality | Races | Wins | Pts | Pos |
|---|---|---|---|---|---|
| Rubens Barrichello | Brazilian | 18 | - | 30 | 7th |
| Jenson Button | British | 18 | 1 | 56 | 6th |

## THE TEAM

| | |
|---|---|
| Team principal: | Nick Fry |
| President of Honda Racing Development: | Yasuhiro Wada |
| Sporting director: | Gil de Ferran |
| Senior technical director: | Shuhei Nakamoto |
| Deputy technical director: | Gary Savage |
| Chief designer: | Kevin Taylor |
| Chief aerodynamicist: | Mariano Alperin |
| Chief engineer: | Jacky Eeckelaert |
| Team manager: | Ron Meadows |
| Test drivers: | Christian Klien & James Rossiter |
| Chassis: | RA107 |
| Engine: | Honda V8 |
| Tyres: | Bridgestone |

**Nothing much was expected of Honda and Ronnie Bucknum on their debut**

# JENSON BUTTON

**No longer do we have to ask when Jenson will claim that first win, for the job was done last year, and in some style. That Honda's form at the end of 2006 was improving must give Jenson enormous optimism that more wins might follow.**

Sir Frank Williams knows all about driving ability. He has had some of the best drivers, Jenson included. That's why people listened last February, a month ahead of the opening round, when he said that Jenson would become a winner before the year was out. And how right he was.

Certainly, at that time, Jenson and Honda Racing were regularly topping the pre-season testing time sheets. Yet there was more to Jenson last year, now aware that he must work flat-out to get in a winning position and then go even harder to grab victory. And that happened at the Hungarian Grand Prix, not that it was easy winning from 14th on the grid on a track which famously offers scant chance to pass, although that made his winning all the better. Drivers of the past, including 1996 World Champion Damon Hill, lined up afterwards to say that this win would herald many more. And they may be proved right this year because Honda looks like a

Jenson was smiling in 2006. Will he have an even bigger grin this this year?

team heading in the right direction. On top of this, Jenson got on well with his new team-mate Rubens Barrichello last year,

though that's easy when you're picking up the better results.

Jenson is locked in a contract to keep him at Honda until the end of 2008 which appears to suit him just fine. Indeed, if they can raise their game together, he might not want to leave.

## TRACK NOTES

| | |
|---|---|
| **Nationality:** | BRITISH |
| **Born:** | 19 JANUARY 1980, FROME, ENGLAND |
| **Website:** | WWW.JENSONBUTTON.COM |
| **Teams:** | WILLIAMS 2000, BENETTON/RENAULT 2001-02, BAR/HONDA 2003-07 |

**CAREER RECORD**

| | |
|---|---|
| **First Grand Prix:** | 2000 AUSTRALIAN GP |
| **Grand Prix starts:** | 119 |
| **Grand Prix wins:** | 1 |
| | 2006 Hungarian GP |
| **Poles:** | 3 |
| **Fastest laps:** | 0 |
| **Points:** | 223 |
| **Honours:** | 1999 MACAU FORMULA THREE RUNNER-UP, 1998 FORMULA FORD FESTIVAL WINNER, BRITISH FORMULA FORD CHAMPION & McLAREN AUTOSPORT BRDC YOUNG DRIVER, 1997 EUROPEAN SUPER A KART CHAMPION, 1991 BRITISH CADET KART CHAMPION |

## HIS GREATEST WIN

Like team-mate Barrichello, there have been wins all the way since he started racing karts. The Formula Ford Festival was won in his first year in cars, more followed in Formula Three and it was expected that it was a matter of when, not if, once he reached Formula One with Williams in 2000. But the team was no longer at its best, while Benetton and Renault were rediscovering themselves when he raced there. A run of podium finishes for BAR in 2004 suggested a win was imminent. However, it took until Jenson's 114th Formula One start last year for that win to come. And what a win. It came at the Hungaroring, a circuit on which overtaking is notoriously limited, and Jenson started 14th on the grid. Changeable weather conditions made matters tricky, but Jenson made no mistakes. He was helped by Kimi Raikkonen crashing and Fernando Alonso retiring from the lead, but it was a masterclass in controlled excellence.

# RUBENS BARRICHELLO

**Rubens struggled to settle in after joining Honda Racing last year, finding the car difficult to drive. However, there are signs that his second campaign for Honda will be considerably more competitive and he ought to be up on the podium again.**

For any driver changing teams from Ferrari it's going to be a step-down, particularly with the team in its pomp at the start of the twenty-first century. However, for this likeable Brazilian it was harder than expected, largely due to inflated expectations which were soon deflated.

Through winter testing, Rubens' hopes soared as he and new team-mate Jenson Button topped the time sheets. Sadly for them, this all changed when they turned up at the opening grand prix in Bahrain and found that Ferrari, Renault and McLaren had the beating of them.

Rubens came down with a crash, really struggling with the brakes. This was sorted after the first three races, but he took a while longer to become comfortable with Honda's traction control system, finding it hard to know just how hard he could push the car. Fortunately, Jenson wasn't racking up top results either, and both enjoyed a turn-around in form come mid-season. Jenson's win in Hungary will have helped the team's confidence, too. No podiums

Will Rubens win again in 2007 to prove there can be life after Ferrari?

came Rubens' way, though, with fourth place at Monaco and at the Hungaroring being his best results, but there's every reason to be confident. The team certainly is, and it has moved forward significantly

since that famous wet day in Hungary.

Other reasons why Rubens should be excited about 2007 include the fact that he gets on well with Jenson, has friend and compatriot Gil de Ferran as the team's sporting director, and general optimism is coursing through the team's veins. So, visits to the podium should be on, and a race win isn't out of the question.

## TRACK NOTES

| | |
|---|---|
| **Nationality:** | BRAZILIAN |
| **Born:** | 23 MAY 1972, SAO PAULO, BRAZIL |
| **Website:** | WWW.BARRICHELLO.COM.BR |
| **Teams:** | JORDAN 1993-96, STEWART 1997-99, FERRARI 2000-05, HONDA 2006-07 |

**CAREER RECORD**

| | |
|---|---|
| **First Grand Prix:** | 1993 SOUTH AFRICAN GP |
| **Grand Prix starts:** | 235 |
| **Grand Prix wins:** | 9 |
| | 2000 German GP, 2002 European GP, Hungarian GP, Italian GP, US GP, 2003 British GP, Japanese GP, 2004 Italian GP, Chinese GP |
| **Poles:** | 13 |
| **Fastest laps:** | 15 |
| **Points:** | 519 |
| **Honours:** | FORMULA ONE RUNNER-UP, 2002 BRITISH FORMULA THREE CHAMPION, 1991 EUROPEAN FORMULA OPEL CHAMPION, 1990 BRAZILIAN KART CHAMPION, 1988 |

## HIS GREATEST WIN

It was garlands all the way in Rubens' early career, rewarding the businessmen who identified his talent in karting and backed him to move to Europe. Formula Opel and Formula Three came and went, Formula 3000 was more of a struggle, but, once he reached Formula One at 20, Rubens produced his best drive. It wasn't one of his nine wins, but seven years before the first of those on a wet day when Donington Park hosted the European GP. It was Rubens' third outing and he qualified in 12th place. The track was wet and, while everyone watched Senna storm from third to first on lap 1, few spotted Rubens climbing to fourth. Drivers started popping into the pits as conditions changed, but after 50 laps Rubens had reached second, giddy heights for a Jordan. After two more pit stops, Rubens was third with just six laps to go when his Hart engine failed.

# BMW SAUBER

Last March we had become accustomed to the white cars with the dark blue flanks, BMW's first full entry into Formula One. The personnel were Sauber of old, but the ethos was very much a new one and BMW is now firmly established.

**Nick Heidfeld will be aiming for more than one podium finish in 2007**

BMW is German and cutting-edge. Sauber was Swiss and quirky; slightly anonymous in many ways, solid and worthy. Not at the front, but not at the back, and that's where they would have remained had BMW not bought them out. Now, with BMW's corporate slickness and, more importantly, millions of euros, the transformed team have the tools to make frequent podium appearances and even the possibility of getting their first win, something of which Sauber could only dream.

It's not just a boost to the team's budget which has made the difference, but a transformation of its leading personnel. At the top is Mario Theissen, a thrusting, hungry and ambitious BMW man who's very different to the taciturn team chief of old, Peter Sauber. While many of the staff have stayed, with Willy Rampf still technical director, you can be sure that Theissen will drive them harder than they've ever been driven before.

And don't forget that Rampf and his team have more "toys" to play with as they shape the 2007 challenger, the BMW F1.07. Rampf is also supported by a greatly changed design team. Willem Toet joined early last year as the team's chief aerodynamicist, with Seamus Mullarkey continuing as chief designer. Then, a few months

## HISTORIC MOMENT

On the back of their successes running Mercedes' sports car racing programme, Sauber broke into Formula One in 1993 with a pair of Mercedes-powered cars for JJ Lehto and Karl Wendlinger, with Ilmor-badged Mercedes engines in the back. Not a lot was expected of the unsponsored cars, but Lehto placed his sixth on the grid for their debut in the South African GP. The Finn was fourth at the end of lap 1, one place ahead of Wendlinger who'd jumped the start from tenth, helped by Damon Hill spinning on his Williams debut. However, an unscheduled pit stop on lap 6 left Lehto last. As others dropped out, including Wendlinger from sixth in mid-race, Lehto kept fighting his way up the order to make it back to fifth after passing Gerhard Berger's failed Ferrari a lap from home, albeit finishing two laps down on race winner Alain Prost's McLaren. Fortunate this may have been, as only seven cars were classified as finishers, but the team which would become BMW Sauber in 2006 had its first points on the board. In a year dominated by Williams, Sauber would go on to rank sixth at year's end, equal with former champion team Lotus.

later, former Williams technical organiser Jorg Zander signed up, with Theissen saying he was "essential" to the team's future. The team also welcomed Mercedes F1 engine development chief Markus Duesmann to head its engine division in the summer, giving him the role formerly filled by Heinz Paschen. The final change was Klaus Drager's promotion from within to take over as head of research and development from Burkhard Goeschel.

Looking back at last year, BMW Sauber propelled two drivers – Nick Heidfeld and Robert Kubica – to podium finishes which emphasised just how much progress had been made. Considerable work had gone on behind the scenes to integrate a considerable number of new personnel into the ranks, and Theissen was extremely impressed with the way the new regime gelled with the old.

If there was one dark cloud over BMW Sauber's 2006 campaign, their rear wings were suspected of being too flexible. Matters came to a head at the Canadian GP in June. A week later, the sport's governing body made the team make them stiffer and undoubtedly this will have cost the team straight-line speed. As if to divert attention from this, the F1.06 next turned out at Magny-Cours with some astonishing-looking vertical wings out of the top of the nose. Effective they might have been, but attractive they were not. However, the FIA stepped in again and banned them lest they impair vision.

The driving line-up is going to be the same as it was at the end of last season, when Robert Kubica had been elevated to the team ahead of Jacques Villeneuve, with Heidfeld nominally the number-one driver. However, Heidfeld knows that he will have to perform to be around in 2008 because Theissen and BMW are very keen on rewarding youthful talent, with 19-year-old Sebastian Vettel having signed up as the team's third driver after some stunning outings when he became third driver on Kubica's promotion towards the end of last year.

For now, though, it looks as if Kubica will be the driver who takes the team forward through the 2007 campaign. As Theissen is quick to point out, the Pole's aggressive speed is backed up by great mental capacity.

The repositioning of teams is more than a re-branding exercise. Indeed, BMW would never have entered into this if they felt that a couple of years down the line they would be running little more than a re-liveried Sauber. Fortunately, they are not and BMW Sauber are fast becoming one of the top teams, one that will chase developmental progress all year, unlike the Sauber of old.

JJ Lehto finished fifth on the Sauber team's Formula One debut

## FOR THE RECORD

| | |
|---|---|
| Country of origin: | Switzerland |
| Team base: | Hinwil, Switzerland |
| Telephone: | (41) 1937 9000 |
| Website: | www.bmw-sauber-f1.com |
| Active in Formula One: | From 1993 (as Sauber until 2005) |
| Grands Prix contested: | 235 |
| Wins: | 0 |
| Pole positions: | 0 |
| Fastest laps: | 0 |

## 2006 DRIVERS & RESULTS

| Driver | Nationality | Races | Wins | Pts | Pos |
|---|---|---|---|---|---|
| Nick Heidfeld | German | 18 | - | 23 | 9th |
| Robert Kubica | Polish | 6 | - | 6 | 16th |
| Jacques Villeneuve | Canadian | 12 | - | 7 | 15th |

## THE TEAM

| | |
|---|---|
| Team principal: | Mario Theissen |
| Technical director: | Willy Rampf |
| Chief designer: | Jorg Zander |
| Chief aerodynamicist: | Willem Toet |
| Head of track engineering: | Mike Krack |
| Team manager: | Beat Zehnder |
| Test driver: | Sebastian Vettel |
| Chassis: | F1.07 |
| Engine: | BMW V8 |
| Tyres: | Bridgestone |

# NICK HEIDFELD

**This is a make-or-break year as BMW has made it plain that it wants to promote youth, and Nick will turn 30 this spring. With Robert Kubica putting him under pressure late last year, Nick has to deliver if he is to remain on board for 2008.**

Here is a driver whose career ought to have brought him more than it has. Just two years ago, when he lost his ride with Jordan, it seemed as though Nick had been sidelined until BMW came along and saved him. A ride with the BMW-powered Williams and then the chance to lead the BMW Sauber attack last year put Nick back on track. He even produced a great drive to finish third in the Hungarian GP. So why is there a cloud on the horizon? Because the next generation of talent has arrived and it's lining up to depose him.

Life with Jacques Villeneuve was acceptable at the start of last year, with Nick's fourth place in Melbourne his best result in the first half of the year. However, the threat to his future arrived when Robert Kubica stepped up from being the team's third driver on Villeneuve's departure, and the Polish driver immediately showed that he was at least the equal of Nick. Furthermore, when Sebastian Vettel took Kubica's place as the third driver, he hinted at being every bit as good.

His car will be better for 2007, but will Nick resist the challenge from within?

A public image has always been a problem for the largely reticent Nick, and Nico Rosberg has already moved ahead of him and Ralf Schumacher in the affections of German Formula One fans, according to an internet poll to find out whom they would support following Michael Schumacher's retirement. At face value this isn't too much of a slight, but the PR people at BMW would surely prefer someone else more promotable, so Nick had better make certain the results start flowing if he wants to keep his ride.

## TRACK NOTES

| | |
|---|---|
| **Nationality:** | GERMAN |
| **Born:** | 10 MAY 1977, MOENCHENGLADBACH, GERMANY |
| **Website:** | WWW.ADRIVO.COM/NICKHEIDFELD |
| **Teams:** | PROST 2000, SAUBER 2001-03, JORDAN 2004, WILLIAMS 2005, BMW 2006-07 |

**CAREER RECORD**

| | |
|---|---|
| **First Grand Prix:** | 1999 AUSTRALIAN GP |
| **Grand Prix starts:** | 117 |
| **Grand Prix wins:** | 0 |
| | best result: second, 2005 Monaco GP and European GP |
| **Poles:** | 1 |
| **Fastest laps:** | 0 |
| **Points:** | 79 |
| **Honours:** | 1999 FORMULA 3000 CHAMPION, 1998 FORMULA 3000 RUNNER-UP, 1997 GERMAN FORMULA THREE CHAMPION, 1995 GERMAN FORMULA FORD RUNNER-UP, 1994 GERMAN FF1600 CHAMPION |

## HIS GREATEST WIN

A star in karting circles, then a champion in Formula Ford, Nick moved up to Formula Three in 1996, hoping to keep on winning. And though he did for Bertram Schafer Racing, the man of the moment was Jarno Trulli, doing some cross-border raiding from Italy to lift the title. Nick came good to keep his career momentum going with a double win at the Nurburgring towards the end of the season, followed by another at the following round at Magny-Cours. With a best result up to this point of second place at the same circuit earlier in the season, Nick beat Trulli in both races, with Manuel Giao twice finishing third. This helped Nick rank third overall behind Trulli, and cemented his seat for the following year when Nick raced to the title to graduate to Formula 3000 and a battle royal with Juan Pablo Montoya for the 1998 title.

# ROBERT KUBICA

**A podium finish on only his third attempt was the icing on the cake for this startlingly quick young Pole who had already done more than enough to convince BMW that he was worthy of their second race seat for the 2007 campaign.**

Many Formula One fans must have been asking just where he came from when Robert Kubica burst on to the scene with BMW Sauber last year. First, he started banging in lap times that left him top of the timesheets in the Friday practice sessions. Certainly, the third drivers tended to put the regular racers in the shade because they got time for more running and also had light tanks. But anyone outpacing the likes of Williams' Alexander Wurz and Honda Racing's Anthony Davidson is worthy of attention.

What really made people sit up and take notice, though, was Robert's speed when promoted to race alongside Nick Heidfeld at the Hungarian GP, filling Jacques Villeneuve's seat. Even taking into account a couple of mistakes, he was still good for seventh, although this was annulled because his car was underweight. Robert reacted by trying harder and raced to a podium finish third time out, at Monza, impressing with his aggressive style. Talk

**Get to know this face, as Robert has only one aim, to become the world champion**

about natural talent ...

It's safe to say that Poland doesn't have a long history in Formula One, with just one Pole trying to race in it before. Trying and

failing actually, with Mikko Kozarowitsky not making the grade on two attempts in a RAM Racing March in 1977 when the country was still run by a communist government. So Robert is breaking new ground and the nation loves him for it. In fact, Poland is already trying to work out how to fund and build a circuit so that it can have a grand prix of its own, although this will certainly take a year or two.

## TRACK NOTES

| | |
|---|---|
| **Nationality:** | POLISH |
| **Born:** | 7 DECEMBER 1984, CRACOW, POLAND |
| **Website:** | WWW.KUBICA.PL |
| **Teams:** | BMW SAUBER 2006-07 |

**CAREER RECORD**

| | |
|---|---|
| **First Grand Prix:** | 2006 HUNGARIAN GP |
| **Grand Prix starts:** | 6 |
| **Wins:** | 0 |
| | best result: third, 2006 Italian GP |
| **Pole positions:** | 0 |
| **Fastest laps:** | 0 |
| **Points:** | 6 |
| **Honours:** | 2005 WORLD SERIES BY RENAULT CHAMPION, 1999 GERMAN & ITALIAN KARTING CHAMPION, 1999 MONACO KART CUP WINNER, 1998 ITALIAN KARTING CHAMPION, 1998 MONACO KART CUP WINNER, 1997 POLISH KARTING CHAMPION |

## HIS GREATEST WIN

Following an illustrious karting career, Robert broke into car racing in 2001 and, after two years in Formula Renault, made the move to European Formula Three series. Well, he would have done but he'd been a passenger in a road accident and broke his arm. That's why he started his campaign at the seventh of the 20 races, the first leg of a double-header at the Norisring street circuit in Nuremburg. Having qualified third for the Prema Powerteam behind ASM Racing's Alex Premat and Olivier Pla, Robert raced to victory when they clashed, leading home future Jordan Formula One driver Timo Glock and Pla. Taking second place in the second race suggested a star had been born, but this dream start wasn't followed by visits to the podium, and it was only when he reached the World Series with Renault, after a further year in Formula Three, that he realised his potential, winning four races and the title.

# TOYOTA

**Last year was a disappointment to Toyota after they rose so high in 2005. There were green shoots of promise but also, too often, retirements. The drivers are the same, but the loss of technical director Mike Gascoyne might hit them hard.**

**Will Jarno Trulli give Toyota their first win in 2007?**

Such was the expected trajectory last year that people were reckoning that Toyota might be able to trouble Formula One's big three of Ferrari, Renault and McLaren. But Formula One isn't as easy as that. If it was, former greats like Williams wouldn't have tumbled down the order.

The first reason why Toyota not only failed to advance from its ranking of fourth overall in 2005, but retreated to sixth, is that the team switched from Michelin to Bridgestone. The drivers found the tyres great in high temperatures but less than competitive when they dipped. Furthermore, their ranking of fourth in 2005 meant that they were no longer able to run a third driver, so limiting the data that they could acquire on Fridays at grand prix meetings. Test drivers Ricardo Zonta and Olivier Panis continued to offer excellent feedback, but only from the test track, which was useful in the general scheme of things, but not to any particular race weekend.

The second reason is that technical director Mike Gascoyne was up and off, quitting the team as early as mid-April after a disagreement with his boss, executive vice-president Yoshiaki Kinoshita. This hampered the team's form through 2006 and will most likely have an effect on this year's car. Despite this loss, and that of chief designer Gustav Brunner in late 2005, neither were replaced directly as Toyota's hierarchy repeated the mantra that a design division in Formula One is no longer about just one person, with Pascal Vasselon (head of vehicle design and development) taking over as the design leader. Brunner spent the winter contesting what he considered to be unfair dismissal, even turning down a £1m compensation offer, saying the terms of his departure prevent him from returning to Formula One. By mid-August, Toyota had coaxed former Jaguar Racing designer Mark Gillan to return to the sport from academia as head of aerodynamics.

The third reason why Toyota lost ground was that Formula One simply became more competitive. Indeed, while gathering 88 points in 2005, Toyota was 1s per lap slower than champions Renault, and as much as 1.5s off the pacy but fragile McLaren, their average difference to the fastest teams in 2006 being closer to 0.5s slower, yet they came away with

a meagre tally of just 35 points.

The arrival of the TF106B, a car designed specifically around Bridgestone tyres with a new monocoque and front suspension in time for the Monaco GP, brought an upturn in form, with Jarno Trulli particularly singing its praise, and looking all set for third place until a hydraulic problem struck right at the end. However, the TF106B still struggled to get heat into its tyres until further modifications arrived in time for the French GP at Magny-Cours. Perhaps the biggest disappointment was Trulli retiring from third place early on in the finale at Interlagos because Bridgestone tyres were definitely the ones to have that day.

That drive of Trulli's at Monaco was enough to convince the team's hierarchy to keep him on with Ralf Schumacher. Indeed, they have given him the security of a three-year deal. Supporting Ralf and Jarno in 2007 will be long-time Renault-tester turned Super Aguri-racer last year, Franck Montagny, taking over from Zonta who moves to test for Renault, and

Panis who is returning to racing to lead Peugeot's Le Mans 24 Hours sports car project.

At the end of 2005, Toyota said that wins were fundamental to its 2006 programme. They didn't come, so it's hard to know what will satisfy the ambitious team this time around, but wins really ought to be on the cards for an immensely well-funded outfit that is beginning its

sixth campaign in Formula One.

This year, of course, Toyota has another team using its V8s, with Williams planning to show the works team just what its engines can achieve. It will be interesting to see which team uses them better, although you can't help but feel that Williams will get a higher profile as Toyota continues to be largely anonymous.

## FOR THE RECORD

| | |
|---|---|
| Country of origin: | Germany |
| Team base: | Cologne, Germany |
| Telephone: | (49) 2234 1823444 |
| Website: | www.toyota-f1.com |
| Active in Formula One: | From 2002 |
| Grands Prix contested: | 88 |
| Wins: | 0 |
| Pole positions: | 2 |
| Fastest laps: | 1 |

## 2006 DRIVERS & RESULTS

| Driver | Nationality | Races | Wins | Pts | Pos |
|---|---|---|---|---|---|
| Ralf Schumacher | German | 18 | - | 20 | 10th |
| Jarno Trulli | Italian | 18 | - | 15 | 12th |

## THE TEAM

| | |
|---|---|
| Chairman & team principal: | Tsutomo Tomita |
| President: | John Howett |
| General manager, engine: | Luca Marmorini |
| General manager, chassis: | Pascal Vasselon |
| Technical co-ordinator: | Noritoshi Arai |
| Head of aerodynamics: | Mark Gillan |
| Team manager: | Richard Cregan |
| Chief engineer: | Dieter Gass |
| Test driver: | Franck Montagny |
| Chassis: | Toyota TF107 |
| Engine: | Toyota V8 |
| Tyres: | Bridgestone |

**Mika Salo scored on Toyota's debut in Australia in 2002**

# RALF SCHUMACHER

**Michael Schumacher is no longer in Formula One, but few feel that brother Ralf will come out of his shadow. Indeed, according to an internet poll, 19.9 per cent of German fans would rather support no one than Ralf following Michael's retirement.**

Such a cruel finding must be incredibly dispiriting for even the most thick-skinned of public figures, but it sums up the near universal response to Ralf Schumacher.

There's no doubting that he's quick in a car, but he's not the quickest. To make matters worse, he drives for Toyota, a team that struggles to develop any discernible image and which, in 2006, had such sketchy form that it could be virtually discounted. Worst of all, though, Ralf has always been petulant with the media, making it hard to present a loveable side to his complex character. Last year he even said that he didn't really know his brother.

The major change for Ralf in 2006, as Toyota fought to rediscover its promising form of 2005, was breaking away from the stable of his long-time manager, Willi Weber, and appointing Hans Mahr to manage his career and try to project him back into a winning team. No deal was achieved for 2007, so Ralf will see out the final year of his three-year Toyota deal, but many things

**Ralf might enjoy the year ahead without Michael and may yet shine again**

must change before he starts to appeal to any of the major teams again, especially with the whole crop of new talent.

Ralf's ten-year Formula One career produced six wins when he raced for Williams, but precious little since 2003. Last year did produce a podium finish, in the curious, see-sawing Australian GP, but this was against the run of play and Ralf, like team-mate Jarno Trulli, struggled as Toyota tried to get up to speed on its Bridgestone tyres, with fourth in the French GP the only other result of note.

## TRACK NOTES

| | |
|---|---|
| **Nationality:** | GERMAN |
| **Born:** | 30 JUNE 1975, KERPEN, GERMANY |
| **Website:** | WWW.RALF-SCHUMACHER.DE |
| **Teams:** | JORDAN 1997-98, |
| | WILLIAMS 1999-2004, TOYOTA 2005-07 |

**CAREER RECORD**

| | |
|---|---|
| **First Grand Prix:** | 1997 AUSTRALIAN GP |
| **Grand Prix starts:** | 164 |
| **Grand Prix wins:** | 6 |
| | 2001 San Marino GP, Canadian GP, |
| | German GP, 2002 Malaysian GP, |
| | 2003 European GP, French GP |
| **Poles:** | 6 |
| **Fastest laps:** | 8 |
| **Points:** | 314 |

**Honours:** 1996 FORMULA NIPPON CHAMPION, 1995 GERMAN FORMULA THREE RUNNER-UP & MACAU GP WINNER, 1993 GERMAN FORMULA JUNIOR RUNNER-UP

## HIS GREATEST WIN

With a father who ran a karting circuit and a brother who was scything his way through the junior races, it's no surprise that Ralf took to four wheels. Graduating to cars was the natural thing to do after being runner-up in the national karting series. Although runner-up to Norberto Fontana in German Formula Three in 1995, Ralf played his trump card by matching brother Michael's feat of winning the Macau street race, beating Jarno Trulli, Pedro de la Rosa and Fontana, in the process making his own name so that he wasn't just the "brother of". This enabled Ralf to race in Japan's high-profile Formula Nippon series in 1996, and he made huge strides in winning that before graduating to Formula One with Jordan in 1997. Moving to Williams was the making of Ralf, with his first win coming in the 2001 San Marino GP, but the wins dried up after 2003 and he moved on to Toyota for 2005.

# JARNO TRULLI

**Just when it looked as though this talented Italian had refound his touch, Toyota went off the boil, with his few drives of promise being hit by poor reliability. How he bounces back in 2007 will be make or break for a driver who needs top results.**

How Jarno must have wished that he'd been able to stay on at Renault as they raced to glory in 2005 and 2006. Finally, they had a car that could win races on a regular basis and he was no longer there, having been dropped at the end of 2004. Then, to make matters worse, just as Toyota looked as though they might start challenging for wins after reaching the podium in 2005, the team lost ground and points became an achievement rather than a right.

Things even looked rocky for Jarno's future last May when team president John Howett hinted that Toyota would change its driver line-up. With team-mate Ralf Schumacher signed until the end of 2007, that left Jarno feeling the draught. Fortunately, a series of strong drives, including being deprived of third place at Monaco by a late-in-the-race mechanical failure, meant Jarno kept his seat with a new contract that will keep him with Toyota until the end of 2009.

Jarno must keep the positives from 2006

**Jarno will be hoping that reliability won't be a factor with his Toyota in 2007**

– being good enough for a podium finish at Monaco, Magny-Cours and Interlagos – and go on from there.

If the results he craves don't start to

flow this year, the sport's insiders might start to carp again, with their favourite jibe being that Jarno is a choker, a driver who falls away in races and fails to collect the due reward. He's great in qualifying they say, pointing to the three pole positions that he has claimed in cars that weren't necessarily the pick of the pack, but not the real ticket when the race gets under way. Mechanical failure has been the excuse on many an occasion, but still Jarno has to prove them wrong.

## TRACK NOTES

| | |
|---|---|
| **Nationality:** | ITALIAN |
| **Born:** | 13 JULY 1974, PESCARA, ITALY |
| **Website:** | WWW.JARNOTRULLI.COM |
| **Teams:** | MINARDI 1997, PROST 1997-99, |
| | JORDAN 2000-01, RENAULT 2002-04, |
| | TOYOTA 2005-07 |

| CAREER RECORD | |
|---|---|
| **First Grand Prix:** | 1997 AUSTRALIAN GP |
| **Grand Prix starts:** | 167 |
| **Grand Prix wins:** | 1 |
| | 2004 Monaco GP |
| **Poles:** | 3 |
| **Fastest laps:** | 0 |
| **Points:** | 175 |
| **Honours:** | 1996 GERMAN FORMULA THREE |
| | CHAMPION, 1994 WORLD KART CHAMPION |

## HIS GREATEST WIN

Like Fernando Alonso, Jarno was World Karting Champion, claiming the title two years before the Spaniard, with his big day coming in 1994. And, like Alonso, he flew through the junior categories, moving direct to Formula Three and beating Nick Heidfeld to the German title in 1996. So, after just a year and a half in cars, Jarno graduated to Formula One with Minardi. His skill was clear for all to see, and he even led the Austrian GP after replacing the injured Olivier Panis at Prost, before retiring. This was typical of Jarno, with startling flashes of speed but few race results, and it was the same when he was at Jordan, but it finally all came right when he won the 2004 Monaco GP for Renault. He claimed pole position, held the lead into Ste Devote and was never headed, except when he pitted, although Jenson Button gave him little rest. For once, too, nothing broke and the monkey was off his back.

# RED BULL RACING

**This team has money aplenty, an Adrian Newey-designed chassis and Renault engines, so it really ought to start to make progress and put an end to its loss of form through 2006 that saw it fade to the very tail end of the midfield.**

David Coulthard will relish the Adrian Newey-designed chassis

Dietrich Mateschitz is a man of almost unimaginable wealth and even more towering ambition. Blessed with the squillions his Red Bull energy drink have earned him, he wants to win in Formula One. Just being there was enough to start with when he backed Sauber, but that is not enough now that he has his own team. Well, two teams actually, with the Scuderia Toro Rosso squad which was formed from Minardi of old last year, helping him to double his chances of success.

Realising that to be the best you need to hire the best, he opened his chequebook to coax leading technical director Adrian Newey away from McLaren, helped in no small part by his number-one driver David Coulthard encouraging his old friend to cross the divide from the establishment to the arrivistes. Another change that may help Coulthard, and new signing Mark Webber, achieve the sort of results that were all but alien to Red Bull Racing last year is its new engine supplier. Put off by the inconsistency of the V8s it received from Ferrari in 2006, the team sought to transfer the second year of its deal to its junior team, Scuderia Toro Rosso, with the incoming Newey pressing for Renault V8s for 2007. And he won the battle, suggesting that if his RB3 – designed in conjunction with

## HISTORIC MOMENT

The Monaco GP of 1997 was only Stewart Grand Prix's fifth race, but the team with tartan-festooned cars came good and not only scored the first points for Jackie Stewart and the crew, but Rubens Barrichello collected a scintillating second place on this most famous street circuit, in front of its ranks of VIPs. He'd started tenth, but a stunning opening lap on a wet track promoted him to fifth. On the second lap, David Coulthard spun his McLaren at the Chicane and stalled, while team-mate Mika Hakkinen got caught up behind and bounced into Jean Alesi's Benetton. This became fourth a lap later when Williams' pole-sitter Heinz-Harald Frentzen struggled for grip on intermediate tyres. He demoted Frentzen's similarly shod team-mate Jacques Villeneuve three laps later, then got past Giancarlo Fisichella's Jordan a lap after that. And there Rubens stayed all the way to the finish, crossing the line 53s behind Michael Schumacher but well clear of Eddie Irvine in the second Ferrari. Monaco continued to be a happy hunting ground in all of the team's three phases, with Irvine finishing third for Jaguar Racing in 2001 and then Coulthard claiming third for Red Bull Racing last year.

former McLaren aerodynamicist Peter Prodromou – is as good as people reckon it is, then Coulthard and Webber ought to be in the points at every race and pushing for podium placings. Fabrice Lom has transferred from Renault to look after its new supply of French engines,

Can they succeed? It depends on whether the RB3 is suited to the Bridgestone spec tyres, with the team and five others – Renault, McLaren, Honda Racing, BMW Sauber and Scuderia Toro Rosso – also having to learn how to get the best out of Bridgestone rubber, putting them at a disadvantage against the likes of Ferrari, Toyota and Williams who ran them last season. This switch of tyre supplier will make having untroubled track time over the close-season all the more important.

Having a fast and experienced driver pairing will be welcome,

too, after last year's indecision over Christian Klien who had a trial mid-season which unnerved him. That he failed the test, largely blamelessly to most onlookers, was made clear when he was replaced by test driver Robert Doornbos for the final three grands prix, helping no one, certainly not Doornbos because the car was not at its best at the season's end. Running two experienced drivers this year ought to ensure car development is more effective, too.

What's not in doubt is, first, that the team will be anxious to avoid the cooling problems which it had last year, before the off, holding back the team in the opening grands prix which are often the easiest ones to gather points when other teams are struggling to find their feet with their new cars. Second, that sporting director Christian

Horner won't be tempted to make any wagers about diving naked into swimming pools should one of his drivers finish on the podium, as he did at Monaco last year. And third, that the "big rig" paddock hospitality will continue to dwarf those of its rivals, not just in size but entertainment

value. There will still be assorted celebrities dropping in. There may even be another tie-in, promoting a major feature film, as happened with *Superman Returns* at Monaco last year. But this is just the dressing because the real thrust of Red Bull Racing is increasingly about winning.

## FOR THE RECORD

| | |
|---|---|
| **Country of origin:** | England |
| **Team base:** | Milton Keynes, England |
| **Telephone:** | (44) 1908 279700 |
| **Website:** | www.redbullracing.com |
| **Active in Formula One:** | From 1997 (as Stewart until 2000 then Jaguar Racing until 2004) |
| **Grands Prix contested:** | 171 |
| **Wins:** | 1 |
| **Pole positions:** | 1 |
| **Fastest laps:** | 0 |

## 2006 DRIVERS & RESULTS

| Driver | Nationality | Races | Wins | Pts | Pos |
|---|---|---|---|---|---|
| **David Coulthard** | British | 18 | - | 14 | 13th |
| **Robert Doornbos** | Dutch | 3 | - | - | n/a |
| **Christian Klien** | Austrian | 15 | - | 2 | 18th |

## THE TEAM

| | |
|---|---|
| **Chairman:** | Dietrich Mateschitz |
| **Sporting director:** | Christian Horner |
| **Technical operations director:** | Adrian Newey |
| **Technical director:** | Mark Smith |
| **Head of race engineering:** | Paul Monaghan |
| **Chief designer:** | Rob Marshall |
| **Head of development:** | Anton Stipinovich |
| **Chief aerodynamicist:** | Peter Prodromou |
| **Team manager:** | Jonathan Wheatley |
| **Test driver:** | tba |
| **Chassis:** | Red Bull RB3 |
| **Engine:** | Renault V8 |
| **Tyres:** | Bridgestone |

Michael won the 1997 Monaco GP, but Rubens (left) had the bigger smile

# DAVID COULTHARD

**For the first time since he left McLaren, David can be compared with a team-mate of calibre in Mark Webber, so it will be interesting to see who comes out on top. If Red Bull advances, much of it will be thanks to David, for he is more than just a driver.**

If Adrian Newey produces one of his best chassis in this year's Red Bull RB3, and the team works its way out of the midfield mire to join the front-running teams like Ferrari, Renault and McLaren, David will deserve the accolades.

Newey said early last year that the 34-year-old Scot, a friend from the years they spent together at McLaren, was key to his joining the team. They have won together before, and team owner Dietrich Mateschitz will be praying that they can work the magic together to propel his team into the big time. Certainly, last May, there were thoughts that the team had got there when David finished third at Monaco in front of the great and the good. However, this result was something of a fluke and, apart from a flawless drive to fifth place in the wet at the Hungaroring, he had little to smile about.

Indeed, by the year's end, he wasn't smiling at all and even antagonised some of the team with comments about

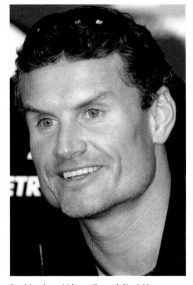

**David enjoyed his podium visit at Monaco so much that he wants many more in 2007**

their technical prowess that left him and Robert Doornbos scratching around with the minnows in the closing races. Let's hope that any such rifts have healed

over winter. However, in sporting director Christian Horner, David has a firm ally who appreciates his combination of speed and experience as well as his desire to spend more time on the podium.

## TRACK NOTES

| | |
|---|---|
| **Nationality:** | SCOTTISH |
| **Born:** | 27 MARCH 1971, TWYNHOLM, SCOTLAND |
| **Website:** | WWW.DAVIDCOULTHARD-F1.COM |
| **Teams:** | WILLIAMS 1994-95, McLAREN |
| | 1996-2004, RED BULL 2005-07 |

**CAREER RECORD**

| | |
|---|---|
| **First Grand Prix:** | 1994 SPANISH GP |
| **Grand Prix starts:** | 212 |
| **Grand Prix wins:** | 13 |
| | 1995 Portuguese GP, 1997 Australian GP, Italian GP, 1998 San Marino GP, 1999 British GP, Belgian GP, 2000 British GP, Monaco GP, French GP, 2001 Brazilian GP, Austrian GP, 2002 Monaco GP, 2003 Australian GP |
| **Poles:** | 12 |
| **Fastest laps:** | 18 |
| **Points:** | 513 |
| **Honours:** | 2001 FORMULA ONE RUNNER-UP, 1991 BRITISH FORMULA THREE RUNNER-UP & MACAU GP WINNER, 1989 McLAREN AUTOSPORT YOUNG DRIVER OF THE YEAR & BRITISH JUNIOR FORMULA FORD CHAMPION, 1988 SCOTTISH KART CHAMPION |

## HIS GREATEST WIN

**Aspiring drivers should note that almost every driver who reaches Formula One has been the man to beat in the junior categories. David is a good example because he waltzed through Formula Ford, Formula Opel and Formula Three. The final step before Formula One, then known as Formula 3000, proved harder but graduation to a Williams race seat after Ayrton Senna's death, in 1994, was the making of him. A little over a year later, he was a winner. But his best win came at the 2000 British GP. He'd won it the year before but this one was special. David qualified fourth and dived inside McLaren team-mate Mika Hakkinen at the first corner. He passed Heinz-Harald Frentzen's Jordan when it pitted, then closed on to the tail of Rubens Barrichello's Ferrari at the halfway point, slipstreaming it down the Hangar Straight and taking the lead around the outside at Stowe to send the crowd wild with delight.**

# MARK WEBBER

**You couldn't but help feel sorry for Mark last year. If there was speed to be extracted from the Williams, he would find it, but top results were denied him through poor reliability. He's now pinning his hopes on a ride with Red Bull Racing.**

Some might question whether this move was sensible because had Mark stayed with Williams, he'd now have Toyota engines. However, Red Bull expects more from its Renault engines this year than it got from its Ferraris in 2006. And you can be sure that this incredibly fit Australian will be giving his all to make sure that Red Bull outperforms Williams at the very least.

Last year, Mark's name was mentioned in connection with replacing Fernando Alonso at Renault, mainly due to his having the same manager, Flavio Briatore. But his name was on a Red Bull contract by August, with Mark attracted by the thought of getting his hands on this year's Adrian Newey-designed RB3.

Encouragingly for Mark, Red Bull mastermind Dietrich Mateschitz says that Mark is a character who exactly fits Red Bull's profile, and the pressure that he'll exert on established team leader David Coulthard will help the team score more points. In truth, this is inevitable because Red Bull tailed off terribly in the second half

No one doubts that Mark is a trier, but will a team change make him a winner?

of 2006, with all development of the RB2 being curtailed to concentrate the design team's efforts on this year's challenger. It had better be worth it because Mark is entering the sixth year of his Formula One

career, and needs to be going for that first win if he is to continue at the top level.

Being the newcomer in a team is seldom easy, even though he knows many of this crew from when the team was Jaguar Racing when he raced there, but one of Mark's strengths is that he is level-headed and gives 100 per cent, something that any team would find appealing as they put in the hours on behalf of their drivers.

## TRACK NOTES

| | |
|---|---|
| **Nationality:** | AUSTRALIAN |
| **Born:** | 27 AUGUST 1976, QUEANBEYAN, AUSTRALIA |
| **Website:** | WWW.MARKWEBBER.COM |
| **Teams:** | MINARDI 2002, JAGUAR 2003-04, WILLIAMS 2005-06, RED BULL RACING 2007 |

**CAREER RECORD**

| | |
|---|---|
| **First Grand Prix:** | 2002 AUSTRALIAN GP |
| **Grand Prix starts:** | 87 |
| **Grand Prix wins:** | 0 |
| | best result: third, 2005 Monaco GP |
| **Poles:** | 0 |
| **Fastest laps:** | 0 |
| **Points:** | 69 |
| **Honours:** | 2001 FORMULA 3000 RUNNER-UP, 1998 FIA GT RUNNER-UP, 1996 BRITISH FORMULA FORD RUNNER-UP & FORMULA FORD FESTIVAL WINNER |

## HIS GREATEST WIN

The biggest problem in Mark's career, when he headed to Europe after starring on the Australian Formula Ford scene, was a lack of money. Encouraged by his victory in the 1996 Formula Ford Festival at Brands Hatch, a timely injection of cash arrived to enable him to move up to Formula Three in 1997 and back at Brands Hatch he got a win. This was for the fourth round of the season, and his best result until then had been a pair of sixth places. But he put pace-setters Jonny Kane and Peter Dumbreck in his wake at the Kent circuit and won by a couple of seconds. Money remained tight, but rugby legend David Campese helped out and Mark was on his way to race in the FIA GT Championship for Mercedes and then to Formula 3000 and, eventually, to Formula One in 2002 with Minardi. This win – his only one of 1997 – made all the difference.

# WILLIAMS

**Seemingly nothing went right for Williams last year but, for 2007, the team has Toyota power to harness. Expect results to improve, Nico Rosberg to make forward moves in his second season and Alexander Wurz to relish racing again.**

Nico Rosberg and Alexander Wurz are hoping for great things

Secrets in Formula One are few and far between, but seemingly everyone in the paddock, and even beyond, knew of Williams' engine supplier for 2007. Then, finally, at the German GP late last July, the announcement was made that the team was to have works power again, with Toyota supplying its motivation.

Having had to pay for Cosworth engines in 2006 – which were perfectly competitive but less than reliable as proved by an engine failure for each driver in practice at the European GP – made a dent in the team's budget. So this deal with Toyota is a great advance for this once great team which has underachieved of late (newer fans may not even be aware that Williams was once the team, the one to be beaten before McLaren, Williams, Ferrari and, recently, Renault took control. Add to this the signing of a new lead sponsor, American telecoms giant AT&T, and you can't help but think that things are about to improve.

The personnel are key to this and crucial changes have been made to the team's structure to ensure that a superior car-engine-tyres package can be crafted. To this end, technical director Sam Michael is having his job reclassified so that he doesn't have to perform seemingly every task at the grands prix. In fact, he is to be factory-based to take a firmer grip on the technical department. Having been saddled last year with the FW28, a car that notably didn't set new standards in aerodynamic efficiency but produced an acceptable level of downforce, Jon Tomlinson has been brought in from Renault to head the aerodynamics division, with McLaren also being raided for the services of Amit Chakraborty, with Loic Bigois continuing to work in this department.

Frank Williams reckons that poor mechanical reliability cost the team as many as 30 championship points in 2006, which would have propelled them from their dismal ranking of eighth out of 11 to fifth, ahead of BMW Sauber and Toyota. To this end, following Jorg Zander's departure to BMW Sauber after a seven-month stay, Ed Wood has been appointed as the team's new chief designer and he will be supported by ex-Jaguar Racing designer John Russell, who worked at Williams long ago.

Looking at the strength of these appointments, you can see that Williams and director of engineering, Patrick Head, have decided to give it their best shot to get the team back in front, where it used to be in the 1980s and 1990s when they were both hands-on in every department, bursting with their fighting attitude.

One of the keys to ironing out the worst of the problems was to get the Toyota V8 integrated quickly and then have a full winter of testing. Narain Karthikeyan was kept on for this purpose, and worked with long-time tester Alexander Wurz who stepped up to fill one of the race seats after Mark Webber's departure for Red Bull Racing. An FW28 was adapted especially for this purpose so that testing could start immediately.

It'll be interesting to see how Wurz gets on in place of Webber alongside Nico Rosberg in 2007 because he was an impressive driver for Benetton in the late 1990s before he lost his ride

and became a test driver with McLaren from 2001-05 before joining Williams last year. And don't forget that he finished third at Imola when he stood in for Juan Pablo Montoya in 2005, and was frequently top of the Friday practice sessions last year.

So, with engines from Toyota, good drivers in Rosberg and Wurz, although perhaps not quite from the top drawer, a year's experience of Bridgestone

tyres and, it is hoped, a more balanced technical line-up, perhaps Williams will start to flex its muscles again and prove that this once great team isn't on a downward spiral as its front men Williams and Head grow ever older than the drivers and staff. At a time when manufacturers hover over the sport, it's imperative for the soul of Formula One that real people succeed.

## FOR THE RECORD

| Country of origin: | England |
| --- | --- |
| Team base: | Grove, England |
| Telephone: | (44) 01235 777700 |
| Website: | www.williamsf1.com |
| Active in Formula One: | From 1972 |
| Grands Prix contested: | 533 |
| Wins: | 113 |
| Pole positions: | 125 |
| Fastest laps: | 129 |

## 2006 DRIVERS & RESULTS

| Driver | Nationality | Races | Wins | Pts | Pos |
| --- | --- | --- | --- | --- | --- |
| Nico Rosberg | German | 18 | - | 4 | 17th |
| Mark Webber | Australian | 18th | - | 7 | 14th |

## THE TEAM

| | |
| --- | --- |
| Team principal: | Sir Frank Williams |
| Director of engineering: | Patrick Head |
| Chief executive officer: | Adam Parr |
| Technical director: | Sam Michael |
| Chief designer: | Ed Wood |
| Head of aerodynamics: | Jon Tomlinson |
| Team manager: | Tim Newton |
| Test drivers: | Narain Karthikeyan & Kazuki Nakajima |
| Chassis: | Williams FW29 |
| Engine: | Toyota V8 |
| Tyres: | Bridgestone |

Smoking in the pitlane was still common when Pescarolo raced in 1972

# NICO ROSBERG

**Sir Jackie Stewart described Nico early last year as "the next global megastar" and it was easy to understand why. But Nico lost his way and crashed too much, and needs to show that he might match his father Keke and become world champion.**

Doing too well too soon can be a curse not a boost. So, when Nico stormed last year's opening round in Bahrain, pitting for a new nose after an early clash and then setting the race's fastest lap as he stormed up the order to finish seventh on his Formula One debut, it was assumed that a star had been born and that the 2005 GP2 champion would go on to win races before long.

Of course, Formula One doesn't work like that, success proving considerably harder to achieve, and it proved a flash in the pan because Williams was unable to challenge, let alone match, Renault and Ferrari after that. Or even McLaren. Indeed, experts soon realised that the cooler-than-expected temperatures at the Bahrain desert track had led to a tyre which wasn't graining, and was able to tolerate Nico's style of driving, drifting the car where possible. At subsequent races, where the weather conditions were guessed more accurately and the tyre compound was pre-selected

Nico knows that the team expects solid results in his second campaign

with greater accuracy, the tyre choice failed to assist him and his drifting style counted against him, graining his tyres.

There were mistakes, too, like his accidents in the German and Brazilian GPs, with the latter being the more embarrassing because he took out his own team-mate, Mark Webber.

However, Nico is known for his brains as well as his film-star looks, and he is sure to spend the winter working out what is needed to make him more effective in this second season in the big time. A Toyota V8 behind his shoulders should certainly help as will being able to carry a year of experience into the season ahead.

## TRACK NOTES

| | |
|---|---|
| **Nationality:** | GERMAN |
| **Born:** | 27 JUNE 1985, WIESBADEN, GERMANY |
| **Website:** | WWW.NICOROSBERG.COM |
| **Teams:** | WILLIAMS 2006-07 |

| CAREER RECORD | |
|---|---|
| **First Grand Prix:** | 2006 BAHRAIN GP |
| **Grand Prix starts:** | 18 |
| **Grand Prix wins:** | 0 |
| | best result: seventh, 2006 Bahrain GP, European GP |
| **Poles:** | 0 |
| **Fastest laps:** | 1 |
| **Points:** | 4 |
| **Honours:** | 2005 GP2 CHAMPION, 2002 FORMULA BMW CHAMPION |

## HIS GREATEST WIN

Put into karts at an early age by his father – 1982 World Champion Keke – Nico scorched to the Formula BMW title in his first year of car racing in 2002. Solid development followed in European Formula Three series over the course of the next two years. But it was what happened in Formula One's feeder formula – GP2 – that put his name up in lights in 2005. He was driving for Nicolas Todt's crack ART team, but Heikki Kovalainen was pre-season favourite and set the early pace. However, Nico started winning by mid-season and they both went to the final round in Bahrain with a shot at the title. Nico displayed Keke's mettle, though, and won both races to claim the championship. It was small wonder that Williams – the team with which Keke won his world title – snapped him up on a multi-year deal. He rewarded them almost immediately on his return to Bahrain for the first race of 2006 when he set fastest lap and was the star of the race.

# ALEXANDER WURZ

He's back, but some may say that he's never been away since he was dropped by Benetton. Indeed, Alex has seldom been out of a Formula One car since. It's just that, until 2006, he plied his craft in private tests rather than in grands prix.

When Williams became aware that Mark Webber's manager Flavio Briatore was looking to move the Australian across to Renault once Fernando Alonso had made public his signing for McLaren for 2007, Sir Frank Williams started looking around for a driver of similar calibre. And he found one right under his nose, a driver whom he had described in January last year as "the best in the business". This was Alexander Wurz.

Alex had been with Williams only for a year but, since 2001, had been pounding the test tracks for McLaren except when he stood in for the injured Juan Pablo Montoya at the 2005 San Marino GP and promptly proved that he hadn't lost his ability to race by finishing in fourth place, which became third when Jenson Button (who'd finished third) was disqualified. No wonder the team had no qualms about promoting him.

In fact, when he was given his Formula One break midway through 1997 by Benetton, when fellow Austrian Gerhard Berger missed a few races through ill

No longer will Alex have to watch from the sidelines, as he's racing again

health, he made a major impact. He stepped up from testing duties to finish third on his third outing, at Silverstone. He then matched team-mate Giancarlo Fisichella in 1998, but was edged out over the following two years and forced to seek employment as a test driver. Now that Alex is back in the driving seat, he has got a chance to put his name back in lights. He has certainly timed his arrival well because Williams gets Toyota power for 2007. Combine this with his top-rate technical input and even the works Toyota team will have to watch out. Whatever happens, it's good that this rapid gentleman is back.

## TRACK NOTES

| | |
|---|---|
| **Nationality:** | AUSTRIAN |
| **Born:** 15 FEBRUARY 1974, WAIDHOFEN, AUSTRIA | |
| **Website:** | WWW.WURZ.COM |
| **Teams:** BENETTON 1997-2000, McLAREN 2005, WILLIAMS 2007 | |

| CAREER RECORD | |
|---|---|
| **First Grand Prix:** | 1997 CANADIAN GP |
| **Grand Prix starts:** | 53 |
| **Grand Prix wins:** | 0 |
| | best result: third, 1997 British GP |
| **Poles:** | 0 |
| **Fastest laps:** | 1 |
| **Points:** | 32 |
| **Honours:** 1996 LE MANS 24 HOURS WINNER, 1994 GERMAN FORMULA THREE RUNNER-UP, 1993 AUSTRIAN FORMULA THREE CHAMPION, 1992 GERMAN & AUSTRIAN FORMULA FORD CHAMPION | |

## HIS GREATEST WIN

A world champion on two wheels, in BMX, before turning to four and starring in Formula Ford, Alex's career reached a turning point after his second year in the German Formula Three series in 1995 when he slumped to sixth after finishing as runner-up in his rookie season. He turned to touring cars and failed to shine for Opel, but the 1996 Le Mans 24 Hours went like a dream and he won the world's most famous sports car race at his first attempt in a Joest-run Porsche WSC95, beating the works 911s in something of an upset result, partnered by American Davy Jones and Germany's Manuel Reuter. Alex became the event's youngest ever winner at the age of 22. Suitably impressed, Mercedes snapped him up for its GT campaign for 1997 and, before the year was out, he'd broken into Formula One with Benetton and finished third in the British GP, kicking off a relationship which lasted until 2000.

# SCUDERIA TORO ROSSO

Thanks to their shared sponsorship, last year's Scuderia Toro Rosso racing cars looked like the Red Bulls. This year, the similarity will be greater still, but the Toro Rossos will have Ferrari engines in their tails and be out for points.

The drivers will be hoping that points finishes will be the norm

## FOR THE RECORD

| | |
|---|---|
| Country of origin: | Italy |
| Team base: | Faenza, Italy |
| Telephone: | (39) 546 696111 |
| Website: | www.scuderiatorosso.com |
| Active in Formula One: | From 1985 (as Minardi until 2005) |
| Grands Prix contested: | 359 |
| Wins: | 0 |
| Pole positions: | 0 |
| Fastest laps: | 0 |

## DRIVERS' 2006 STATISTICS

| Driver | Nationality | Races | Wins | Pts | Pos |
|---|---|---|---|---|---|
| Vitantonio Liuzzi | Italian | 18 | - | 1 | 19th |
| Scott Speed | American | 18 | - | - | n/a |

## THE TEAM

| | |
|---|---|
| Team owners: | Dietrich Mateschitz & Gerhard Berger |
| Team principal: | Franz Tost |
| General director: | Gianfranco Fantuzzi |
| Technical director: | Alex Hitzinger |
| Chief designer: | Ben Butler |
| Chief engineer: | Laurent Mekies |
| Team manager: | Massimo Rivola |
| Test driver: | tba |
| Chassis: | Scuderia Toro Rosso STR02 |
| Engine: | Ferrari V8 |
| Tyres: | Bridgestone |

The metamorphosis of tail-ender Minardi into Scuderia Toro Rosso was a remarkable one last year. Many of the personnel were the same, but the livery made the cars look like mid-grid Red Bulls, and the ambition was to move forward. More to the point, the ambition was backed up with money, something that was always short in the Minardi days, but something of which Red Bull owner Dietrich Mateschitz has a prodigious amount.

Gerhard Berger, former grand prix winner and co-owner of the team, has a three-year plan to take the team to the top. This is year two. To this end, Toro Rosso is planning to run the same chassis as its sister team Red Bull Racing, that's to say the latest Adrian Newey design. There were disputes over intellectual property, but the outcome is that Toro Rosso will have a cutting-edge chassis with Ferrari power. No longer will they stand out alone for using restricted V10s against every other team's V8s.

Berger is the main man, but Franz Tost is in charge of the day-to-day running. Alex Hitzinger has taken over from Gabriele Tredozi as technical director, and Jim Wright has arrived from Williams to upgrade the commercial side. The drivers will remain the same, with Berger keen to build on a stable base.

# VITANTONIO LIUZZI

**This flamboyant Italian has proved his ability in Formula One and now wants the machinery to help him shine.**

Kept on tenterhooks by Red Bull Racing in 2005, when he was given just four race outings, Vitantonio enjoyed last year when he was allowed to race from start to finish. And race he did, going as well as the machinery beneath him would allow. In his case, it was a car sourced from the 2005 Red Bull but run by the Minardi team of old, now under the name of Scuderia Toro Rosso. Unusually, it was allowed to race on with a V10 engine with all rival teams changing to V8s.

Whatever the situation, Vitantonio put some shine back on the strong reputation he'd brought with him from Formula 3000 with a trio of tenth-place finishes, but most of all eighth at the United States GP, the team's only point all year. The low point of the year was having a 170mph crash when testing for the senior Red Bull team at Silverstone, and any hopes of graduating to Red Bull were blocked by Mark Webber joining from Williams, but he'll effectively have the same chassis as Webber in 2007, albeit with Ferrari rather than Renault power.

*Correct at the time of going to press.*

# SCOTT SPEED

**Despite the flashes of speed in Scott's maiden year, this will be the season when we find out how good he is.**

How frustrating it must have been for this young American in his rookie year of Formula One, as few could evaluate his performance. For starters, he was driving for a team that used to be Minardi, and driving a car that used to be a Red Bull. In addition, he was driving with a (restricted) V10 engine and everyone else bar his team-mate Vitantonio Liuzzi was using a V8. Indeed, Liuzzi was his only benchmark and, by the end of the season, they were pretty close on form. Unlike his team-mate, Scott failed to score, although he had a point taken away from him after being demoted from eighth to 11th in the Australian GP for overtaking under yellow flags. He then added to his feisty reputation - there were crashes, and his collision with Ralf Schumacher in the British GP stands out - by picking up a $5,000 fine for arguing with the stewards.

*Correct at the time of going to press.*

# SPYKER MF1 RACING

The Spyker MF1 team has a new look for 2007 and, impressively, its cars will be powered by Ferrari horsepower. In addition, leading technical mastermind Mike Gascoyne has been added to help improve the team's technical progress.

There were no points in 2006, but this may change in 2007

There has seldom been such a time of change for the teams in the drop zone behind Formula One's midfield, but Minardi changed last year to Scuderia Toro Rosso and what was Jordan became Midland and then Spyker MF1 after Michiel Mol orchestrated a take-over from former owner Alex Shnaider. This year is when the changes to this Silverstone-based team will become truly apparent, with the new Dutch owner – the Spyker sports car company – helping to land a deal to replace its Toyota V8s with Ferrari motors for 2007.

The livery is fresh and new, too, but it will be what happens beneath the skin that really counts with former Toyota technical director now running the technical side, effectively joining up with some of the crew who stayed on from when the team was Jordan, including technical director James Key. Unusually, he's not being bullish, reckoning that their best chance of moving up the order will come in 2008 when the regulations change. The fact that he couldn't join the team until last October, when his Toyota contract had run its course, means his input into this year's chassis is less than the team would have liked.

Colin Kolles stays on as the team principal, but Johnny Herbert is no longer sporting director and will return to the cockpit in sports car racing.

## FOR THE RECORD

| | |
|---|---|
| Country of origin: | England |
| Team base: | Silverstone, England |
| Telephone: | (44) 01327 850800 |
| Website: | www.spykerf1.com |
| Active in Formula One: | From 1991 (as Midland until 2006) |
| Grands Prix contested: | 268 |
| Wins: | 4 |
| Pole positions: | 2 |
| Fastest laps: | 2 |

## DRIVERS' 2006 STATISTICS

| Driver | Nationality | Races | Wins | Pts | Pos |
|---|---|---|---|---|---|
| Christijan Albers | Dutch | 18 | - | - | n/a |
| Tiago Monteiro | Portuguese | 18 | - | - | n/a |

## THE TEAM

| | |
|---|---|
| Team owner: | Michiel Mol |
| Team principal: | Colin Kolles |
| Chief technical officer: | Mike Gascoyne |
| Technical director: | James Key |
| Head of design: | John McQuilliam |
| Head of aerodynamics: | Simon Phillips |
| Chief engineer: | Dominic Harlow |
| Team manager: | Andy Stevenson |
| Test driver: | tba |
| Chassis: | Spyker MF1 2007 |
| Engine: | Ferrari V8 |
| Tyres: | Bridgestone |

# CHRISTIJAN ALBERS

**Christijan deserves a break. Having compatriot Michiel Mol bring money to the team might be just what he needs.**

This is the second time that Christijan has had reason to thank Michiel Mol. Last year, after a solid but unspectacular campaign with Minardi in 2005, he found himself without a drive when the team was sold. In stepped Mol and bought him a ride with Midland. Then, before the year was out, he bought the team and brought in money from the Spyker car company. Christijan owes him big time.

Christijan is looking forward to the team having money to develop its car this year and, it is hoped, that'll cure the lack of reliability that appeared to hit him particularly hard last year. A pair of tenth-place finishes in Australia and Hungary were a decent reward for driving hard, but he craves points. And real points, unlike the four he earned for finishing fifth in the 2005 United States GP when only six cars started.

Perhaps the main reason that a rare smile ought to creep on to Christijan's face is that Mike Gascoyne joined last November as chief technical officer, and all changes are likely to be positive. Having a Ferrari V8 engine behind his shoulders ought to be a thrill – even with the rev limiters that are mandatory for 2007.

# ADRIAN SUTIL

**Michael Schumacher has retired, so now it's time for the next generation of German drivers to come through.**

Adrian is one such driver, a bright light who has waltzed through the junior formulae and impressed sufficiently when he had a trio of runs as the Midland team's third driver last year. The person he impressed the most was team principal Colin Kolles, a man who happened to give Adrian his Formula Three break back in 2004.

The key to Adrian taking the second seat as team-mate to Christijan Albers is his potential. Simply comparing his age, 23 to Monteiro's 30, is one way of doing this. But his CV is superior too, with strong form shown in his second year of Formula Three when he finished as runner-up to new McLaren signing Lewis Hamilton, before going on to win last year's Japanese Formula Three title. Add to this the way that he took first to Germany's A1GP car and then to last year's Midland Formula One car showed that he can handle powerful single-seaters and has the ability to build upon.

# SUPER AGURI RACING

**It came, it saw, it took part and it survived. Best of all, it advanced. This year, with the luxury of a little planning, Super Aguri will do even better. Adding Anthony Davidson to the driving force should provide the team with speed and focus.**

Takuma Sato really enjoyed the challenge of 2006

It was on, it was off, then it was on again, and it was called Super Aguri Racing after founder and former grand prix driver Aguri Suzuki. Honda helped with the engines and this year will be helping with the chassis it used in 2006, no doubt tweaked to keep it different in the eyes of its rivals. It will be a step up from the hurriedly upgraded version of the 2002 Arrows A23 it had at the start of last year, before upgrading to the SA06 mid-season. With this improved pedigree, derived from the car that won last year's Hungarian GP don't forget, the SA07 will be a huge step forward.

Lead driver Takuma Sato will welcome the upturn in potential,

as will Anthony Davidson, a driver who knows this car intimately, having been Honda's test driver last year. For 2007, Super Aguri plans to field just the two drivers, not four like through the course of the World Championship last year.

There have been a host of staff moves, with Mark Preston promoted from chief technical officer to technical director, and chief race engineer Graham Taylor becoming sporting director, rewarding those who helped move Super Aguri from being 7 per cent off the leading pace when they started to 3 per cent. Indeed, there was no clearer illustration of their progress than Sato's run to tenth place in the final round in Brazil.

## FOR THE RECORD

| | |
|---|---|
| Country of origin: | England |
| Team base: | Witney, England |
| Telephone: | (44) 0993 871600 |
| Website: | www.saf1.com |
| Active in Formula One: | From 2006 |
| Grands Prix contested: | 18 |
| Wins: | 0 |
| Pole positions: | 0 |
| Fastest laps: | 0 |

## DRIVERS' 2006 STATISTICS

| Driver | Nationality | Races | Wins | Pts | Pos |
|---|---|---|---|---|---|
| Yuji Ide | Japanese | 4 | - | - | n/a |
| Franck Montagny | French | 7 | - | - | n/a |
| Takuma Sato | Japanese | 18 | - | - | n/a |
| Sakon Yamamoto | Japanese | 7 | - | - | n/a |

## THE TEAM

| | |
|---|---|
| Team principal: | Aguri Suzuki |
| Managing director: | Daniele Audetto |
| Technical director: | Mark Preston |
| Sporting director: | Graham Taylor |
| Chief designer: | Peter McCool |
| Team manager: | Mick Ainsley-Cowlishaw |
| Test driver: | Giedo van der Gardo |
| Chassis: | Super Aguri SA07 |
| Engine: | Honda V8 |
| Tyres: | Bridgestone |

# TAKUMA SATO

**Takuma worked wonders with a brand-new team, and he will be praying that the progress continues into 2007.**

Takuma is a delightful individual with a ready smile, but the mega-watt grin that illuminated his face after the final round at Interlagos last October was one of the sights of the season. This was because he had finished tenth, effectively as the best of the rest after the top five teams. Behind him came Scuderia Toro Rosso, Red Bull Racing and Spyker MF1. And that, ladies and gentlemen, marked a considerable advance for the team which was only just ready for the opening round, starting its campaign with an updated 2002 chassis. Super Aguri Racing had arrived.

The Japanese understand and appreciate the concept of a challenge and Takuma's image will have been transformed from that of the driver who wasn't quite the ticket at Jordan then BAR, with Jenson Button outscoring him 38 points to one in 2005.

Takuma's aim for 2007 is to build on this improvement and to remain the top dog within the team when former Formula Three team-mate Anthony Davidson is expected to push him very hard indeed. It's more than possible that the challenge from within will force better form still from Takuma.

## TRACK NOTES

| Nationality: | JAPANESE |
| --- | --- |
| **Born:** | 28 JANUARY 1977, TOKYO, JAPAN |
| **Website:** | WWW.TAKUMASATO.COM |
| **Teams:** | JORDAN 2002, BAR 2003-05, |
| | SUPER AGURI RACING 2006-07 |

### CAREER RECORD

| First Grand Prix: | 2002 AUSTRALIAN GP |
| --- | --- |
| **Grand Prix starts:** | 72 |
| **Grand Prix wins:** | 0 |
| | best result: third, 2004 US GP |
| **Poles:** | 0 |
| **Fastest laps:** | 0 |
| **Points:** | 40 |
| **Honours:** | 2001 BRITISH FORMULA |
| | THREE CHAMPION |

# ANTHONY DAVIDSON

**At long last, Anthony is being given a full season and a chance to show that he can race as well as drive fast.**

Every driver wants to have his talents respected, and Anthony's certainly are. It's just that he wants to be seen as a racing driver and not just a test driver, even if he is a test driver par excellence.

Anthony is going to embrace the second Super Aguri seat, and he certainly has a strong knowledge of the car because the Super Aguri SA07 is unlikely to be significantly different from the Honda RA106 which he tested again and again last year, and in which he was frequently the fastest in the Friday sessions as he battled with Alex Wurz and Robert Kubica to be fastest of the teams' third drivers.

Apart from an all-but-abortive race with BAR in Malaysia in 2005 and two outings for Minardi in 2002, Anthony hasn't raced since 2001 when he drove in British Formula Three and all but overcame his team-mate then, who will be his team-mate now, Takuma Sato.

## TRACK NOTES

| Nationality: | BRITISH |
| --- | --- |
| **Born:** | 18 APRIL 1979, HEMEL HEMPSTEAD, ENGLAND |
| **Website:** | WWW.ANTHONYDAVIDSON.INFO |
| **Teams:** | MINARDI 2002, BAR 2005, |
| | SUPER AGURI 2007 |

### CAREER RECORD

| First Grand Prix: | 2002 HUNGARIAN GP |
| --- | --- |
| **Grand Prix starts:** | 3 |
| **Wins:** | 0 |
| **Pole positions:** | 0 |
| **Fastest laps:** | 0 |
| **Points:** | 0 |
| **Honours:** | 2000 McLAREN AUTOSPORT BRDC |
| YOUNG DRIVER & FORMULA FORD FESTIVAL WINNER | |

# THE RISE OF THE YOUNG GUNS

Formula One can be something of a closed shop to the young and talented, but there are signs that the best of the young guns are being groomed for stardom by the major teams and will get their chance.

There had been a spell in the 1980s when there was almost no movement in the driver market. Gerhard Berger, Nigel Mansell, Nelson Piquet, Alain Prost and Ayrton Senna were happy to stay where they were, enjoying the financial rewards but making Formula One stale in the process. Death on the track was by then no longer a factor, reducing the opportunities for drivers wanting to break into the top category. Many had to bide their time, and many didn't graduate. Now, things are very different and Formula One is open to young hopefuls like never before, even though there are just 22 race seats. And that's thanks to the manufacturers.

As a way of maximising their financial commitment, the manufacturers are getting the best young drivers on their books to ensure that none of their rivals picks a potential world champion. It's a long-term policy, with some drivers needing two or three years of development before they are ready, but the benefits to the manufacturers can be huge.

Renault didn't bring Fernando Alonso to Formula One but took over his management when he raced for Minardi in 2001, used him as a test driver in 2002 and the rest is history, with his first world title in the bag by 2005 at just 24 years of age. They're now hoping that Heikki Kovalainen, a driver they've nurtured since his second year of car racing in 2002, will hit the big time.

Renault (like most other teams) does not just finance the climb through the junior ranks or run juniors in endless tests, but teaches them the skills required to be a top driver, including fitness and diet instruction, dealing with the media, and how to work with a team of engineers. Renault put Argentina's Jose Maria Lopez and Brazil's Lucas di Grassi under its Renault driver development scheme in GP2 in 2006, but neither shone as brightly as champion Lewis Hamilton (more of whom later) or

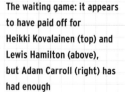

The waiting game: it appears to have paid off for Heikki Kovalainen (top) and Lewis Hamilton (above), but Adam Carroll (right) has had enough

Three to watch: Robert Kubica (above, on right) showed the way for the new generation with third on his third outing, while Sebastian Vettel (right) and Nelson Piquet Jr have testing contracts

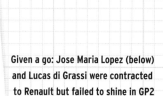

Given a go: Jose Maria Lopez (below) and Lucas di Grassi were contracted to Renault but failed to shine in GP2

runner-up Nelson Piquet Jr, with the latter being rewarded with a Renault testing contract. Robert Kubica, who starred late last year with BMW Sauber, was once a Renault development driver, but it was his speed in his inaugural Formula One test with Renault that led BMW to snap him up as its 2006 test driver. Third place in just his third grand prix proved that BMW had stolen a march on Renault.

BMW – a manufacturer with more of a background in touring car racing – concentrate on the entry-level, single-seater Formula BMW, offering a Formula One test to the winner of its end-of-season World Finals. BMW has already propelled 2004 German Formula BMW champion Sebastian Vettel into its test line-up with spectacular results.

German rival Mercedes will be hoping that McLaren's investment in Lewis Hamilton will yield similar success. McLaren and Hamilton go way back, with Lewis having had the guts to approach McLaren boss Ron Dennis at an awards ceremony (when Lewis was still racing karts) and ask, "How about it?" Mercedes also gave Michael Schumacher a leg-up in the 1990s when they picked him for their sports car team as he struggled to

finance his graduation from Formula Three. Without that, who knows what might have become of the driver who became Formula One's most titled racer?

Honda and Toyota also have young drivers on their books but, amazingly, last year Adam Carroll asked to be released from his contract with Honda. To many, this was career suicide, but he reckoned that there weren't enough rides available with Honda, and that he was limiting his options. In the hope of greater things, he won't be the last to get out of a multi-year deal.

Perhaps because Ferrari is Formula One's most established manufacturer, they have never brought along talent. True, Felipe Massa was nurtured as a test driver in 2005, but this was largely because his career was being managed by the son of the Ferrari supreme, Jean Todt.

# KNOW THE TRACKS 2007

**Subtle tweaks have given this year's FIA Formula One World Championship a different feel. Germany will no longer host two grands prix, and Italy has lost its second one, the one which is run as the San Marino GP. There are no new venues for 2007, although the return of Japan's Fuji Speedway after a 30-year gap and a major revamp make it all but new.**

After a succession of new countries have been added to the Formula One roster over the past decade, with Turkey following Bahrain, China and Malaysia, it's good to note that the major change for 2007 is the return of the Fuji Speedway circuit, used just twice by Formula One. The first of these occasions, in 1976, was one of the most famous championship finals in memory, between James Hunt and Niki Lauda in the pouring rain. The following year's race resulted in the death of a marshal and a spectator. The Japanese GP remained off the calendar until Suzuka claimed the race in 1987. Now, having been reshaped at considerable expense by Toyota,

Fuji is back, an exciting circuit on the slopes of one of Japan's most emblematic landmarks, Mount Fuji. Honda-owned Suzuka does not plan to stay on the sidelines for long, though, with talk of it hosting a Pacific GP in the future.

It's also worth noting that countries aren't finding it so easy to host one grand prix under their own name and a second under a courtesy title. Germany has just lost one of its two races, the European GP, with Nurburgring (above) getting the nod to host the German GP this year as the start of a taking-it-in-turns arrangement.

Ferrari fans will no longer be treated specially either, with Italy failing to hold on to its pair of races, despite Imola agreeing to modernise and extend its pits and paddock so that it could continue to hold the San Marino GP.

As for the other 14 grands prix on the calendar, the Australian GP has regained its position as the season's opening event, with the Bahrain GP dropping behind the Malaysian GP. This trio of venues emphasises how much variety there is in the Formula One circus, with a temporary circuit in a city park followed by a pair of purpose-built ones in rainforest heat and humidity, followed by one in the heat and aridity of a desert.

Each circuit visited has a unique format and particular atmosphere, with Barcelona's Circuit de Catalunya having become a cauldron of excitement since Fernando Alonso hit the big time. Monaco couldn't be more different with its tight circuit past the casino and along the waterfront, under the noses of the glitterati. Then comes a brief break from the European heart of the World Championship with a North American double-header. The island-bound Circuit Gilles Villeneuve in Montreal couldn't be more different to the infield circuit with its flat-out blast around the Turn 1 banking at the fabled Indianapolis Motor Speedway. All team owners and sponsors cheered last summer that a good show was put on in front of the American fans after the six-car débâcle of 2005.

The high-speed open layouts of Magny-Cours and Silverstone are succeeded by the increasingly tight confines of the Nurburgring and the Hungaroring, with the Hungarian venue praying that lightning will strike in the same place twice and produce a race even half as good as last year's wet classic in which Jenson Button scored his first win.

Turkey was in disgrace for irregularities in its podium ceremony when politics tried to piggy-back itself on the event, but no race fan would want it to be lost because the Istanbul Park circuit has proved a major hit since its debut in 2005. After Monza, hallelujah, the magnificent Spa-Francorchamps is back to wave the banner as Formula One's finest venue and bring down the curtain on the European sector.

The vastness of the Shanghai International Circuit and the mountainside beauty of Fuji Speedway add a cosmopolitan difference, before the down-at-heel but full-of-passion Interlagos brings the championship trail to its conclusion with a blast of Brazilian heat to contrast with the northern European autumn.

Among the nations clamouring to land a grand prix is Poland, a former communist country hugely excited by the meteoric rise of Robert Kubica on to the world stage. A site outside Gdansk has been earmarked, but the trick is to have the considerable finance in place. Too many organisers have been let down the hard way.

# MELBOURNE

**Back as the season-opener, this is the circuit on which the drivers hope that their teams' labours through the winter months will enable them to make a winning start.**

In 2006, Formula One came to Albert Park for the third grand prix of the season to avoid clashing with the Commonwealth Games in Melbourne, but in 2007 it resumed its traditional position as the opening race of the season. This is the meeting above all others at which the markers are laid down for the season ahead.

The first corner produces trouble year after year. It's an openish right feeding into a similar left, and the gravel traps are usually visited by several cars on the opening lap. The drivers' view then narrows on the run down the concrete barrier-lined and tree-overhung straight to Turn 3, a tight right that catches out more than a few. There was incident aplenty at Turn 3 last year, with cars bouncing off each other at this tight right. Good exit speed is vital before drivers plunge back into darkness under an avenue of trees.

The nature of the track changes after Turn 6 as the trees drop away as the track opens out on to a stretch between the golf course and lake with a long, arcing left after a tight chicane. Things get hairy at Turns 11 and 12, and Turn 13 was the scene of Christian Klien's dramatic departure in 2006, after which there's a return to overhanging trees and 90-degree bends to complete the lap, with the final corner famously tricky, as Michael Schumacher discovered last year.

One thing that keeps the teams on their toes is the weather, as a swing in temperature can change the level of grip enormously.

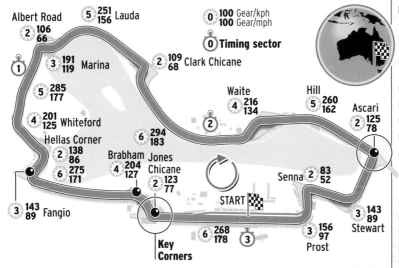

**2006 POLE TIME: Button (Honda)**
1m25.229s, 139.178mph/223.975kph
**2006 FASTEST LAP: Raikkonen (McLaren)**
1m26.045s, 137.863mph/221.859kph

**2006 WINNER'S AVERAGE SPEED:**
119.297mph/191.981kph
**LAP RECORD: M Schumacher (Ferrari)**
1m24.125s, 141.016mph/226.933kph, 2004

# SEPANG

## The drivers really have to work for their living in the heat and humidity of Malaysia, but they all love the circuit for the overtaking opportunities it offers.

Nobody watching the Malaysian GP from the comfort of an armchair can get close to imagining how hostile is the environment. Hot doesn't even start to cover it. Body-sapping is the norm, but it's the humidity that is the killer, making walking more than a handful of paces enough to make you feel as though you're melting. So, drinking as much as possible and taking salt is the order of the day, for drivers and mechanics.

The track itself is one of Hermann Tilke's best. It's sinuous, flowing, fast and varied. Even better, it's unusally wide so there's plenty of overtaking. The first likely place comes right at the start of the lap, at Turn 1, a corner that turns back on itself and a good line in doesn't always become a good line

out as rivals try to dive down the inside and collisions are a constant danger, with nose wings often taking a battering.

Positioning a car for entry to Turn 2 is vital because it dictates your speed through the twisting run down to Turn 4, Langkawi. This is a really tricky, sharp corner, with a rising entry and a flattening exit. The track flows beautifully through two fast and sweeping corners to Turn 7, with overtaking possible into the Turn 9 hairpin given a good exit out of Turn 8.

After a series of futher twists, with the gently downhill Turn 12 quite a shocker, you need a good exit from Turn 14 to give a good run up the back straight for a shot at passing into the final hairpin.

**Local attractions:** For buzzing city life, few places can top Kuala Lumpur. It's a combination of sky-scraping office blocks with modern malls and ramshackle markets. The view from the top of the Menara TV Tower – so high up it's like being in a plane just after take-off – gives a clear indication of the pace of change. Langkawi Island is also well worth a visit, and you might find a driver or two 'acclimatising' on the beach.

**Best view:** Anywhere there's shade, given the soaring temperatures. But best of all is the view from the pit exit at the end of the main grandstand, taking in the cars as they brake from 180mph into Turn 1, before they twist through Turn 2 and head off again.

**Best for action:** Turns 1 and 2 always produce a mêlée of action on the opening lap, but the place that delivers, lap after lap, is the entrance to the final corner, Turn 15. Look down from the shady grandstand as driver after driver attempts to prove the master of late-braking into this left-hand hairpin. The track is wide on entry and exit, allowing room for experimentation.

**0** 100 Gear/kph
**0** 100 Gear/mph

**Ⓞ Timing sector**

**Key Corners**

2 103
64 Langkawi

5 255
160 Genting
Turn 5 4 174
109

3 123
77 Turn 3

2 85
53

Turn 2 1 78
49

🏁 START

2 106
66

Turn 7
4 193
120

Pangkor Laut chicane 6 303
190

3

1 76
47

4 200
125 Klia

Sunway Lagoon 2 114
71

3 193
120 Turn 10

Turn 12 5 247
154

2

Turn 11 2 124
77

| 2006 POLE TIME: **Fisichella (Renault)** | 2006 WINNER'S AVERAGE SPEED: |
|---|---|
| **1m33.480s, 132.632mph/213.440kph** | **128.373mph/206.587kph** |
| 2006 FASTEST LAP: **Alonso (Renault)** | LAP RECORD: **Montoya (Williams)** |
| **1m34.803s, 131.554mph/211.706kph** | **1m34.223s, 131.595mph/211.772kph, 2004** |

# BAHRAIN

This will be Formula One's fourth visit to the desert-bound Bahrain International Circuit, an ultra-modern circuit set against a stark and rocky backdrop.

Fifty years ago, the grands prix scene used to be set in a world of straw bales, officials in blazers and the smell of Castrol R. Nowadays, Formula One heroes are just as likely to go into action in an ultra-modern setting like this Middle Eastern desert circuit.

As with every brand-new circuit that has joined the World Championship roster in the past decade, the one at Bahrain came from the offices of the German architect Hermann Tilke. That's immediately obvious with his trademark start/finish straight into a tight right-hander, then a slow second corner like the ones at Sepang and Shanghai. But what's notable here is that there's then a distinct change of scene as

the drivers blast down the straight to Turn 4, leaving the "oasis" section of the track with the pits, paddock and grandstands, to enter the desert area.

Although more rocky than sandy, this sector is prone to dust blowing across the track making some of the corners a lottery, especially when the wind direction changes, with drivers really having to focus on the fifth-gear Turns 5 and 6.

Good traction is vital out of the tighter corners such as Turn 10 and Turn 13 because they all lead on to appreciable straights, right the way through to Turn 14. This leads back into the "oasis" sector with its grassed verges and shaded grandstands, and on to the start/finish straight.

## INSIDE TRACK

**BAHRAIN GRAND PRIX**

| | |
|---|---|
| Date: | **15 April** |
| Circuit name: | **Bahrain InternationalCircuit** |
| Circuit length: | **3.366 miles/5.417km** |
| Number of laps: | **57** |
| Telephone: | **00 973 406222** |
| Website: | **www.bahraingp.com.bh** |

PREVIOUS WINNERS

| 2004 | **Michael Schumacher** FERRARI |
|---|---|
| 2005 | **Fernando Alonso** RENAULT |
| 2006 | **Fernando Alonso** RENAULT |

**Local attractions:** If you love blue skies and beach weather, you'll love Bahrain, although a few more trees would make the coastal resorts less exposed. With Bahrain being made up of 36 islands, there's certainly plenty of waterfront. For more fun, and a far more authentic taste of old Bahrain, go to the souk for the pure Arabic shopping experience. If you want glitzy and gaudy, head for Dubai, with its modern shopping malls and even an indoor ski slope.

**Best view:** No question, it's the view down from the nine-storey tower at the pit exit, giving a panorama over the entire circuit to the stone-strewn hills beyond. However, the tower is for VIPs and race officials only, so the view from the top row of the grandstand overlooking the startline is the next best place, especially as it gives a view over the pit buildings to the high-speed sweepers of Turns 5/6 and 12.

**Best for action:** That's Turns 1 and 14, with both being excellent places for the sort of overtaking that all motor sport fans crave. On balance, Turn 1 is best because it's guaranteed to deliver some excitement on the opening lap. However, if Hollywood was writing the scripts, Turn 14 would come first for delivering the move that sees the hero complete his fightback drive through the field to capture the lead from a scurrilous rival at the final corner of the very last lap of the grand prix.

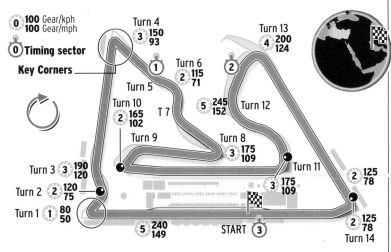

2006 POLE TIME: **M Schumacher (Ferrari)**
1m31.431s, 132.533mph/213.281kph
2006 FASTEST LAP: **N Rosberg (Williams)**
1m32.408s, 131.773mph/212.058kph

2006 WINNER'S AVERAGE SPEED:
128.761mph/207.211kph
LAP RECORD: **M Schumacher (Ferrari)**
1m30.252s, 134.260mph/216.061kph, 2004

Making a break: pole man Fernando Alonso keeps his Renault ahead of Kimi Raikkonen's McLaren and Michael Schumacher's Ferrari at the start

# BARCELONA

## All Formula One drivers know this Spanish circuit like the backs of their hands from the considerable amount of testing they do here, but do they really love it?

Some circuits start well but their presence falls away, whereas the Circuit de Catalunya has got better and better in recent years thanks to one man, Fernando Alonso, the first racing driver to become a national hero in Spain.

Before the 2005 World Champion started winning, the Circuit de Catalunya was another workaday circuit, with sparsely filled grandstands providing little atmosphere. Its popularity with the teams owed more to the attractions of Barcelona, the promise of good weather and the in-depth knowledge of every metre of its length from endless testing here. Now the organisers have to keep adding grandstands, and there's a real buzz.

A lap of the circuit offers a straight that dips from the startline down to Elf. This 90-degree right feeds almost immediately into a more open left. Then it's uphill, arcing right through the long, long Renault corner before dipping down again to Repsol. Downhill on entry, uphill on exit, the track rises to Seat then dives through a kink to a key corner. Good exit speed out of this left helps a driver carry more speed through the blind Campsa corner – the highest point of the lap – and on to the back straight. Bending back on itself at La Caixa, the track feeds through a sequence of four right-handers before hitting the start of the long, main straight, and carrying momentum through New Holland is vital if a driver is to hit 200mph and go for a passing manoeuvre.

## INSIDE TRACK

**SPANISH GRAND PRIX**

| | |
|---|---|
| Date: | **13 May** |
| Circuit name: | **Circuit de Catalunya** |
| Circuit length: | **2.875 miles/4.627km** |
| Number of laps: | **66** |
| Telephone: | **00 34 93 5719771** |
| Website: | **www.circuitcat.com** |

| PREVIOUS WINNERS | |
|---|---|
| 1997 | **Jacques Villeneuve** WILLIAMS |
| 1998 | **Mika Hakkinen** McLAREN |
| 1999 | **Mika Hakkinen** McLAREN |
| 2000 | **Mika Hakkinen** McLAREN |
| 2001 | **Michael Schumacher** FERRARI |
| 2002 | **Michael Schumacher** FERRARI |
| 2003 | **Michael Schumacher** FERRARI |
| 2004 | **Michael Schumacher** FERRARI |
| 2005 | **Kimi Raikkonen** McLAREN |
| 2006 | **Fernando Alonso** RENAULT |

**Local attractions:** The Catalan countryside is lovely, but Barcelona is even better. Just a short train or car journey to the south, it has something for everyone, from the old town by the Ramblas and Gaudi's architecture to the Olympic port and Montjuich Park, home of the Spanish GP in 1969, 1971, 1973 and 1975.

**Best view:** Campsa corner is the highest point on the circuit, and the view from the banking on the outside before the turn-in point offers a view of the track climbing to the apex and the long straight dropping to La Caixa, as well as a sight of the main straight as it approaches Elf, the circuit's first corner.

**Best for action:** Elf remains the best place for overtaking action. In fact, it's almost the only place for overtaking action. The long straight before it enables a driver to get into the tow of the car in front, then the right-left sequence offers the choice of fast-in, slow-out or vice-versa. The gravel traps give the best chance of photographing drivers' expressions as they climb out of their crashed cars.

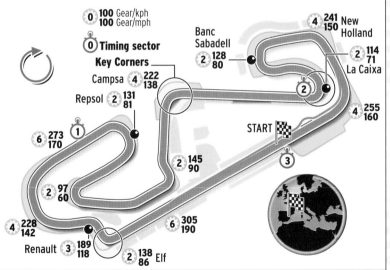

2006 POLE TIME: **Alonso (Renault)**
1m14.648s, 141.737mph/228.093kph
2006 FASTEST LAP: **Massa (Ferrari)**
1m16.648s, 135.036mph/217.309kph

2006 WINNER'S AVERAGE SPEED:
131.777mph/212.065kph
LAP RECORD: **Fisichella (Renault)**
1m15.641s, 136.840mph/220.212kph, 2005

# MONACO

## It's unique and not very challenging from the drivers' perspective, but a win on this fabled street circuit here provides more kudos than any other track.

One of the hardest mental images to conjure is Monaco's bucking strip of blacktop without its grand surroundings. Try swapping its buildings and rooftops with alpine meadows – think of the A1-Ring – and the image would be bizarre, but it would debunk the mystique that Monaco is a tricky circuit. It isn't. Since manual gearshifting was scrapped, it's not even testing, and drivers aren't even subjected to many lateral forces. However, it's hard to race because the merest slip means you'll clatter off the barriers, and overtaking has to be worked out by the team strategist.

The first corner, Sainte Devote, remains tight and blind on entry but it does offer a rare chance of overtaking. The climb to Massenet is even steeper than it looks on TV, and is tighter and certainly bumpier. Indeed, it's always bumpy because for the other 51 weeks of the year the surface is pounded by local delivery trucks. This is not a pristine surface.

Casino Square is always a marvellous sight before the flow tightens up with the Mirabeau and Grand Hotel hairpins, and the descent to Portier. Then it's fast, fast, fast through the arcing tunnel and back into daylight. The harbour front is tight, but flows better than it used to around Piscine, tightening only for La Rascasse and Anthony Noghes, the corner that Michael Schumacher so famously failed to negotiate in the final minutes of qualifying last year.

## INSIDE TRACK

### MONACO GRAND PRIX

| | |
|---|---|
| Date: | **27 May** |
| Circuit name: | **Monte Carlo** |
| Circuit length: | **2.075 miles/3.339km** |
| Number of laps: | **78** |
| Telephone: | **00 377 93152600** |
| Website: | **www.acm.mc** |

### PREVIOUS WINNERS

| | |
|---|---|
| 1997 | **Michael Schumacher** FERRARI |
| 1998 | **Mika Hakkinen** McLAREN |
| 1999 | **Michael Schumacher** FERRARI |
| 2000 | **David Coulthard** McLAREN |
| 2001 | **Michael Schumacher** FERRARI |
| 2002 | **David Coulthard** McLAREN |
| 2003 | **Juan Pablo Montoya** WILLIAMS |
| 2004 | **Jarno Trulli** RENAULT |
| 2005 | **Kimi Raikkonen** McLAREN |
| 2006 | **Fernando Alonso** RENAULT |

**Local attractions:** It's hard to know where to start because Monaco, and the centre in particular, offers so much. Try your luck at the casino and you may well then be able to afford a drink or two at Jimmy'z nightclub.

**Best view:** Down from the parapets of the old town, to the track and harbour below. Forget those expensive grandstands that line the harbourside, for the view from up here is magnificent, giving sight of the cars from the moment they burst into the Nouvelle Chicane until they accelerate up the start/finish straight. And, for the bits you can't see, there's a giant screen on the far side of the harbour.

**Best for action:** Ste Devote remains the most likely place for overtaking, not only on the opening lap, but any time in the race. Grandstand seats are limited here, so you'll just have to flick through your phonebook until you find a friend with an apartment overlooking the corner, which is safer since the pit exit was moved, now being after the corner and not before it.

### Track map

**0** 100 Gear/kph
100 Gear/mph

**0** Timing sector

**Key Corners**

Sainte Devote ② 112 / 70

Massenet ② 94 / 58

START
③

Anthony Noghes ② 88 / 55

Beau Rivage ⑥ 273 / 170

Casino Square ② 128 / 80

Mirabeau ② 80 / 50

② 143 / 89

Grand Hotel ① 45 / 30

3 193 / 120   Piscine

4 204 / 127   Louis Chiron

2 56 / 35   Nouvelle chicane

② 

② 128 / 80   La Rascasse

Tunnel ⑥ 264 / 165

② 64 / 40   Portier

---

**2006 POLE TIME: Alonso (Renault)**
1m13.962s, 100.998mph/162.533kph
**2006 FASTEST LAP: M Schumacher (Ferrari)**
1m15.143s, 99.430mph/160.010kph

**2006 WINNER'S AVERAGE SPEED:**
93.640mph/150.692kph
**LAP RECORD: M Schumacher (Ferrari)**
1m14.439s, 100.373mph/161.527kph, 2004

# MONTREAL

**There's more to this circuit than just straights and chicanes, as any driver who has raced here will tell you. It's a full-bore acceleration, heavy-braking car-breaker.**

The Circuit Gilles Villeneuve, named after Canada's most emblematic racer, is different. Very different. For starters, it's on an island, and the island is little larger than the track itself. Second, it shares the honour with Monaco of having a casino in its infield. Third, it has its own fauna, with little marmots known to pop their heads out of their holes around the track even when the cars are racing by. And, finally, it's one of the few with its own rail link. Now part of a North American double-header over a couple of weekends with the US Grand Prix, Canada's race is one of the few based in a major city, and it provides a stunning backdrop across the St Lawrence River.

After a gentle kink to the right, the first corner is a gentle turn to the left, but it feeds directly into a long right-hander, the Island Hairpin, where there is first-lap action every year. The drivers then accelerate on to the back section, a tricky series of esses where they have to work for their living. Everything slows at Turn 6, a tighter left and then again at Turn 8, a fiddly right.

The far end of the lap is marked by a tight hairpin right at the feet of a packed grandstand. Out of here, the drivers get on to the power as early as possible as they accelerate on to the lap's longest straight back towards the pits, with a very tricky right-left chicane spitting the cars back out on to the start/finish straight and, sometimes, into the wall. Some years you could swear that wall was magnetic, drawing in even the very best of the drivers.

## INSIDE TRACK

**CANADIAN GRAND PRIX**

| | |
|---|---|
| Date: | **10 June** |
| Circuit name: | **Circuit Gilles Villeneuve** |
| Circuit length: | **2.710 miles/4.361km** |
| Number of laps: | **70** |
| Telephone: | **001 514 350 0000** |
| Website: | **www.grandprix.ca** |

PREVIOUS WINNERS

| | |
|---|---|
| 1997 | **Michael Schumacher** FERRARI |
| 1998 | **Michael Schumacher** FERRARI |
| 1999 | **Mika Hakkinen** McLAREN |
| 2000 | **Michael Schumacher** FERRARI |
| 2001 | **Ralf Schumacher** WILLIAMS |
| 2002 | **Michael Schumacher** FERRARI |
| 2003 | **Michael Schumacher** FERRARI |
| 2004 | **Michael Schumacher** FERRARI |
| 2005 | **Kimi Raikkonen** McLAREN |
| 2006 | **Fernando Alonso** RENAULT |

**Local attractions:** It's hard to know where to start with Montreal, a buzzing city with so much to do. Try the viewpoint in the park above the city, the shopping, eating in Jacques Villeneuve's restaurant or jet-boating on the river.

**Best view:** L'Epingle hairpin at the far end of the circuit is a magnificent place to watch. Not only can you see the cars coming straight at you, sometimes trying to overtake, but you can then watch them power away down the Droit du Casino towards the final chicane. Better still, there's the magnificent city backdrop. Nigel Mansell is not a fan because in 1991 he waved to the fans when leading on the final lap and his engine stalled, handing victory to his team-mate Nelson Piquet.

**Best for action:** The Island Hairpin on the opening lap virtually guarantees action as the track tightens just where the drivers are fighting for position. Anyything that happens from the front end of the grid, through the first corner, the hairpin itself and the accelerating stretch to Turn 3 is visible from the grandstand.

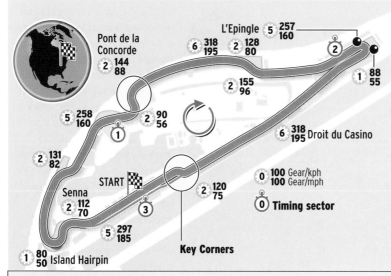

Pont de la Concorde — L'Epingle — Droit du Casino — START — Senna — Island Hairpin

Key Corners — Timing sector — Gear/kph — Gear/mph

2006 POLE TIME: **Alonso (Renault)**
1m14.942s, 130.181mph/209.496kph
2006 FASTEST LAP: **Raikkonen (McLaren)**
1m15.841s, 128.633mph/207.005kph

2006 WINNER'S AVERAGE SPEED:
120.825mph/194.440kph
LAP RECORD: **Barrichello (Ferrari)**
1m13.622s, 132.511mph/213.246kph, 2004

# INDIANAPOLIS

## It has history, banked corners and a double life, hosting both the Indianapolis 500 on its full oval course and Formula One mainly on its infield.

Formula One and the USA have had an on-off relationship. However, despite the blip of 2005 when only six cars took the start after a tyre problem, last year's race put Formula One firmly back on the agenda at Indianapolis.

The first thing that Formula One fans must know is that the Indianapolis Motor Speedway is famed chiefly for its annual 500-mile race which dates back almost a century. This, and the post-1994 NASCAR race are its crown jewels around the legendary 2.5-mile oval. Although the history books show that Formula One arrived here only in 2000, the World Championship's connection actually covers the period 1950-60 when the Indy

500 counted as a championship round, even though no Formula One teams made the journey to race in it.

The circuit used by Formula One takes in only one of the oval's four banked corners and its start/finish straight, both being used in the opposite direction to normal. From the Turn 1/2 complex, the track feeds through a sequence of tightish corners to the infield. None is notable, but Turn 7 is important because it feeds the cars on to the back straight. Overtaking is possible into Turn 8, but perhaps the most critical corner is Turn 11 where a fast exit speed provides better entry speed as the cars hit the banking at Turn 12 and rise up it at 185mph, through Turn 13, on to the main straight.

## INSIDE TRACK

### UNITED STATES GP

| | |
|---|---|
| Date: | 17 June |
| Circuit name: | Indianapolis Motor Speedway |
| Circuit length: | 2.606 miles/4.195km |
| Number of laps: | 73 |
| Telephone: | 001 317 481 8500 |
| Website: | www.my.brickyard.com |

### PREVIOUS WINNERS

| 2000 | **Michael Schumacher** FERRARI |
|---|---|
| 2001 | **Mika Hakkinen** McLAREN |
| 2002 | **Rubens Barrichello** FERRARI |
| 2003 | **Michael Schumacher** FERRARI |
| 2004 | **Michael Schumacher** FERRARI |
| 2005 | **Michael Schumacher** FERRARI |
| 2006 | **Michael Schumacher** FERRARI |

**Local attractions:** The Indianapolis Motor Speedway itself, and the museum on the infield that charts the Indy 500 back to its beginning in 1911. The city centre is something of an architectural desert, but it's fine for shopping and sports in general, with stadia for baseball, football, ice hockey and basketball, and further racing on the Indianapolis Raceway Park dirt oval.

**Best view:** Without a doubt, the best view is is from the balcony on top of the glass tower above the pits, but access is restricted to race officials and VIPs. Instead, try the grandstand at Turn 13 (Turn 1 of the oval), with its view down to where the cars hit the banking at Turn 12, and then all the way down the main straight to Turn 1. If you sit high enough up, you can also see much of the infield.

**Best for action:** Nothing can match what you can see at Turns 1 and 2. This is because the track is fast and extremely wide on the approach, the drivers ought to have been able to catch a tow, and there's overtaking throughout the race. The first lap is always hairy - just ask Nick Heidfeld what it was like last year when he was pitched into a series of rolls at Turn 2.

---

**100** Gear/kph
**100** Gear/mph

**(0) Timing sector**

Turn 12 **5 250 156**

Turn 11 **3 130 81**

Turn 9 **3 140 37**

**2**

Turn 5 **2 115 71**  Turn 7 **2 115 71**

**6 290 181**

Turn 4 **2 130 81**

**1**

Hulman Boulevard

**2 90 56** Turn 10

**3 120 75** Turn 11

Turn 2  Turn 6

**Key Corners**

**5 225 140**
Turn 3

START

Turn 13

Turn 1 **2 90 56**

**6 335 209**  **3**

**6 305 190**

---

| 2006 POLE TIME: **M Schumacher (Ferrari)** | 2006 WINNER'S AVERAGE SPEED: |
|---|---|
| **1m10.832s, 132.449mph/213.145kph** | **120.619mph/194.108kph** |
| 2006 FASTEST LAP: **M Schumacher (Ferrari)** | LAP RECORD: **Barrichello (Ferrari)** |
| **1m12.719s, 128.951mph/207.517kph** | **1m10.399s, 133.207mph/214.366kph, 2004** |

# MAGNY-COURS

**This isn't the best place to pick up points if the car's got a hint of a problem with its chassis set-up. This most technical of tracks demands total perfection.**

Poor old Magny-Cours: nobody loves it, not even the French. While 2006's attendance was the best for years, with the likelihood of a Renault win, its rural location will always restrict the numbers. And the teams hate the lack of hotels which can lead to a long drive in every morning.

The track itself is fine, actually quite a challenge, and includes every kind of corner making the chassis set-up a real nightmare. The lap certainly gets off to a cracking start, with the Grand Courbe left-hander quite a challenge in top gear. The track dips away from here to Estoril corner where it starts to bend right, and keeps on bending until it spits the cars on to the circuit's longest straight. The straight is kinked in two places, but is a flat-out, uphill run on which all cars top 180mph. Then it's hard on the anchors for the Adelaide hairpin which is very tight but with ample run-off for the inevitable incidents.

Coming back downhill, the drivers are faced with the first of two testing esses, with one called Nurburgring having to be negotiated before the tightish 180-degree turn sends them on an uphill course.

The Imola esses are perhaps even trickier than those at Nurburgring, then everything slows again for the tight right at Château d'Eau. It's sharply downhill from here to the recently revised final corner complex with a sharp right, and then a chicane on to the start/finish straight.

## INSIDE TRACK

**FRENCH GRAND PRIX**

| | |
| --- | --- |
| Date: | **1 July** |
| Circuit name: | **Magny-Cours** |
| Circuit length: | **2.741 miles/4.411km** |
| Number of laps: | **70** |
| Telephone: | **00 33 3 86218000** |
| Website: | **www.magny-cours.com** |

PREVIOUS WINNERS

| | | |
| --- | --- | --- |
| 1997 | **Michael Schumacher** | FERRARI |
| 1998 | **Michael Schumacher** | FERRARI |
| 1999 | **Heinz-Harald Frentzen** | JORDAN |
| 2000 | **David Coulthard** | McLAREN |
| 2001 | **Michael Schumacher** | FERRARI |
| 2002 | **Michael Schumacher** | FERRARI |
| 2003 | **Ralf Schumacher** | WILLIAMS |
| 2004 | **Michael Schumacher** | FERRARI |
| 2005 | **Fernando Alonso** | RENAULT |
| 2006 | **Michael Schumacher** | FERRARI |

**Local attractions:** Like Silverstone, Magny-Cours is in the middle of the countryside but, unlike Silverstone, Magny-Cours is deep in the heart of nowhere. The closest town, Nevers, offers little. Unless you like the bucolic life, your best bet is to visit the circuit museum and go for a race on the neighbouring kart track.

**Best view:** Sit in the grandstand at the Imola esse and it's hard to imagine a more dynamic view. The cars come into view from your left, turning right as they fly over a kerb, drop into a dip, turn left as they do so and, in a trice, they're gone again. In the background, you can also see the track as it comes down the hill from the Adelaide hairpin.

**Best for action:** The Adelaide hairpin is undoubtedly the best place for overtaking. Certainly, the Grande Courbe-Estoril sequence on the opening lap might produce the odd passing move, but the long, arcing straight up the hill to this tight hairpin is tailor-made for overtaking. And Adelaide seldom disappoints, at any stage of the race.

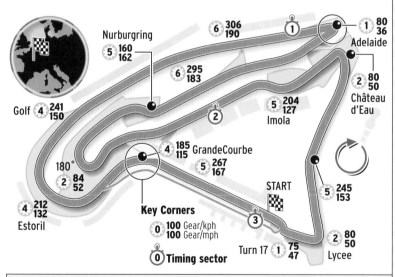

Nurburgring
6 306/190
5 160/162
1
1 80/36
Adelaide
6 295/183
2 80/50
Château d'Eau
5 204/127
Imola
Golf 4 241/150
4 185/115 GrandeCourbe
2
5 267/167
180°
2 84/52
START
5 245/153
4 212/132
Estoril

**Key Corners**
0 100 Gear/kph
100 Gear/mph
0 Timing sector

Turn 17 1 75/47
3
2 80/50
Lycee

**2006 POLE TIME: M Schumacher (Ferrari)**
**1m15.493s, 130.709mph/210.346kph**
**2006 FASTEST LAP: M Schumacher (Ferrari)**
**1m17.111s, 127.960mph/205.922kph**

**2006 WINNER'S AVERAGE SPEED:**
**124.875mph/200.958kph**
LAP RECORD: **M Schumacher (Ferrari)**
**1m15.377s, 130.910mph/210.669kph, 2004**

# SILVERSTONE

## It was the venue for the first World Championship grand prix and is one of the most popular tracks with the drivers, but its future remains in the balance.

The World Championship is a fabulous mix of circuits old and new, and Silverstone definitely belongs to the former. It hosted the opening round of the inaugural World Championship in 1950, but there is still indecision about its future development, something that Formula One ringmaster Bernie Ecclestone says is a "must" if it's to continue hosting a grand prix. Damon Hill is now at the helm, and it's hoped that the 1996 World Champion will oversee its redevelopment, making it a centre of world motorsport.

The lap of the circuit has remained largely unchanged over the years, save for the odd realignment. The first corner, Copse, remains one of the most fearsome, being taken in sixth gear at 175mph. But the highlight is the sequence of corners that starts with Maggotts and then feeds into the Becketts sweepers which are widely acknowledged as one of the best sequences in Formula One.

Then there's the flat-out blast along the Hangar Straight to Stowe, one of the better overtaking positions before the track dips into Vale. The Abbey chicane is the slow-point before heavy acceleration through the dip into Bridge, and into the stadium section ringed by grandstands.

The end of the lap is less flowing as it follows two slow lefts with two slow rights, with a clean exit from Luffield vital for a quick run down to the Copse.

## INSIDE TRACK

**BRITISH GRAND PRIX**

| | |
|---|---|
| Date: | **8 July** |
| Circuit name: | **Silverstone** |
| Circuit length: | **3.194 miles/5.140km** |
| Number of laps: | **60** |
| Telephone: | **01327 857271** |
| Website: | **www.silverstone-circuit.co.uk** |

**PREVIOUS WINNERS**

| | |
|---|---|
| 1997 | **Jacques Villeneuve** WILLIAMS |
| 1998 | **Michael Schumacher** FERRARI |
| 1999 | **David Coulthard** McLAREN |
| 2000 | **David Coulthard** McLAREN |
| 2001 | **Mika Hakkinen** McLAREN |
| 2002 | **Michael Schumacher** FERRARI |
| 2003 | **Rubens Barrichello** FERRARI |
| 2004 | **Michael Schumacher** FERRARI |
| 2005 | **Juan Pablo Montoya** McLAREN |
| 2006 | **Fernando Alonso** RENAULT |

**Local attractions:** Situated amid rolling Northamptonshire countryside, there's little to do, but a short drive south-west to Oxford provides a fine, historical sideshow.

**Best view:** Stand on the banking at Maggotts, and you can see the drivers hanging on to their cars as they power through Copse. Turn your head as they pass you and you'll see them scrabble for traction through the right-left-right of Becketts.

**Best for action:** Stowe always used to be the place to watch the opening lap where the cars raced abreast down the Hangar Straight before diving for position into the braking zone for the right-hander. Even though the reshaped corner offers little more than one line through it, limiting some of the more speculative attempts, it's still the circuit's most likely overtaking point. Look left from the grandstands and you have the added bonus of seeing the cars through the Vale, turn into Club and blast back towards Abbey.

### Track Map

Woodcote 5 260 162
Luffield 3 160 100
Bridge 5 245 154
Farm
START
6 290 181
Copse 5 226 140
3 (center)
2 (center)
3 155 97 Priory
Club 4 200 125
6 285 178
2 120 75 Abbey
Maggotts 6 285 178
0 100 Gear/kph 100 Gear/mph
0 Timing sector
2 80 50 Vale
Becketts 4 210 131
**Key Corners**
5 276 172
6 305 190
Stowe 4 180 112
1 (center)
Chapel 5 235 147

---

**2006 POLE TIME: Alonso (Renault)**
1m20.253s, 143.277mph/230.571kph
**2006 FASTEST LAP: Alonso (Renault)**
1m21.599s, 140.934mph/226.801kph

**2006 WINNER'S AVERAGE SPEED:**
133.886mph/215.459kph
**LAP RECORD: M Schumacher (Ferrari)**
1m18.739s, 146.059mph/235.048kph, 2004

# NURBURGRING

**The Nurburgring has the honour of kicking off an alternation of venues for the German Grand Prix with Hockenheim and it's a circuit that offers a challenge.**

It has now been 31 years since the World Championship last visited the full Nurburgring circuit. The drivers had been campaigning for improved safety long before that, and they were graphically proved right when leading campaigner Niki Lauda was nearly burned to death on the treacherous Nordschleife in 1976. So it wasn't until 1984 that Formula One returned to race on a revised, shortened and sanitised track. Nowhere near as popular as the Nordschleife circuit of old, it was ironically starting to get a good press just when it's now about to be culled because Germany isn't allowed two grands prix a year.

Run until last year under the convenience title of the European GP, the race moves from spring to summer and offers the drivers a bit of everything.

The start of the lap used to be through a fast esse. Now the Mercedes Arena is a tight right that feeds through two lefts and another right-hander, this one being slightly banked, on to the section that takes it downhill through a fifth-gear left and a slower right. At the foot of the hill, the Dunlop Kehre, the track doubles back and climbs through the Audi-S to the crest at Michelin. From Bit Kurve, the cars dive through the Hatzenbach Bogen and then climb to the NGK Chicane and on, up to the Coca-Cola Kurve, before heading down the gently sloping start/finish straight.

## INSIDE TRACK

**GERMAN GRAND PRIX**

| | |
|---|---|
| Date: | **22 July** |
| Circuit name: | **Nurburgring** |
| Circuit length: | **3.198 miles/5.148km** |
| Number of laps: | **60** |
| Telephone: | **00 49 2691 923060** |
| Website: | **www.nuerburgring.de** |

| PREVIOUS WINNERS | |
|---|---|
| 1996 | **Jacques Villeneuve** WILLIAMS |
| 1998* | **Mika Hakkinen** McLAREN |
| 1999 | **Johnny Herbert** STEWART |
| 2000 | **Michael Schumacher** FERRARI |
| 2001 | **Michael Schumacher** FERRARI |
| 2002 | **Rubens Barrichello** FERRARI |
| 2003 | **Ralf Schumacher** WILLIAMS |
| 2004 | **Michael Schumacher** FERRARI |
| 2005 | **Fernando Alonso** RENAULT |
| 2006 | **Michael Schumacher** FERRARI |

\* As the Luxemburg Grand Prix

**Local attractions:** Deep in the Eifel forests, your only likely entertainment is going to be hiking around the 14 miles of the Nordschleife, camping and making log fires. If you'd rather someone else did the cooking, head for the nearby village of Nurburg beneath the castle.

**Best view:** For those who still revere the Nordschleife circuit that feeds into the woods behind the circuit, any vantage point that takes in its majesty is a must. The one from the grandstands over the NGK Chicane is popular, especially as drivers always try some outbraking of a rival into there.

**Best for action:** Like so many Tilke-designed tracks, the first corner is tight. In fact few are as tight as this, and drivers have been stumbling over each other ever since it was redesigned for 2002. The opening lap has guaranteed fireworks, with even those who hug the inside not certain of becoming involved as the track doubles back on itself.

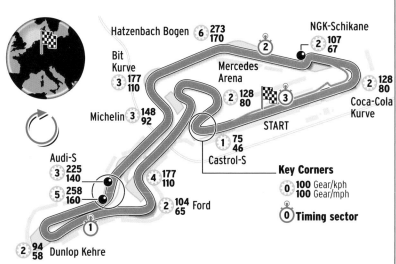

Hatzenbach Bogen 6 273/170

NGK-Schikane 2 107/67

Bit Kurve 3 177/110

Mercedes Arena 2 128/80

Michelin 3 148/92

2 128/80 3

Coca-Cola Kurve 2 128/80

START

1 75/46

Audi-S 3 225/140 / 5 258/160

4 177/110

Castrol-S

**Key Corners**

0 100 Gear/kph
0 100 Gear/mph

0 Timing sector

2 104/65 Ford

2 94/58 Dunlop Kehre

1

2006 POLE TIME: **Alonso (Renault)**
1m29.819s, 128.178mph/206.273kph
2006 FASTEST LAP: **M Schumacher (Ferrari)**
1m32.099s, 125.005mph/201.166kph

2006 WINNER'S AVERAGE SPEED:
119.981mph/193.082kph
LAP RECORD: **M Schumacher (Ferrari)**
1m29.468s, 128.719mph/207.144kph, 2004

# HUNGARORING

**The city of Budapest is magnificent, but the circuit is quite the opposite. It's the worst Formula One track. No question, although it produced a classic in 2006.**

Racing circuits mean many things to many people, from the drivers to teams to fans. The Hungaroring is great for fans as most vantage points give good views of much of the circuit, but the drivers come away feeling short-changed as there are few high-speed corners through which they can show off their skills. For side-by-side action, it's a non-starter.

Built across a valley east of Budapest 21 years ago, the Hungaroring starts high on the southern side before running across the valley floor and mounting the opposite side of the valley, then doing the reverse journey. The first corner is an open hairpin that drops from entry to exit. The best line is from out wide, but this is no good on the first lap when every driver has to compromise his line in the hope of making up a place or two.

The descent continues through Turns 2 and 3 before the track bottoms out and climbs to Turn 4. This is a fast kink that's followed by uphill Turn 5, after which the track runs on the level through a series of esses to Turn 11 before a sharp right tips the track down into the valley again. Turn 12, where the track starts to rise, is tight, but most important of all is a clean exit from Turn 14 giving momentum down the start/finish straight. In fact, with only one straight the drivers have little time to relax, the heat and humidity of high summer not helping.

## INSIDE TRACK

**HUNGARIAN GRAND PRIX**

| | |
|---|---|
| Date: | **5 August** |
| Circuit name: | **Hungaroring** |
| Circuit length: | **2.722 miles/4.381km** |
| Number of laps: | **70** |
| Telephone: | **00 36 2 844 1861** |
| Website: | **www.hungaroring.hu** |

PREVIOUS WINNERS

| 1997 | **Jacques Villeneuve** WILLIAMS |
|---|---|
| 1998 | **Michael Schumacher** FERRARI |
| 1999 | **Mika Hakkinen** McLAREN |
| 2000 | **Mika Hakkinen** McLAREN |
| 2001 | **Michael Schumacher** FERRARI |
| 2002 | **Rubens Barrichello** FERRARI |
| 2003 | **Fernando Alonso** RENAULT |
| 2004 | **Michael Schumacher** FERRARI |
| 2005 | **Kimi Raikkonen** McLAREN |
| 2006 | **Jenson Button** HONDA |

**Local attractions:** Take your pick of the twin cities of Buda and Pest, to either side of the mighty Danube. The architecture is diverse thanks to occasional sackings, with Pest the more modern. Bars and restaurants are plentiful, and their fare is superior to the offerings when Formula One came here when it was behind the Iron Curtain. The thermal baths at Gellert Hotel are a highlight.

**Best view:** Sitting high in the grandstands at Turn 14, or towards the other end of the main straight close to Turn 1, gives the best views because you can look across the valley without being blinded by the sun.

**Best for action:** This is another circuit where the best chance of overtaking comes at the first corner, when a straight feeds into a tight bend. Running clockwise, like most tracks, this is a right-hander but, unusually, it has a gradient, and you can get a great view to the action below. Overtaking is possible here at any time because it's the only likely place for making a pass.

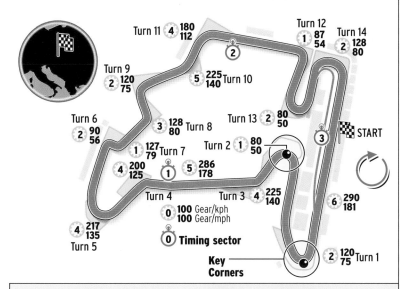

Turn 11 — 4 — 180 / 112
Turn 12 — 1 — 87 / 54
Turn 14 — 2 — 128 / 80
Turn 9 — 2 — 120 / 75
Turn 10 — 5 — 225 / 140
Turn 6 — 2 — 90 / 56
Turn 8 — 3 — 128 / 80
Turn 13 — 2 — 80 / 50
Turn 7 — 1 — 127 / 79
Turn 2 — 1 — 80 / 50
— 4 — 200 / 125
— 5 — 286 / 178
START — 3
— 6 — 290 / 181
Turn 4 — Turn 3 — 4 — 225 / 140
Turn 5 — 4 — 217 / 135
0 — 100 Gear/kph / 100 Gear/mph
0 — **Timing sector**
Turn 1 — 2 — 120 / 75
**Key Corners**

| 2006 POLE TIME: **Raikkonen (McLaren)** | 2006 WINNER'S AVERAGE SPEED: |
|---|---|
| **1m19.599s, 123.107mph/198.112kph** | **101.769mph/163.774kph** |
| 2006 FASTEST LAP: **Massa (Ferrari)** | LAP RECORD: **M Schumacher (Ferrari)** |
| **1m23.516s, 117.333mph/188.820kph** | **1m19.071s, 123.828mph/199.461kph, 2004** |

# ISTANBUL

## This Turkish circuit proved an instant hit on its debut in 2005, and the drivers know that if they're going to shine, this could be the place. It can be a scorcher.

The German architect Hermann Tilke has been behind most of the new circuits over the past decade, and they all carry his imprint, but he broke new ground when the Turks asked him to design a circuit. He truly went the extra mile to produce something more than a little bit special.

Like Interlagos and Imola, the Istanbul Park Circuit takes the unusual course of running in an anti-clockwise direction. And like Interlagos, the first corner is a left-hand bend – as it would be on an anti-clockwise circuit – and drops away from its entry to exit. Then, after an arcing run to Turn 3, the flow is slow until Turn 6 where, before Turn 7, it feeds back on itself towards Turn 8.

This is perhaps the Big Daddy of the bends, Turn 8 being a triple-apex corner through which it's very hard for a driver to position the car at 150mph. Indeed, many blow their lap time by running wide over the kerbs and on to the run-off beyond. There's little to hit, but dust aplenty to coat their tyres and thus delay progress.

Turn 9 is tight, but then the track really finds its legs for the blast down to the tight left at Turn 12, with passing more than possible under the heavy braking required to slow the cars from 185mph. The final sector is fiddly, with a quick exit out of Turn 14 being vital if anyone's going to pull off an overtaking move at the far end of the start/finish straight.

## INSIDE TRACK

**TURKISH GRAND PRIX**

| | |
|---|---|
| Date: | **26 August** |
| Circuit name: | **Istanbul Park Circuit** |
| Circuit length: | **3.293 miles/5.299km** |
| Number of laps: | **58** |
| Telephone: | **00 90 216 418 5222** |
| Website: | **www.formula1-istanbul.com** |

PREVIOUS WINNERS

| | |
|---|---|
| 2005 | **Kimi Raikkonen** McLAREN |
| 2006 | **Felipe Massa** FERRARI |

**Local attractions:** Ankara might be the capital of Turkey, sited in the middle of this huge country, but Istanbul is the centre of everything that's fun and historic. Straddling the River Bosphorus, the city formerly known as Constantinople buzzes day and night at the point where Europe meets Asia Minor. Make sure that your visit includes a side-trip to the magnificent Blue Mosque.

**Best view:** It may seem a heresy, but cars teetering on the edge of adhesion can be every bit as entertaining as those trying to overtake each other. The Becketts sweepers at Silverstone and the Imola esses at Magny-Cours prove that. In turn, Istanbul Park has its own sequence of corners with the sweeping esses from Turn 3 to Turn 6. Best of all, stand high on the banking on the outside of the track at Turn 6 and you can spin around and watch the drivers piling into the daunting high-speed-entry-and-hang-on-for-dear-life Turn 8.

**Best for action:** To catch the majority of attempted passing manoeuvres head for the spectator banking at Turn 12. From there, you can look down at the drivers as they approach the tight left-hander at speed and then line up an overtaking move, and watch them negotiate the tight and twisting Turns 13 and 14 before heading off down the start/finish straight.

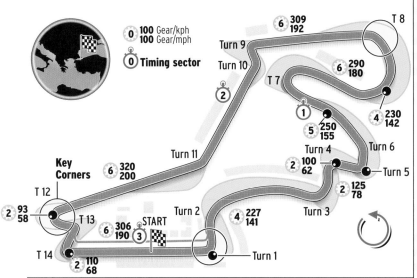

| 0 | **100** Gear/kph |
|---|---|
| | **100** Gear/mph |
| (0) | **Timing sector** |

**Key Corners**

| 6 | **309** |
| | **192** |

T 8

Turn 9

Turn 10

| 6 | **290** |
| | **180** |

T 7

| 2 | |

| 4 | **230** |
| | **142** |

| 1 | |

| 5 | **250** |
| | **155** |

Turn 4    Turn 6

| 2 | **100** |
| | **62** |

Turn 5

| 2 | **125** |
| | **78** |

Turn 11

| 6 | **320** |
| | **200** |

T 12

| 2 | **93** |
| | **58** |

T 13

| 6 | **306** |
| | **190** |

START (3)

Turn 2

| 4 | **227** |
| | **141** |

Turn 3

T 14

| 2 | **110** |
| | **68** |

Turn 1

---

**2006 POLE TIME: Massa (Ferrari)**
1m26.907s, 137.443mph/221.184kph
**2006 FASTEST LAP: M Schumacher (Ferrari)**
1m28.005s, 135.729mph/218.424kph

**2006 WINNER'S AVERAGE SPEED:**
129.829mph/208.930kph
**LAP RECORD: Montoya (McLaren)**
1m24.770s, 138.096mph/222.167kph, 2005

# MONZA

**Its history, prestige and wild tifosi make this a magical circuit, and it's even better if you triumph at the wheel of one of the tifosi's beloved Ferraris.**

In use ever since 1922, the Autodromo Nazionale at Monza is a track that excites. It looks fast even without a car on it, with its wide open straights slashing across its parkland setting. Some of the fastest races ever were held here, as well as some of the most exciting.

The key to a good lap of Monza used to mean having a car that's rocket quick in a straight line, a trick achieved by running with as little wing angle as possible. But since chicanes were added in 1972, the ability to take corners or vault the kerbs has become part of the mix which ensures that the teams' engineers are forced to find a compromise that trades off straightline speed against some wing angle for downforce required through the slower corners.

The lap starts with a blast to the Variante del Rettifilo, a right-left chicane that inevitably produces thrills and spills, with many a driver being taken out by another's accident. There's scope for more collisions at the second chicane, the Variante della Roggia, that's even trickier than the first chicane due to its blind entry.

After this, the lap settles down with the pair of Lesmo bends, and the charge back under the bridge over which the old banked circuit flows, heading for Ascari. This is the site of the third chicane, and a good exit is critical for a fast run down the straight to Parabolica.

## INSIDE TRACK

**ITALIAN GRAND PRIX**

| | |
|---|---|
| Date: | **9 September** |
| Circuit name: | **Monza** |
| Circuit length: | **3.600 miles/5.793km** |
| Number of laps: | **53** |
| Telephone: | **00 39 39 24821** |
| Website: | **www.monzanet.it** |

PREVIOUS WINNERS

| | |
|---|---|
| 1997 | **David Coulthard** McLAREN |
| 1998 | **Michael Schumacher** FERRARI |
| 1999 | **Heinz-Harald Frentzen** JORDAN |
| 2000 | **Michael Schumacher** FERRARI |
| 2001 | **Juan Pablo Montoya** WILLIAMS |
| 2002 | **Rubens Barrichello** FERRARI |
| 2003 | **Michael Schumacher** FERRARI |
| 2004 | **Rubens Barrichello** FERRARI |
| 2005 | **Juan Pablo Montoya** McLAREN |
| 2006 | **Michael Schumacher** FERRARI |

**Local attractions:** The town of Monza is fine, and the royal park in which the circuit is situated has good walks. But it's to Milan that everyone should head. There's La Scala for opera, the Duomo shopping arcade for haute couture (clothes even smarter than a Ferrari beanie hat), and restaurants beside the canal.

**Best view:** The most magical view at Monza is from the grandstand opposite the pit exit. Although not close to the first corner, the Variante del Rettifilo, there are good views of cars flashing past at way over 200mph, of the magnificent old control tower, of the crumbling old banking on the infield, and of the Alps in the background. Pure magic.

**Best for action:** The first chicane always provides action, at any stage of the race, but some of the best passing moves are carried out on the final corner of the lap, the Parabolica, where drivers try to slow from over 200mph, overtake without compromising their exit speed by going in too deep, and fire back on to the main straight without being overtaken.

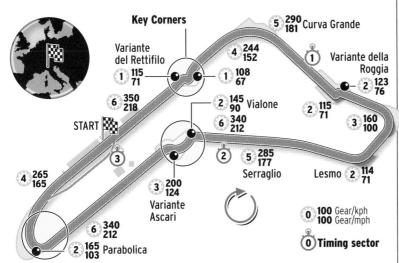

**Key Corners**

Variante del Rettifilo
Curva Grande
Variante della Roggia
Vialone
Serraglio
Lesmo
Variante Ascari
Parabolica
START

0 100 Gear/kph
0 100 Gear/mph

0 Timing sector

---

**2006 POLE TIME: Raikkonen (McLaren)**
1m21.484s, 159.050mph/255.954kph
**2006 FASTEST LAP: Raikkonen (McLaren)**
1m22.559s, 156.979mph/252.621kph

**2006 WINNER'S AVERAGE SPEED:**
152.749mph/245.814kph
LAP RECORD: Barrichello (Ferrari)
1m21.046s, 159.899mph/257.321kph, 2004

# SPA-FRANCORCHAMPS

## Dropped from last year's calendar at the eleventh hour, fans and drivers are delighted that this great track is back for 2007. It offers a huge challenge.

It's hard to know where to start when describing Spa-Francorchamps. Like Monza and Silverstone, the circuit is blessed with a long, illustrious history. It's also blessed with majestic scenery because it sits high in the Ardennes forests, giving a circuit of grandeur. Better still, its lap includes a couple of the best corners in Formula One.

The uphill start is a short blast to La Source hairpin, then it's a steep dive past the old pits into the most famous corner of all, Eau Rouge. The track bottoms, snaps left then immediately right as it appears to be slammed into the drivers' faces before veering up in an incredibly steep climb to Raidillion. The cars feel incredibly light here when the track crests the slope and

jinks left, with the drivers having to hang on and keep the throttle planted.

A good exit from Raidillion often means catching a tow up the long ascent to Les Combes, where a right-left esse pitches the track to the downhill Rivage hairpin. Then it's down, down, down to the double-apex Pouhon, a notably tricky corner.

The next stretch of open corners is fast but bland before the track reaches its lowest point at Stavelot and starts its ascent to the finish.

Blanchimont remains fearsomely fast, followed by the gentle Bus Stop chicane which has been reprofiled for 2007 and offers a less vicious final sting in the tail than it used to.

## INSIDE TRACK

**BELGIAN GRAND PRIX**

| | |
|---|---|
| Date: | 16 September |
| Circuit name: | Spa-Francorchamps |
| Circuit length: | 4.333 miles/6.973km |
| Number of laps: | 44 |
| Telephone: | 00 32 8727 5138 |
| Website: | www.spa-francorchamps.be |

PREVIOUS WINNERS

| | | |
|---|---|---|
| 1995 | Michael Schumacher | BENETTON |
| 1996 | Michael Schumacher | FERRARI |
| 1997 | Michael Schumacher | FERRARI |
| 1998 | Damon Hill | JORDAN |
| 1999 | David Coulthard | McLAREN |
| 2000 | Mika Hakkinen | McLAREN |
| 2001 | Michael Schumacher | FERRARI |
| 2002 | Michael Schumacher | FERRARI |
| 2004 | Kimi Raikkonen | McLAREN |
| 2005 | Kimi Raikkonen | McLAREN |

**Local attractions:** The resort town of Spa, a short drive to the north, is the most civilised spot in the Ardennes, with its spa facilities, casino and refined restaurants and patisseries. And the surrounding Ardennes forests are a treat if you like country rambling or fishing. For petrolheads, there's a kart track and metal toboggan run at the funfair at Coo.

**Best view:** There are so many supreme views at Spa-Francorchamps that it's hard to choose, but one that's special is from the hillside above the left-hand kink after Rivage, from where the track below looks great. You can also see the cars race all the way down to Pouhon and flash in and out of view as they power though the trees on the climb from Stavelot to Blanchimont.

**Best for action:** If you get high on overtaking, make the long climb to Les Combes and take a seat in the grandstands on the outside of the track, looking down on to the braking zone as the cars complete their blast up the hill from Eau Rouge.

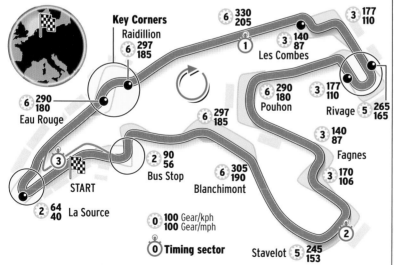

**Key Corners**

Raidillion — 6 | 297 / 185

330 / 205 — 6

177 / 110 — 3

1 — 140 / 87 — 3 — Les Combes

290 / 180 — 6 — Eau Rouge

290 / 180 — 6 — Pouhon — 177 / 110 — 3

297 / 185 — 6 — Rivage — 5 | 265 / 165

140 / 87 — 3 — Fagnes

90 / 56 — 2 — Bus Stop

3 — START — La Source — 2 | 64 / 40

305 / 190 — 6 — Blanchimont — 170 / 106 — 3

0 | 100 / 100 — Gear/kph / Gear/mph

0 — Timing sector

Stavelot — 5 | 245 / 153

2

| 2005 POLE TIME: **Montoya (McLaren)** | 2005 WINNER'S AVERAGE SPEED: |
|---|---|
| 1m46.391s, 146.618mph/235.947kph | 127.119mph/204.569kph |
| 2005 FASTEST LAP: **R Schumacher (Toyota)** | LAP RECORD: **Raikkonen (McLaren)** |
| 1m51.453s, 140.019mph/225.328kph | 1m45.108s, 148.407mph/238.827kph, 2004 |

# SHANGHAI

## It has got the corners, and the facilities. Now all the Shanghai circuit needs is its grandstands to be packed and noisy to produce buckets of atmosphere.

Shanghai is a city like no other, bursting forth and expanding in every direction. It's big, bold and brassy, and it's only fitting that this, the entrepreneurial and commercial centre of China, was given a circuit to match. Built outside the city limits, it took circuit facilities to a new planet, the sheer scale of everything taking your breath away.

The circuit, yet again from Hermann Tilke's crew, drew gasps from the city elders when they saw the plans because, fortuitously, it replicated the Shang symbol, part of the city's name.

The first corner has a curving entry that tightens and tightens as it mounts a slight slope, before turning back on itself and sliding back down the incline. This is where many try to overtake through the dipping left-hander.

Turning from right to left as it goes, the lap then opens out on to a straight up to a second-gear hairpin at Turn 6. The next corner, Turn 7, is a sweeping sixth-gear left into a fifth-gear right. An open hairpin feeds the cars on to a straight before a sequence of bends that mirrors the one that opens the lap, this time feeding on to a long straight. Overtaking is very possible going into the hairpin at its end, especially as the track is wide, with a final left-hander onto the start/finish straight made all the more impressive as the track drops away at the exit, catching out the less wary.

## INSIDE TRACK

### CHINESE GRAND PRIX

| | |
|---|---|
| Date: | **30 September** |
| Circuit name: | **Shanghai International Circuit** |
| Circuit length: | **3.390 miles/5.450km** |
| Number of laps: | **57** |
| Telephone: | **00 86 2162520000** |
| Website: | **www.f1china.com.cn** |

PREVIOUS WINNERS

| | |
|---|---|
| 2004 | **Rubens Barrichello** FERRARI |
| 2005 | **Fernando Alonso** RENAULT |
| 2006 | **Michael Schumacher** FERRARI |

**Local attractions:** Shanghai is a combination of the sci-fi film "Blade Runner" and the 1930s. The elegant bank headquarters along the Bund remain, but they are now dwarfed by the surrounding glass and steel buildings, each of which attempts to outstrip those built 12 months before. Only Chicago in the 1930s had skscraper fever to a similar degree. The old markets remain, but for how much longer?

**Best view:** Sit in the far end of the main grandstand opposite the pits, at the end closest to Turn 1, and you'll see the pitlane action, everything that happens into the first corner, and the cars twisting through Turns 2 to 4 before accelerating into the distance. You also get the shade under the huge, wing-shaped walkway that bridges the track there, and a good view of the sheer scale of the circuit's mind-boggling architecture.

**Best for action:** The back-straight from Turn 13 is so long that drivers can practically read a book as they power down it, but their attention has to be 100 per cent when they reach its end at Turn 14. This right-hand hairpin is the prime overtaking spot on the entire lap, with drivers diving out of a rival's slipstream and attempting to dive down the inside to snatch the position. Fortunately, there's enough run-off there to make it worth having a go.

### Key Corners

| 3 | 175 / 109 |
| 6 | 310 / 193 |
| 2 | 125 / 78 |
| 3 | |
| 5 | 250 / 155 |
| 1 | |
| 6 | 290 / 180 |
| 2 | 70 / 44 |
| 0 | 100 Gear/kph / 100 Gear/mph |
| 0 | **Timing sector** |
| 3 | 165 / 102 |
| 2 | |
| 3 | 175 / 109 |
| 2 | 88 / 55 |
| 2 | 85 / 53 |
| 6 | 326 / 202 |
| 4 | 250 / 155 |

**START**

---

**2006 POLE TIME: Alonso (Renault)**
1m44.360s, 116.941mph/188.190kph
**2006 FASTEST LAP: Alonso (Renault)**
1m37.586s, 124.957mph/201.089kph

**2006 WINNER'S AVERAGE SPEED:**
116.603mph/187.646kph
**LAP RECORD: M Schumacher (Ferrari)**
1m32.238s, 132.202mph/212.749kph, 2004

# FUJI

## It's all-change for this year's Japanese GP with Suzuka losing out to the old favourite, Fuji Speedway, a circuit that sits on the slopes of Japan's most famous volcano.

Formula One fans of a certain age well remember their first sight of the Fuji Speedway in autumn, 1976. It was the climax of that year's nip-and-tuck title battle between Ferrari's Niki Lauda and McLaren's James Hunt. It was wet, very wet, and Hunt did just enough to claim the crown after Lauda withdrew just after the start, blinded by the spray and unable to blink due to facial burns. Few recall that Mario Andretti won for Lotus.

Inspired by the success of that inaugural grand prix in Japan, Formula One returned in 1977, but a marshal and a spectator who had strayed into an out-of-bounds area were killed and that was that until Suzuka picked up the threads in 1987. The Honda-owned track has now had to give way to Fuji Speedway, whose Toyota owners have funded its major overhaul. Even so, it's very recognisable from that late-1970s epic.

The start/finish straight is still long, almost 1 mile, but the key change is that it's approached by a tight sequence of corners rather than the long, open right-hander of old, thus cutting speeds down the straight. The first corner is still a tight right, with the track then dropping down a gentle incline to the loop that contains 100R and the hairpin behind the paddock. It's fast out of here, with a drop to a tight right, from which it rises to a right, a left-hand hairpin and then the right-hand hairpin to complete the lap.

## INSIDE TRACK

**JAPANESE GRAND PRIX**

| | |
|---|---|
| Date: | **30 September** |
| Circuit name: | **Fuji Speedway** |
| Circuit length: | **2.852 miles/4.563km** |
| Number of laps: | **67** |
| Telephone: | **00 81 550 781234** |
| Website: | **www.fsw.tv/english** |

| PREVIOUS WINNERS | |
|---|---|
| 1976 | **Mario Andretti** LOTUS |
| 1977 | **James Hunt** McLAREN |

**Local attractions:** The most arresting feature of this part of the Shizuoka prefecture, to the west of Tokyo, is Mount Fuji, with the track located on its flanks. Japan's talismanic volcano is snow-capped and picture perfect, and on days when its summit is not obscured by cloud, with autumnal colours kicking in, the setting is absolutely stunning. Don't expect the local town of Gotemba to provide high jinks, but if you want a taste of authentic Japan, it's fine. Make sure, though, that you choose a restaurant where the food is pictured to ensure that you know what to expect.

**Best view:** If you want to have a great view of the racing and still be close to the action around the paddock, you could do worse than sit on the banking overlooking the hairpin after 100R. The view to the valley below can be breathtaking on a sunny day, being not dissimilar to the views from the mountainside around Austria's A1-Ring.

**Best for action:** The grandstand overlooking Turn 1 is the best for fans. That long straight into the hairpin provides overtaking aplenty as cars dive out of each other's slipstream. Better still, the sight of the original banked curve cut into the mountainside beyond makes fans long to have been here from the circuit's opening in 1965 until 1974 when it was judged too dangerous.

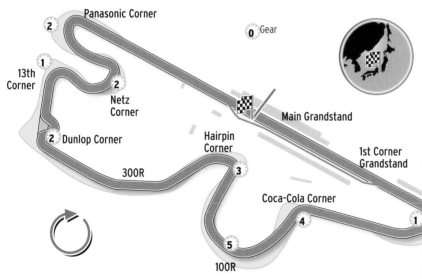

**1977 POLE TIME: Andretti (Lotus)** 1m12.230s, 135.019mph/217.281kph

**1977 FASTEST LAP: Scheckter (Wolf)** 1m14.300s, 131.257mph/211.228kph

**1977 WINNER'S AVERAGE SPEED:** 129.167mph/207.864kph

**LAP RECORD: Scheckter (Wolf)** 1m14.300s, 131.257mph/211.228kph, 1977

# INTERLAGOS

**Some tracks have character, some score a zero, but the home of the Brazilian GP is packed with it and its grandstands are brim full with the noisiest fans of all.**

Interlagos's facilities would be rejected if a European country requested a grand prix with a track in similar condition, but this is Formula One's only slot in South America. The regulars are prepared to forgo a few of the luxuries on which they normally insist, though things get a bit OTT with the occasional car-jacking.

Unusual in being run anti-clockwise, a lap of Interlagos dives straight into Curva 1, the track dropping left and steeply down towards the Senna S, where it kinks right before settling through the Curva do Sol.

The appreciable straight – the only straight one in the entire lap – that follows down to Descida do Lago sees a lot of jockeying for position, with overtaking

at its end a near certainty. Then, from the bottom of the hill – with the banking of the original circuit still visible in the background – the track climbs to Ferra dura, a tricky double-apex corner on the crest of the hill.

The track then dips down at Laranja then drops to Pinheirinho before rising to Cotovelo and plunging again to Mergulho, out of which the drivers are accelerating hard through a series of uphill left-hand kinks that unfold past the packed grandstands into the start/finish straight. The drivers feel dwarfed by high concrete walls on either side before bursting back into the light at Curva 1, leaving the enclosing concrete behind.

## INSIDE TRACK

**BRAZILIAN GRAND PRIX**

| | |
| --- | --- |
| Date: | **22 October** |
| Circuit name: | **Interlagos** |
| Circuit length: | **2.667 miles/4.292km** |
| Number of laps: | **71** |
| Telephone: | **00 55 11 813 5775** |
| Website: | **www.interlagos.com** |

| PREVIOUS WINNERS | |
| --- | --- |
| 1997 | **Jacques Villeneuve** WILLIAMS |
| 1998 | **Mika Hakkinen** McLAREN |
| 1999 | **Mika Hakkinen** McLAREN |
| 2000 | **Michael Schumacher** FERRARI |
| 2001 | **David Coulthard** McLAREN |
| 2002 | **Michael Schumacher** FERRARI |
| 2003 | **Giancarlo Fisichella** JORDAN |
| 2004 | **Juan Pablo Montoya** WILLIAMS |
| 2005 | **Juan Pablo Montoya** McLAREN |
| 2006 | **Felipe Massa** FERRARI |

**Local attractions:** Sao Paulo bustles like no other city, save perhaps Mexico City, but it has also acquired a leisurely side from the laidback attitude of the Paulistas. For red-blooded carnivores, head for any of the churascerias for an evening of meat consumption. Remember to turn the disc on your table from green to red when you have had enough or the meat will keep on coming.

**Best view:** The best view is in the grandstand at Curva 1. Not only is it a tricky, dipping corner that offers much of the overtaking, but you can also see the Senna S-Curva do Sol sequence. Another big plus is that you'll be surrounded by Brazilian fans who treat the day like a carnival, singing and blowing horns even before the cars hit the track.

**Best for action:** Down at the lowest point of the track, the left-hander called Descida do Lago is the most likely place for passing. You can sit in the grandstands along the outside of the track and watch an overtaking unfold before your eyes.

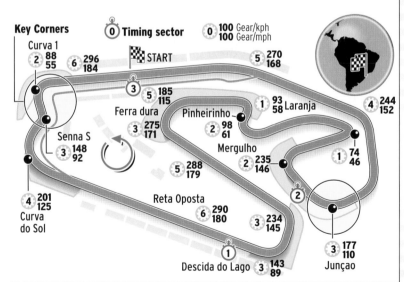

**Key Corners**

Curva 1 — 2 | 88 / 55 — 6 | 296 / 184

(O) Timing sector

🏁 START

0 | 100 Gear/kph / 100 Gear/mph

5 | 270 / 168

3 | — 5 | 185 / 115

Ferra dura — 3 | 275 / 171

Pinheirinho — 1 | 93 / 58 Laranja — 4 | 244 / 152

2 | 98 / 61

Senna S — 3 | 148 / 92

Mergulho — 2 | 235 / 146 — 1 | 74 / 46

5 | 288 / 179

4 | 201 / 125 Curva do Sol

Reta Oposta — 6 | 290 / 180 — 3 | 234 / 145 — 2

3 | 177 / 110 Junção

(1) Descida do Lago — 3 | 143 / 89

**2006 POLE TIME: Massa (Ferrari)**
1m10.680s, 136.356mph/219.423kph
**2006 FASTEST LAP: M Schumacher (Ferrari)**
1m12.162s, 133.550mph/214.918kph

**2006 WINNER'S AVERAGE SPEED:**
124.139mph/199.773kph
**LAP RECORD: Montoya (Williams)**
1m11.473s, 134.867mph/217.038kph, 2004

# NO TWO ALIKE

One of the glories of Formula One is the variety of countries visited, and the range of different circuits. Football stadia may vary, but a pitch is a pitch. That's not true of the circuits. Try comparing Monaco with Indianapolis or Silverstone and you'll get the idea. This is a celebration of the differences.

Compare and contrast (clockwise from top right): Monaco; Montreal; Istanbul; Bahrain; and Shanghai

# REVIEW OF THE 2006 SEASON

**It was Michael Schumacher's last stand and he came within an ace of pulling off his eighth and final world title, but Fernando Alonso held firm to win again for Renault. McLaren came closer, Honda Racing broke its duck, Red Bull ran two teams, Midland changed its name and Super Aguri Racing started from scratch.**

What a year. It wasn't always attractive, with politics and technical wrangling spoiling the show, but it was blessed with some great racing and few can dispute that Fernando Alonso and Renault deserve to be world champions for the second year in a row.

The big question right up until the Italian GP in September was whether Michael Schumacher would announce his retirement. It was initially considered a done deal, to the extent that Ferrari had signed Kimi Raikkonen for 2007, with McLaren lining up

Alonso to move from Renault to replace him. The only problem was that Michael didn't seem to want to hang up his helmet, well, not once his season kicked into top gear with a victory at Imola, and especially not when he closed in on Alonso in the points race. That eighth title looked very possible, but it was only when he announced – after winning at Monza – that he would quit after the final grand prix at Interlagos and spend time at home trying to work out what to do with the rest of his life that everything else

could fall into place. In short, it was a relief when he went public, but Formula One will be very different without him.

Renault and Alonso probably would have won both titles at a canter had not their mass damping system been outlawed mid-season. This took the wind out of their sails and allowed Ferrari to close in, but they responded well. Meanwhile, McLaren and Kimi Raikkonen gave their all, but their chassis–engine package just wasn't good enough, though they might have won in Monaco and China with a bit of luck. Juan Pablo Montoya was no match for Raikkonen and quit the team mid-season to try his hand in NASCAR stock cars in the USA. His replacement, Pedro de la Rosa, also failed to get close to Raikkonen's speed.

Only one other team looked capable of victory. And that was only once, in the wet/dry race at the Hungaroring, when Honda Racing (born as BAR in 1999) took it with both hands. The driver was Jenson Button who became a grand prix winner at the 115th attempt after a flawless drive in tricky conditions from 14th on the grid.

BMW brought money to Sauber and they combined to surprise many, particularly once Robert Kubica stepped up from their test team to replace another driver who quit – Jacques Villeneuve – and showed that he is one to watch by finishing third in only his third grand prix. Toyota progressed after changing to their TF106B

chassis which was made to suit the Bridgestone tyres they were using for 2006, having switched from Michelins. Jarno Trulli was nominally the pick of their drivers, and would have scored more points than Ralf Schumacher but for cruel luck when heading for third place both at Monaco and Magny-Cours. That third place at Monaco was grabbed instead by Red Bull Racing's David Coulthard, but he and the team had little else to smile about, with Christian Klien being made the scapegoat for the team's poor form.

Scuderia Toro Rosso – known as Minardi until bought by Red Bull boss Dietrich Mateschitz at the end of 2005 – proved the best of the three tail-end teams. Midland also received an injection of cash, having being taken over by Spyker, and should now improve while Super Aguri Racing beat all the odds by going from concept to reality in record time.

One factor that added great interest was the tyre war between the teams on Bridgestones and the teams on Michelins, with the advantage swinging according to a minor shift in temperature or a flurry of rain. Sadly, this was the last tyre war for a while because Bridgestone will be supplying all the tyres in 2007.

So, with a few changes to the calendar for the season ahead, we wave goodybye, for now at least, to Imola, Hockenheim and Suzuka, the last being the biggest loss because the drivers loved its challenge.

# BAHRAIN GP

**Honda had been strong in the close-season testing, but reigning champions Renault ruled the roost at the opening round in the Middle East, albeit only after a flash of speed from Michael Schumacher and Ferrari came close to giving them victory.**

Fight to the finish: Fernando Alonso got his world title defence off to a triumphant start, but Ferrari's Michael Schumacher pushed him hard

Nobody likes to be beaten, and it's safe to say that seven-times Formula One World Champion Michael Schumacher enjoys it less than most. After a 2005 season in which he could only pick up scraps as Renault and Fernando Alonso dominated, Michael was delighted with the speed given by the combination of Ferrari's new V8-engine 248 and Bridgestone's latest rubber. Indeed, he and new Ferrari team-mate Felipe Massa lined up first and second on the grid at Bahrain after the first rendition of the new-look qualifying sessions.

The race proved that both Ferrari drivers had qualified with a lighter fuel load than that carried by Renault's reigning champion Alonso, but one small slip in qualifying was all that stood between Michael returning to the track from his second pit stop ahead of

Alonso. There was less than a car length in it: it really was that close.

The slip-up came as Michael did a slow lap and lost a lap of "fuel credit" allowance for the start of the race. It wasn't his fault since he'd been delayed by traffic, but it meant that he would have to come in for his first pit stop at least a lap earlier than rival Alonso – actually, it turned out to be four laps earlier – which meant that the Spaniard was still ahead when Michael emerged from his final stop.

So Alonso, who'd lined up fourth behind the Ferraris and Jenson Button's Honda, made the most of a new set of Michelin tyres to power past Massa and Button at the start, and then hit the front when Michael made his first pit stop on lap 15. Alonso stayed there until he pitted on lap 19, but

there was a new leader when he returned, one who had started the race with even more fuel on board: McLaren's Juan Pablo Montoya. The Colombian's lead was over when he pitted on lap 23 though, and Alonso resumed control.

Alone among the front runners, Kimi Raikkonen had elected to run a one-stop strategy in his McLaren. But the Finn's hand had been forced because he'd had to start from the tail of the grid after he was the first to fall foul of the new qualifying system, being eliminated when his MP4-21's rear suspension failed in the first of the three sectors of qualifying, the resultant damage precluding him from taking part in the second knock-out session to determine the 11th to 16th grid positions.

Fired up by this, Raikkonen drove like a

man possessed and rose from 22nd to 30th place on the opening lap. Not making his pit stop until lap 30, he rose to third, and was able to finish there, moving back up from sixth to third when Button, his own team-mate Montoya and Williams' driver Mark Webber all called in for their second pit stop.

Making his Formula One debut, Nico Rosberg ought to have been right in there with them in his Williams, but a first corner clash with Nick Heidfeld's BMW Sauber resulted in the German having to pit for a new nose, costing him 45s. This might have ruined his race, but the son of 1982 World Champion Keke Rosberg was determined to impress, and impress he did as he fought his way up the order to seventh place, setting the race's fastest lap on the way and demoting Red Bull Racing's Christian Klien with just two laps to go. It was small wonder that three-times World Champion Jackie Stewart described the drive as "the most impressive grand prix debut I can ever remember anyone making".

Not surprisingly, the all-new Super Aguri Racing team brought up the rear in qualifying with their updated Arrows chassis. But, commendably considering how little testing they had done, Takuma Sato took his all the way to the finish.

# BAHRAIN ROUND 01
Date: **12 March 2006** Laps: **57** Distance: **191.716 miles/308.523km**
Weather: **Very hot and bright**

## RACE RESULT

| Position | Driver | Team | Result | Stops | Qualifying Time | Grid |
|---|---|---|---|---|---|---|
| 1 | **Fernando Alonso** | Renault | 1h29m46.205s | 2 | 1m31.702s | 4 |
| 2 | **Michael Schumacher** | Ferrari | 1h29m47.451s | 2 | 1m31.431s | 1 |
| 3 | **Kimi Raikkonen** | McLaren | 1h30m05.565s | 1 | no time | 22 |
| 4 | **Jenson Button** | Honda | 1h30m06.197s | 2 | 1m31.549s | 3 |
| 5 | **Juan Pablo Montoya** | McLaren | 1h30m23.253s | 2 | 1m32.164s | 5 |
| 6 | **Mark Webber** | Williams | 1h30m28.137s | 2 | 1m33.006s | 7 |
| 7 | **Nico Rosberg** | Williams | 1h30m49.248s | 3 | 1m32.620s | 12 |
| 8 | **Christian Klien** | Red Bull | 1h30m52.976s | 2 | 1m33.112s | 8 |
| 9 | **Felipe Massa** | Ferrari | 1h30m56.112s | 2 | 1m31.478s | 2 |
| 10 | **David Coulthard** | Red Bull | 1h31m01.746s | 1 | 1m32.850s | 13 |
| 11 | **Vitantonio Liuzzi** | Toro Rosso | 1h31m12.202s | 2 | 1m33.416s | 15 |
| 12 | **Nick Heidfeld** | BMW Sauber | 1h29m56.330s | 2 | 1m33.926s | 10 |
| 13 | **Scott Speed** | Toro Rosso | 56 laps | 1 | 1m34.606s | 16 |
| 14 | **Ralf Schumacher** | Toyota | 56 laps | 2 | 1m34.702s | 17 |
| 15 | **Rubens Barrichello** | Honda | 56 laps | 2 | 1m32.579s | 6 |
| 16 | **Jarno Trulli** | Toyota | 56 laps | 2 | 1m33.066s | 14 |
| 17 | **Tiago Monteiro** | Midland | 55 laps | 2 | 1m35.900s | 19 |
| 18 | **Takuma Sato** | Super Aguri | 53 laps | 6 | 1m37.411s | 20 |
| R | **Yuji Ide** | Super Aguri | 35 laps/engine | 3 | 1m40.270s | 21 |
| R | **Jacques Villeneuve** | BMW Sauber | 29 laps/engine | 1 | 1m32.456s | 11 |
| R | **Giancarlo Fisichella** | Renault | 21 laps/hydraulics | 2 | 1m33.496s | 9 |
| R | **Christijan Albers** | Midland | 0 laps/driveshaft | 0 | 1m35.724s | 18 |

**FASTEST LAP:** ROSBERG, 1M32.408S, 131.015MPH/210.838KPH, ON LAP 42

# TALKING POINT: RAIKKONEN FALLS FOUL OF NEW QUALIFYING

**As Kimi Raikkonen discovered, the new qualifying format made suspension failure even more of a disaster. He limped back to his pit but, as the first part of the session was only 15 minutes long, his McLaren pit crew were unable to get him back out again, leaving him among the cars from 17th to 22nd who were barred from the second qualifying session. In the latter, only the fastest ten would go through to the final 20-minute session, which would follow after a further five-minute break, with the ones eliminated lining up from 11th to 16th on the grid.**

Kimi Raikkonen did the damage and the timetable left his team insufficient time to get him out again

# MALAYSIAN GP

A refuelling slip-up in qualifying cost Fernando Alonso dear, but he was still able to complete a Renault one-two behind Giancarlo Fisichella – the team's first since 1982 – as Ferrari found its strong Bahrain form had deserted them.

It's party time: Renault team boss Flavio Briatore celebrates with Fisichella and winner Alonso

This was Giancarlo Fisichella's third grand prix victory, and he drove perfectly with Fernando Alonso close on 5s in his wake. However, as with much of his time at Renault, his win had to be put into perspective and, yet again, it was his team-mate Alonso who took the plaudits.

Alonso had qualified in seventh place and had had to work his way forward, while Fisichella had started on pole position and was never troubled by anyone else.

The Renault team wasn't convinced that Alonso's refuelling rig had delivered its load before the Top 10 qualifying shoot-out, which in fact it had, so they gave it another go and effectively double-fuelled his R26. With this extra weight, Alonso did well to lap eighth fastest, helped by Christian Klien deciding not to go for a flier, and engine failure hitting Ralf Schumacher, with the subsequent ten-place penalty dropping the Toyota driver to the wrong end of the grid.

Alonso was then given another helping hand when Michael Schumacher was moved back ten places on the grid for having had an engine change.

So, Fisichella sped away from Jenson Button's Honda at the start. Making the most of Renault's famed speed off the line, Alonso went from a standing start to third into the first corner, while Nico Rosberg went the other direction, dropping from third on the grid to seventh in his Williams.

Once they started lapping in earnest, Button was unable to hold on to second place as Alonso set a series of fastest laps. With all the extra fuel on board following the qualifying mix-up, Alonso made his first pit stop nine laps later than Fisichella and, by the time their second cycle of stops was completed, Renault were running first and second. With Fisichella in control and no one able to challenge them, Renault raced to its first one-two since Rene Arnoux led Alain Prost across the finish line in the 1982 French GP at Paul Ricard.

While everyone at Renault was grinning, Kimi Raikkonen's season continued to be troublesome with the Finn's McLaren being eliminated by contact with Klien at Turn 1 on the opening lap, the Red Bull Racing charger hitting the MP4-21 from behind and breaking its suspension.

At least McLaren got its other car – Juan Pablo Montoya's – to the finish. Rosberg also went out early, his Cosworth V8 failing after just six laps when he was running in sixth place behind Montoya after repassing Nick Heidfeld as he fought to make up ground after his tardy getaway.

Completing a bad day for Williams,

Rosberg's team-mate Mark Webber's FW28 lasted little longer than quarter-distance before it suffered hydraulics problems, promoting Montoya to fourth.

Button proved to be the best of the rest for Honda, but he was already making ominous noises that the Japanese manufacturer's pre-season form was just an illusion as the team's Michelins failed to offer the desired amount of grip. The English driver gave his best, but was edged out of second place by a short head at the second round of pit stops, cursing the fact that he'd been delayed by Scott Speed's Toro Rosso. Button was in good form compared with new team-mate Rubens Barrichello, though, with the experienced Brazilian struggling right through the race and finishing only tenth, a lap down on the Renaults.

Ferrari were less than happy at Sepang, too, with engine failures forcing both drivers to take a ten-place grid penalty, leaving Michael Schumacher to start in 14th and Felipe Massa in 21st. Massa started on a one-stop strategy, and this proved just superior to Michael's two-stop race, with Massa coming home just ahead in fifth for a welcome boost to his confidence. And Super Aguri deserved another pat on the back for again getting one of its hastily updated cars to the finish.

# SEPANG ROUND 02
Date: **19 March 2006**   Laps: **56**   Distance: **192.887 miles/310.407km**
Weather: **Hot and humid**

## RACE RESULT

| Position | Driver | Team | Result | Stops | Qualifying Time | Grid |
|---|---|---|---|---|---|---|
| 1 | Giancarlo Fisichella | Renault | 1h30m40.529s | 2 | 1m33.8402s | 1 |
| 2 | Fernando Alonso | Renault | 1h30m45.114s | 2 | 1m35.747s | 7 |
| 3 | Jenson Button | Honda | 1h30m50.160s | 2 | 1m33.986s | 2 |
| 4 | Juan Pablo Montoya | McLaren | 1h31m19.880s | 2 | 1m34.916s | 5 |
| 5 | Felipe Massa | Ferrari | 1h31m23.783s | 1 | no time | 21* |
| 6 | Michael Schumacher | Ferrari | 1h31m24.383s | 2 | 1m34.668s | 14 |
| 7 | Jacques Villeneuve | BMW Sauber | 1h32m00.990s | 2 | 1m34.752s | 10 |
| 8 | Ralf Schumacher | Toyota | 1h32m01.817s | 3 | no time | 22* |
| 9 | Jarno Trulli | Toyota | 55 laps | 2 | 1m34.702s | 9 |
| 10 | Rubens Barrichello | Honda | 55 laps | 1 | 1m34.683s | 20* |
| 11 | Vitantonio Liuzzi | Toro Rosso | 54 laps | 3 | 1m36.581s | 13 |
| 12 | Christijan Albers | Midland | 54 laps | 2 | 1m37.426s | 15 |
| 13 | Tiago Monteiro | Midland | 54 laps | 2 | 1m37.819s | 16 |
| 14 | Takuma Sato | Super Aguri | 53 laps | 2 | 1m39.011s | 17 |
| R | Nick Heidfeld | BMW Sauber | 48 laps/engine | 2 | 1m34.783s | 11 |
| R | Scott Speed | Toro Rosso | 41 laps/clutch | 1 | 1m36.297s | 12 |
| R | Yuji Ide | Super Aguri | 33 laps/throttle | 1 | 1m40.720s | 18 |
| R | Christian Klien | Red Bull | 26 laps/hydraulics | 2 | 1m38.715s | 8 |
| R | Mark Webber | Williams | 15 laps/hydraulics | 1 | 1m34.672s | 4 |
| R | David Coulthard | Red Bull | 10 laps/hydraulics | 0 | 1m34.614s | 19* |
| R | Nico Rosberg | Williams | 6 laps/engine | 0 | 1m34.626s | 3 |
| R | Kimi Raikkonen | McLaren | 0 laps/accident | 0 | 1m34.983s | 6 |

FASTEST LAP: ALONSO, 1M34.803S, 131.554MPH/211.706KPH ON LAP 45

* TEN-PLACE GRID PENALTY

# TALKING POINT: FURY AT FERRARI'S FLEXIBLE FRIENDS

Formula One wouldn't be the same if there wasn't a rumour bubbling under the surface, and the one at Sepang getting everyone hot under the collar was the flexibility of Ferrari's wings. Many reckoned that the red cars' front wings were too flexible and broke the rules because they weren't fully secured to their mountings, enabling them to lie flatter and thus reduce drag at speed before coming back up again to offer down force at the corners. The sport's governing body, the FIA, gave them the all clear, leaving Honda leading the way as it sought to find out whether it too could run a "flexi" version of its 2006 rear wing.

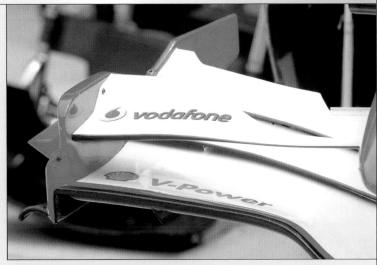

All eyes were on Ferrari's front wings and everyone wanted to know whether they were legal or not

# AUSTRALIAN GP

Unusually low track temperatures made some teams struggle for grip as Renault's Fernando Alonso got the better of Honda's Jenson Button early on, and raced to victory ahead of McLaren's Kimi Raikkonen in a much-interrupted race.

**Flat-out acceleration: Fernando Alonso powers past Jenson Button's Honda at the first of the restarts to take the lead and then race to victory**

It seemed odd to be in Melbourne for the Australian GP with two races having already been run, but that's what happened as the traditional season-opener was moved back nigh on a month to make way for this sports-mad city to host the Commonwealth Games.

As a result, this time around, the event lacked its usual element of surprise as teams pit their all-new racers against each other in earnest for the first time, but there was considerable sorting out and reappraising as cooler than usual weather altered the outcome of the race.

The person to suffer the most was Honda's Jenson Button. He was leading the race, but simply couldn't get enough heat into his tyres at the restart after the first of four safety car periods to resist the challenge of Fernando Alonso, and that was the last he saw of the Renault driver as Alonso simply waltzed away into the lead.

The first safety car period allowed for the retrieval of Felipe Massa's wrecked Ferrari that was sitting in the middle of the track between Turns 1 and 2, after clashing with Christian Klien's Red Bull on the opening lap, with Nico Rosberg's Williams ending up in the mêlée. And that wasn't even the race's first drama because Juan Pablo Montoya had spun his McLaren at the final corner on the way to the grid.

The Colombian's blushes were spared when Giancarlo Fisichella had his anti-stall device go haywire on the grid, cutting his R26's V8 engine and forcing the entire field to go on another formation lap, and allowing him to regain his fifth-grid slot.

For Montoya, more drama was to follow before the race was out, as he made a bad afternoon worse as he spun behind the safety car, falling behind Ralf Schumacher and Mark Webber in the process.

Having lost the lead to Alonso on the first restart, Button then came under pressure from McLaren's Kimi Raikkonen. Webber was also on the move, passing Schumacher's Toyota. Seizing the moment, Montoya dived past as well, with Nick Heidfeld taking a look to see if he could also squeeze by in his BMW Sauber before backing out.

Then the safety car was deployed for a second time on lap 7 after Klien's Red Bull slammed into the wall when under braking for Turn 9, perhaps due to sidepod damage from his lap 1 clash with Massa.

When the safety car withdrew, Raikkonen made the most of Button's Honda struggling on tyres that refused to come back up to temperature, and slotted past into second place into Turn 1. Button tried to fight back and they all but hit each other at Turn 3 before the Finn escaped to chase off after Alonso's Renault.

When the first round of pit stops commenced, Webber stayed out and earned the biggest cheer of the day as he took the lead, only to retire with a gearbox problem.

When this round of pit stops had been completed, Button had lost out and fallen back to fifth place behind Alonso, Raikkonen, Montoya and Heidfeld.

Button's next concern was Michael Schumacher who was reeling him in. The Ferrari driver had also been suffering from an inability to get his car's Bridgestone tyres up to their optimum operating temperature in these cooler than normal conditions, but he had a performance advantage over the Honda and wanted to get by. Except, Michael pushed too hard through the final corner, ran wide, hit a bump and slammed into the wall. Cue his retirement and the third safety car period. Cue, too, a rush for the pits, with everyone eager to make their second and final stop with minimal time penalty.

After the second round of stops, Button had lost a further place as Schumacher's Toyota had climbed to third, assisted by Montoya having called in behind Raikkonen and losing time while McLaren replaced a wing endplate on Raikkonen's car, dropping him from third to sixth. The Colombian's day went from bad to worse when he exited fourth place after a brush with the wall switched off the engine.

# AUSTRALIA ROUND 03
Date: **2 April 2006** Laps: **57** Distance: **191.117 miles/307.574kph**
Weather: **Warm and bright**

## RACE RESULT

| Position | Driver | Team | Result | Stops | Qualifying Time | Grid |
|---|---|---|---|---|---|---|
| 1 | **Fernando Alonso** | Renault | 1h34m27.870s | 2 | 1m25.778s | 3 |
| 2 | **Kimi Raikkonen** | McLaren | 1h34m29.699s | 2 | 1m25.822s | 4 |
| 3 | **Ralf Schumacher** | Toyota | 1h34m52.694s | 3 | 1m26.612s | 6 |
| 4 | **Nick Heidfeld** | BMW Sauber | 1h34m58.902s | 2 | 1m27.579s | 8 |
| 5 | **Giancarlo Fisichella** | Renault | 1h35m06.291s | 2 | 1m25.635s | 2 |
| 6 | **Jacques Villeneuve** | BMW Sauber | 1h35m17.424s | 1 | 1m29.239s | 19* |
| 7 | **Rubens Barrichello** | Honda | 1h35m19.774s | 2 | 1m29.943s | 16 |
| 8 | **David Coulthard** | Red Bull | 1h35m21.853s | 2 | 1m27.023s | 11 |
| 9 | **Scott Speed** | Toro Rosso | 56 laps** | 2 | 1m30.426s | 18 |
| 10 | **Jenson Button** | Honda | 56 laps/engine | 2 | 1m25.229s | 1 |
| 11 | **Christijan Albers** | Midland | 56 laps | 2 | 1m30.226s | 17 |
| 12 | **Takuma Sato** | Super Aguri | 55 laps | 3 | 1m32.279s | 21 |
| 13 | **Yuji Ide** | Super Aguri | 54 laps | 3 | 1m36.164s | 22 |
| R | **Juan Pablo Montoya** | McLaren | 46 laps/electrical | 2 | 1m25.976s | 5 |
| R | **Tiago Monteiro** | Midland | 39 laps/hydraulics | 2 | 1m30.709s | 20 |
| R | **Vitantonio Liuzzi** | Toro Rosso | 37 laps/accident | 2 | 1m27.219s | 12 |
| R | **Michael Schumacher** | Ferrari | 32 laps/accident | 1 | 1m26.718s | 10 |
| R | **Mark Webber** | Williams | 22 laps/transmission | 0 | 1m26.937s | 7 |
| R | **Christian Klien** | Red Bull | 4 laps/accident | 0 | 1m27.591s | 13 |
| R | **Jarno Trulli** | Toyota | 0 laps/accident | 0 | 1m26.327s | 9 |
| R | **Nico Rosberg** | Williams | 0 laps/accident damage | 0 | 1m29.422s | 14 |
| R | **Felipe Massa** | Ferrari | 0 laps/accident | 0 | 1m28.868s | 15 |

**FASTEST LAP:** RAIKKONEN, 1M26.045S, 137.863MPH/221.859KPH ON LAP 57

* TEN-PLACE GRID PENALTY ** INCLUDES 25 SECOND PENALTY FOR OVERTAKING UNDER YELLOW FLAGS

# TALKING POINT: HONDA FINDS ITSELF GOING NOWHERE FAST

**Pole position for Jenson Button ought to have been a cause for celebration, but faces were long by the following afternoon as he parked, his engine smoking, metres short of the finish. The blown engine cost a few points because he had slid to fifth, but the team's concerns were centred more on their tyres. Put simply, the Honda RA106 was failing to get the right amount of heat into its Michelins and Button told the team to sort it out. Team-mate Rubens Barrichello's form continued to disappoint as he also struggled to get used to Honda's traction control system and a lack of feeling when braking.**

The Michelin-shod Honda of Rubens Barrichello had no answer to Massa's Bridgestone-tyred Ferrari

# SAN MARINO GP

A Ferrari victory on home ground always delights the tifosi, but one in which their hero Michael Schumacher guided his Ferrari past reigning world champion Fernando Alonso's Renault sent them home from Imola in paroxysms of delight.

The start of something big: Michael Schumacher's victory for Ferrari demonstrated that Reanult was going to have to fight to retain its title

Besides cut-throat overtaking, everyone wants to see a tactical masterstroke. And that's what Ferrari pulled off on one of their two home circuits - Imola - to beat reigning champions Renault and Fernando Alonso.

Getting pole position was the first important factor, with Alonso stuck in fifth behind the Hondas of Jenson Button and Rubens Barrichello, who'd done well in qualifying, and his own team-mate Felipe Massa. A good getaway from the standing start was also a prerequisite and Michael duly delivered, though his escape into the wild blue yonder was kept in check as the safety car was deployed before the lap was

out to clear wreckage at the second chicane. Yuji Ide had been a little overambitious and his Super Aguri had given Christijan Albers' Midlands a clout, sending it into a spectacular roll. The Dutchman walked away without injury, although his blood pressure was momentarily off the clock with fury.

As ever, Alonso was quick off the line, both he and Massa demoting Barrichello. The Spaniard's next quarry was harder to pass, with Massa remaining ahead until he pitted on lap 19. With Button having reported in four laps earlier, Alonso was up to second. One lap later, Michael pitted from the lead leaving Alonso in front. He pressed all he

could over the next five laps until he was the last of the frontrunners to make their first pit stop of two. Unfortunately for Alonso, he hit traffic on the last two of these five laps and Michael was able to retake the lead.

On his second set of tyres, Alonso fared better than Michael and started carving great chunks out of the German's lead. Then he got stuck, slowed down by the Ferrari, trapped in its wake, and was unable to overtake around the narrow twists of Imola. It was the 2005 race revisited, with their roles reversed. This time, though, there was a pit stop to come and it looked as though Alonso would be able to make his final stop and rejoin in the lead. Except that Renault had short-fuelled him at his first stop and reckoned that he had the fuel to do only one lap more than Michael.

Worried that they might actually pit on the same lap, Renault's tactical mastermind Pat Symonds gambled and brought Alonso in on lap 41, catching Ferrari off guard, but it was a slow in-lap. Reacting immediately, Ross Brawn called Michael in the following lap and he dramatically upped his pace to the extent that his flying in-lap was enough for him to rejoin in the lead. Despite Alonso's best efforts in the final stint, that's how they finished, with Juan Pablo Montoya a distant third, the McLaren driver having moved ahead of Massa by making his final pit stop later. Raikkonen was at the tail of this trio, in fifth.

Such was the Hondas' decline that Button fell to seventh just behind Mark Webber's Williams after losing considerable time at his first pit stop when a wheel wouldn't engage, and then having a worse delay at his second stop when he drove off with the fuel hose still attached. Barrichello also lost out in the pits, losing eight places when his fuel rig failed.

Third place in the Australian GP became a distant memory for Ralf Schumacher as he struggled home in ninth place.

# IMOLA ROUND 04

Date: **23 April 2006** Laps: **62** Distance: **189.897 miles/305.595km**
Weather: **Warm and dry**

## RACE RESULT

| Position | Driver | Team | Result | Stops | Qualifying Time | Grid |
|---|---|---|---|---|---|---|
| 1 | Michael Schumacher | Ferrari | 1h31m06.486s | 2 | 1m22.795s | 1 |
| 2 | Fernando Alonso | Renault | 1h31m08.582s | 2 | 1m23.709s | 5 |
| 3 | Juan Pablo Montoya | McLaren | 1h31m22.354s | 2 | 1m24.021s | 7 |
| 4 | Felipe Massa | Ferrari | 1h31m23.582s | 2 | 1m23.702s | 4 |
| 5 | Kimi Raikkonen | McLaren | 1h31m24.010s | 2 | 1m24.158s | 8 |
| 6 | Mark Webber | Williams | 1h31m44.225s | 2 | 1m24.795s | 10 |
| 7 | Jenson Button | Honda | 1h31m46.121s | 3 | 1m22.988s | 2 |
| 8 | Giancarlo Fisichella | Renault | 1h31m46.686s | 2 | 1m23.771s | 11 |
| 9 | Ralf Schumacher | Toyota | 1h31m51.977s | 3 | 1m23.772s | 6 |
| 10 | Rubens Barrichello | Honda | 1h32m24.337s | 2 | 1m23.242s | 3 |
| 11 | Nico Rosberg | Williams | 1h32m26.161s | 2 | 1m23.966s | 13 |
| 12 | Jacques Villeneuve | BMW Sauber | 1h32m28.856s | 2 | 1m23.887s | 12 |
| 13 | Nick Heidfeld | BMW Sauber | 1h31m14.621s | 2 | 1m24.129s | 15 |
| 14 | Vitantonio Liuzzi | Toro Rosso | 61 laps | 2 | 1m24.520s | 16 |
| 15 | Scott Speed | Toro Rosso | 61 laps | 2 | 1m25.437s | 18 |
| 16 | Tiago Monteiro | Midland | 60 laps | 2 | 1m26.820s | 19 |
| R | David Coulthard | Red Bull | 47 laps/driveshaft | 2 | 1m24.101s | 14 |
| R | Takuma Sato | Super Aguri | 44 laps/accident | 2 | 1m27.609s | 21 |
| R | Christian Klien | Red Bull | 40 laps/hydraulics | 1 | 1m25.410s | 17 |
| R | Yuji Ide | Super Aguri | 23 laps/suspension | 2 | 1m29.282s | 22 |
| R | Jarno Trulli | Toyota | 5 laps/steering | 0 | 1m24.172s | 9 |
| R | Christijan Albers | Midland | 0 laps/accident | 0 | 1m27.088s | 20 |

FASTEST LAP: ALONSO, 1M24.569S, 131.197MPH/211.131KPH ON LAP 23

# TALKING POINT: A NOT QUITE SO SUPER AGURI DRIVER

**Super Aguri Racing's ability to contest the 2006 World Championship was quite a surprise as the plans only came together after the 11th hour. But the selection of Yuji Ide as the new team's number two to Takuma Satowas a shock. With the exception of his 2005 season in which he finished runner-up in Japan's Formula Nippon series, he had been lacklustre. And he'd had virtually no pre-season testing as the team struggled to modify its 2002 Arrows chassis. People sympathised; he'd been flung in at the deep end. By Imola, however, that sympathy had evaporated, especially Christijan Albers'.**

Hampered by a lack of testing or track knowledge, Yuji Ide spent too much time like this...

# EUROPEAN GP

**Ferrari squared up to Renault again, and once more Michael Schumacher beat Fernando Alonso to the chequered flag. It was a classic case of two drivers going flat-out throughout, each hoping his team's tactics would give him a win.**

This race differed from the one before it, at Imola, because Fernando Alonso was not fighting from behind. This time around, Renault had thrown a little more at qualifying and claimed pole position, lapping 0.2s faster than Michael Schumacher to put one over on Alonso's arch-rival.

With Felipe Massa qualifying the second Ferrari third fastest, at least Michael had an ally because Giancarlo Fisichella lined up only 11th in the second Renault after failing to get into the Top Ten qualifying run-off, having been held up on his flying lap by Jacques Villeneuve's BMW Sauber. The normally calm Italian was less than happy at this turn of events.

With Michael getting the power down best at the start, he held on to the lead into and through the tight opening corner.

As happens every year, there was a first-lap accident. This time it involved David Coulthard who had benefited notably in 2005 by avoiding trouble here. On this occasion, his Red Bull was hit by Vitantonio Liuzzi's Toro Rosso which had been pitched into the air by Ralf Schumacher's Toyota. With Liuzzi's car stuck on the racing line, the safety car was deployed for a brief spell. Dietrich Mateschitz, owner of both Red Bull Racing and Scuderia Torro Roso, had even less reason to smile two laps later when Coulthard parked up with accident damage.

Once the race was under way again, Alonso opened out a decent lead, but it didn't give him the luxury of running a three-stop race strategy. Instead, he was the first front-runner to pit, followed in on lap 17 by Massa and by Michael on the following lap, with Michael just failing to get out ahead of Alonso

when he returned. Worrying for all of them, Kimi Raikkonen stayed out and took the lead before pitting on lap 23. The Finn rejoined in fourth place but was clearly becoming a leading player in the day's events.

Ferrari remained confident of glory, though, because they reckoned they'd put more fuel into Michael's car at the first stop than Renault had put into Alonso's. And they were proved right as his second stop was three laps later than the Spaniard's, giving Michael the lead. Well, he was actually in

second place behind Raikkonen but the Finn still had to make his second stop, and dropped back to fourth when he made it.

Having been demoted to second, Alonso realised that he couldn't pass Michael and eased off the revs to save his engine for its second race, at Monaco. This was something that many drivers had to do at certain points in the season due to having to make an engine last for two races. It went counter to their culture as racers, but the risk of pushing it hard and risking a blow-up and the resultant

**Podium fun: Felipe Massa secures his first top-three finish and celebrates by drenching his team leade**

10-place grid penalty made them see sense.

Alonso's reduced pace enabled Massa to close in, with Raikkonen joining in to tail the Brazilian at the finish but not deprive him of his first podium finish. Afterwards, McLaren's CEO Martin Whitmarsh claimed that if the team had selected the correct compound of Michelin, they would have beaten Ferrari. And indeed they might.

Rubens Barrichello proved to be the best of the rest and finished fifth, with Fisichella a frustrated sixth, just ahead of Nico Rosberg. The Williams driver deserved praise as he started 22nd and worked his way into the points. Had the team not been concerned about tyre degradation and changed from a one-stop strategy, he might have finished fifth.

Rosberg's team-mate Mark Webber could also have collected a handful of points, having leapt from 19th to 12th by the first corner, but his car was taken out by a hydraulic failure. Ralf Schumacher and Juan Pablo Montoya also went home empty-handed after retiring.

Following criticism of Yuji Ide's standard of driving in his first-lap accident at the San Marino GP, Franck Montagny replaced him at Super Aguri and wasn't far behind the pace of team leader Takuma Sato. Neither finished the race, though.

# NURBURGRING ROUND 05
Date: **7 May 2006**  Laps: **60**  Distance: **195.167 miles/314.076km**
Weather: **Warm and bright**

## RACE RESULT

| Position | Driver | Team | Result | Stops | Qualifying Time | Grid |
|---|---|---|---|---|---|---|
| 1 | Michael Schumacher | Ferrari | 1h35m58.765s | 2 | 1m30.028s | 2 |
| 2 | Fernando Alonso | Renault | 1h36m02.516s | 2 | 1m29.819s | 1 |
| 3 | Felipe Massa | Ferrari | 1h36m03.212s | 2 | 1m30.407s | 3 |
| 4 | Kimi Raikkonen | McLaren | 1h36m03.644s | 2 | 1m30.933s | 5 |
| 5 | Rubens Barrichello | Honda | 1h37m11.351s | 2 | 1m30.754s | 4 |
| 6 | Giancarlo Fisichella | Renault | 1h37m12.881s | 2 | 1m31.197s | 11 |
| 7 | Nico Rosberg | Williams | 1h37m13.330s | 2 | 1m31.194s | 22* |
| 8 | Jacques Villeneuve | BMW Sauber | 1h37m28.129s | 2 | 1m36.998s | 9 |
| 9 | Jarno Trulli | Toyota | 59 laps | 2 | 1m31.419s | 7 |
| 10 | Nick Heidfeld | BMW Sauber | 59 laps | 2 | 1m31.422s | 13 |
| 11 | Scott Speed | Toro Rosso | 59 laps | 2 | 1m32.992s | 17 |
| 12 | Tiago Monteiro | Midland | 59 laps | 2 | 1m33.658s | 18 |
| 13 | Christijan Albers | Midland | 59 laps | 2 | 1m32.936s | 16 |
| R | Ralf Schumacher | Toyota | 52 laps/engine | 2 | 1m30.944s | 10 |
| R | Juan Pablo Montoya | McLaren | 52 laps/engine | 2 | 1m31.880s | 8 |
| R | Takuma Sato | Super Aguri | 45 laps/hydraulics | 2 | 1m35.239s | 20 |
| R | Franck Montagny | Super Aguri | 29 laps/engine | 1 | 1m46.505s | 21 |
| R | Jenson Button | Honda | 28 laps/engine | 1 | 1m30.940s | 6 |
| R | Christian Klien | Red Bull | 28 laps/transmission | 1 | 1m32.901s | 15 |
| R | Mark Webber | Williams | 12 laps/hydraulics | 0 | 1m33.405s | 19* |
| R | David Coulthard | Red Bull | 2 laps/accident damage | 2 | 1m31.227s | 12 |
| R | Vitantonio Liuzzi | Toro Rosso | 0 laps/accident damage | 0 | 1m31.728s | 14 |

**FASTEST LAP:** MICHAEL SCHUMACHER, 1M32.099S, 125.005MPH/201.166KPH ON LAP 39

* TEN-PLACE GRID PENALTY

## TALKING POINT: COSWORTH BEGINS TO FEEL THE HEAT

**Engine failures in Formula One have never been as costly as in 2006. With an engine expected to last two grands prix, a change spells a 10-place grid demotion. And that's what happened to both Williams drivers after practice at the Nurburgring, leaving them to line up 19th and 22nd on the grid. With Williams still undecided about its engine choice for 2007, it was felt that Cosworth hadn't done itself any favours and its one-year deal with Williams might end, with a subsidised or free Toyota V8s taking over. Indeed, Cosworth was already aware that it might end the year with no deals for 2007.**

After engine changes in practice, it was a long way to the front for both of the Williams drivers

# SPANISH GP

**Fernando Alonso described being presented the winner's trophy by King Juan Carlos as "the best thing that had happened to me in Formula One", his national pride the only thing exceeding his delight at leaving Schumacher in his wake.**

Royal command performance: World Champion Fernando Alonso bends down to be greeted by King Juan Carlos as team-mate Fisichella looks on

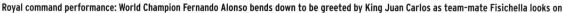

Fernando Alonso really wanted to enjoy his first grand prix on home ground since being crowned World Champion at the end of 2005. Extra grandstands were erected to cope with the demand, and they quickly sold out. His Renault and its Michelin tyres were competitive and, best of all, he took pole position while his team-mate Giancarlo Fisichella qualified second fastest, keeping Michael Schumacher third on the grid.

The Renaults held position at the start, with Felipe Massa holding on to fourth in the second Ferrari, being surprised to find Kimi Raikkonen's McLaren on his tail after Turn 1, the Finn having gone around the outside of both Toyotas and both Hondas. However, the

key to the race was Fisichella being able to keep himself between Alonso and Michael. Well, until the first round of pit stops. Alonso came in first on lap 17, followed by Fisichella on lap 18. Michael and Ferrari were obviously attempting to hit the front and he led until he came in on lap 23.

By this time, he'd done enough to take second place, but Alonso was away, easily in control of proceedings, thankful that he'd been able to pull so far clear in the opening stint. And this was how the top four finished: Alonso, Michael 18.5s behind, Fisichella a further 5.5s back, and then Massa.

Having had their hopes raised by improving form at the previous round at the

Nurburgring, McLaren might have reckoned that they'd be in good shape for the Circuit de Catalunya – one of their happiest hunting grounds in the past decade – but it wasn't to be. Kimi Raikkonen came in a distant fifth, never able to trouble the Renaults and Ferraris. Still, at least he finished, which is more than can be said of team-mate Juan Pablo Montoya who spun off, beaching his McLaren in a gravel trap and ruining what might have been a strong run on a one-stop race strategy.

After qualifying sixth, Toyota's Ralf Schumacher might have reckoned on scoring points, but his day was ruined when he attempted a passing manoeuvre on team-mate, Jarno Trulli, forcing him to pit for a new nose. Worse followed when Ralf had to retire with an electronic problem. Trulli again found his Toyota's handling a problem, and he ended up tenth; he might have scored 43 points in 2005, but in six attempts in 2006 he was still stuck on zero.

Honda again started well up the grid, with Rubens Barrichello fifth and Jenson Button eighth, but Barrichello was pushed back a place at the start by the flying Raikkonen, and he was pushed further back at the first round of stops by Button who had seemingly been delayed by Barrichello, and that's how they finished, in sixth and seventh. The final point went to Nick Heidfeld, the BMW Sauber driver who gained two places over his grid position by the demise of the Toyotas, doing just enough to hold off Mark Webber's Williams at the close.

Red Bull Racing were unusually far from the pace, with Christian Klien finishing ahead of David Coulthard, the Scot having started at the back of the grid. In fact, the Ferrari-powered RB2s were so disappointing that they were fleetingly behind the Toro Rosso sister cars early on, with Scott Speed and Vitantonio Liuzzi starting well before Klien went ahead. Coulthard only got past Liuzzi on the final lap when the Italian's car stopped with hydraulic problems.

# CATALUNYA ROUND 06
Date: **14 May 2006**  Laps: **66**  Distance: **189.677 miles/305.256km**
Weather: **Hot and bright**

## RACE RESULT

| Position | Driver | Team | Result | Stops | Qualifying Time | Grid |
|---|---|---|---|---|---|---|
| 1 | **Fernando Alonso** | Renault | 1h26m21.759s | 2 | 1m14.648s | 1 |
| 2 | **Michael Schumacher** | Ferrari | 1h26m40.261s | 2 | 1m14.970s | 3 |
| 3 | **Giancarlo Fisichella** | Renault | 1h26m45.710s | 2 | 1m14.709s | 2 |
| 4 | **Felipe Massa** | Ferrari | 1h26m51.618s | 2 | 1m15.442s | 4 |
| 5 | **Kimi Raikkonen** | McLaren | 1h27m18.634s | 2 | 1m16.015s | 9 |
| 6 | **Jenson Button** | Honda | 1h27m20.106s | 2 | 1m16.008s | 8 |
| 7 | **Rubens Barrichello** | Honda | 65 laps | 2 | 1m15.885s | 5 |
| 8 | **Nick Heidfeld** | BMW Sauber | 65 laps | 2 | 1m17.144s | 10 |
| 9 | **Mark Webber** | Williams | 65 laps | 2 | 1m15.502s | 11 |
| 10 | **Jarno Trulli** | Toyota | 65 laps | 2 | 1m15.976s | 7 |
| 11 | **Nico Rosberg** | Williams | 65 laps | 2 | 1m15.804s | 13 |
| 12 | **Jacques Villeneuve** | BMW Sauber | 65 laps | 1 | 1m15.847s | 22* |
| 13 | **Christian Klien** | Red Bull | 65 laps | 2 | 1m15.928s | 14 |
| 14 | **David Coulthard** | Red Bull | 65 laps | 2 | no time | 21 |
| 15 | **Vitantonio Liuzzi** | Toro Rosso | 63 laps | 2 | 1m16.661s | 15 |
| 16 | **Tiago Monteiro** | Midland | 63 laps | 2 | 1m17.702s | 17 |
| 17 | **Takuma Sato** | Super Aguri | 62 laps | 3 | 1m18.920s | 19 |
| R | **Christijan Albers** | Midland | 48 laps/spun off | 3 | 1m18.024s | 18 |
| R | **Scott Speed** | Toro Rosso | 47 laps/engine | 1 | 1m17.361s | 16 |
| R | **Ralf Schumacher** | Toyota | 31 laps/electronics | 1 | 1m15.885s | 6 |
| R | **Juan Pablo Montoya** | McLaren | 17 laps/spun off | 0 | 1m15.801s | 12 |
| R | **Franck Montagny** | Super Aguri | 10 laps/driveshaft | 0 | 1m20.763s | 20 |

**FASTEST LAP:** MASSA, 1M16.648S, 135.036MPH/217.309KPH ON LAP 42  * TEN-PLACE GRID PENALTY

## TALKING POINT: EVERYONE WANTS A PIECE OF ALONSO

For years, promoters didn't know how to make Formula One popular in Spain. Motorsport to the Spaniards meant motorcycle racing, which attracted hundreds of thousands to cheer on its numerous world champions in the 1980s. Formula One was the poor cousin, with their only driver of calibre being Alfonso de Portago before he crashed fatally on the Mille Miglia in 1957. The solution was simple: find a Spanish driver capable of taking on the best. Fernando Alonso was the man, as he proved every year after his first win, at Hungary, in 2003. When he became World Champion in 2005, the country went ballistic.

Spain to the fore as local hero Fernando Alonso leads the field through the first sequence of corners

# MONACO GP

**Fernando Alonso was peerless, leading effectively from start to finish. However, the 2006 Monaco GP will long be remembered as the one in which Michael Schumacher darkened his name with an extraordinary and most surprising incident in qualifying.**

Formula One fans won't forget this one. First, Michael Schumacher steered his Ferrari straight at the barriers to block the track and end the final qualifying session with his name top, denying anyone else the chance of beating him, and then countered questions afterwards with a stony face. Then there was Kimi Raikkonen's pursuit of Fernando Alonso, followed by Raikkonen storming off to board his yacht after retiring from the race, and Mark Webber's flaming retirement, and David Coulthard being kitted out with a red Superman cape for the podium ceremony in celebration of Red Bull Racing's first podium finish since it metamorphosed from Jaguar Racing, and to help promote the film "Superman Returns". However, the inescapable outcome of it all was that Alonso strengthened his lead in the drivers' championship, and Renault eased away in the constructors' standings.

It's safe to say that Michael Schumacher's qualifying antics were the talk of Monaco, and he was banished from pole position to the rear of the grid. But he was in masterful form in the race, and worked his way through the field to come within spitting distance of a podium finish. However, the man of the meeting was Alonso. Promoted to pole by Schumacher's demotion, he made a clean start and led into Ste Devote as Webber gave his all to keep Raikkonen from wresting second place from him. He was managing all right, but next time around he slid wide at the same right-hander and the Finn was through to start exerting pressure on the Spaniard, with Webber quickly back in line to make it a threesome. The pressure was relentless until the tail of Raikkonen's

McLaren went up in smoke after 50 laps, just one lap after his second pit stop.

Amazingly, having been harried almost all the way, the pressure completely fell away from Alonso because two laps earlier Webber had dropped out of this trio, triggering a safety car period that sent the remaining two-stop runners diving for the pits when his Williams caught light. Michael

Schumacher had reason to curse the timing of the deployment of the safety car as he'd already made his one and only planned pit stop, having brought it forward because he'd got caught in traffic. Had he stuck to his original plan, he might even have made it to the podium, not that he'd have been popular given his earlier antics.

So McLaren's Juan Pablo Montoya was

**A walk in the park: Kimi Raikkonen didn't feel like admiring the flowers after retiring from the race**

promoted to second place, some way adrift of Alonso with 28 laps to go, but well clear of Rubens Barrichello's Honda. And all the while Michael Schumacher was making up ground. A drive-through penalty for speeding in the pit lane scuppered Barrichello's afternoon, though it no doubt cheered the two-stopping drivers stuck behind his one-stopping Honda early in the race, and up into third place came Jarno Trulli.

The Italian's run of bad luck continued ten laps later when his Toyota pulled up with a hydraulic problem with just five laps of the race remaining.

And so Coulthard, who had not put a foot wrong as he ran a one-stop strategy, continued his ascent for Red Bull Racing, taking over from Trulli in third place. Barrichello soon closed in on him, with Michael Schumacher joining this group, but Monaco isn't an easy passing circuit and this was how they reached the finish, with Coulthard forcing team chief Christian Horner to honour a bet and dive naked into the Red Bull pool. His blushes were spared by a strategically placed Superman cape. Giancarlo Fisichella was the last of the cars on the lead lap, in sixth place, with the final points going to Nick Heidfeld and Ralf Schumacher, with Felipe Massa and Vitantonio Liuzzi not far behind.

# MONACO ROUND 07

Date: **28 May 2006**  Laps: **78**  Distance: **161.880 miles/260.520km**
Weather: **Warm and bright**

## RACE RESULT

| Position | Driver | Team | Result | Stops | Qualifying Time | Grid |
|---|---|---|---|---|---|---|
| 1 | Fernando Alonso | Renault | 1h43m43.116s | 2 | 1m13.962s | 1 |
| 2 | Juan Pablo Montoya | McLaren | 1h43m57.683s | 2 | 1m14.664s | 4 |
| 3 | David Coulthard | Red Bull | 1h44m35.414s | 1 | 1m16.426s | 7 |
| 4 | Rubens Barrichello | Honda | 1h44m36.453s | 2 | 1m15.804s | 5 |
| 5 | Michael Schumacher | Ferrari | 1h44m36.946s | 1 | No time | 22* |
| 6 | Giancarlo Fisichella | Renault | 1h44m45.188s | 2 | 1m17.260s | 9** |
| 7 | Nick Heidfeld | BMW Sauber | 77 laps | 1 | 1m15.137s | 15 |
| 8 | Ralf Schumacher | Toyota | 77 laps | 1 | 1m14.398s | 10 |
| 9 | Felipe Massa | Ferrari | 77 laps | 1 | no time | 21 |
| 10 | Vitantonio Liuzzi | Toro Rosso | 77 laps | 1 | 1m14.969s | 12 |
| 11 | Jenson Button | Honda | 77 laps | 1 | 1m14.982s | 13 |
| 12 | Chistijan Albers | Midland | 77 laps | 2 | 1m15.598s | 16 |
| 13 | Scott Speed | Toro Rosso | 77 laps | 1 | 1m16.236s | 18 |
| 14 | Jacques Villeneuve | BMW Sauber | 77 laps | 2 | 1m15.052s | 14 |
| 15 | Tiago Monteiro | Midland | 76 laps | 2 | 1m15.993s | 17 |
| 16 | Franck Montagny | Super Aguri | 75 laps | 1 | 1m17.502s | 20 |
| 17 | Jarno Trulli | Toyota | 72 laps/hydraulics | 1 | 1m15.857s | 6 |
| R | Christian Klien | Red Bull | 56 laps/transmission | 1 | 1m14.747s | 11 |
| R | Nico Rosberg | Williams | 51 laps/throttle | 2 | 1m16.636s | 8 |
| R | Kimi Raikkonen | McLaren | 50 laps/fire | 2 | 1m14.140s | 3 |
| R | Mark Webber | Williams | 48 laps/fire | 1 | 1m14.082s | 2 |
| R | Takuma Sato | Super Aguri | 46 laps/electrical | 1 | 1m17.276s | 19 |

**FASTEST LAP:** MICHAEL SCHUMACHER, 1M15.143S, 99.430MPH/160.010KPH ON LAP 74

* ALL QUALFYING TIMES DISALLOWED ** THREE-PLACE GRID PENALTY

## TALKING POINT: MICHAEL REDISCOVERS HIS BAD OLD WAYS

**Why, oh why? The most-titled World Champion ever, a driver still at the top of his game, showed a side of his character that was unsporting and unnecessary. His act was one of panic on his final lap as he deliberately hit the barriers at Rascasse to block the track and end the final qualifying session with his name still top of the timesheets as others were winding up to topple him. He was publicly slated but, worst of all, it confirmed that when he manoeuvred into rivals Damon Hill at Adelaide in 1994, and Jacques Villeneuve at Jerez in 1997, it was probably no accident, reminding fans of previous stains on his reputation.**

Michael has long been a master of Monaco, making his accident seem extremely surprising

# BRITISH GP

**Fernando Alonso made it three wins in a row, but the manner of his victory at Silverstone impressed more than the ten points. Michael Schumacher overhauled Kimi Raikkonen to be the best of the rest, but his deficit went out to 23 points.**

**Making a break: pole man Fernando Alonso keeps his Renault ahead of Kimi Raikkonen's McLaren and Michael Schumacher's Ferrari at the start**

Those who were concerned that moving the British GP a month forward from its traditional slot might mean problems with wet weather needn't have worried because the weather was fabulous, while Fernando Alonso gave Renault a double celebration because they were also about to chalk up their 200th start as a works team.

Alonso had lined up in pole position and made a clean getaway, with Kimi Raikkonen holding on to second place through the Copse. Then came Felipe Massa, protecting Michael Schumacher and Giancarlo Fisichella, hoping to help the Renault cause. Through the Becketts they went, but not all made it out the other end into the Hangar Straight as Scott Speed made a do-or-die

dive up the inside of Ralf Schumacher, the Toro Rosso clipping the Toyota. Mark Webber then discovered a further downside of qualifying only 17th, having failed to make the grade to enter the second qualifying session, when he attempted to guide his Williams through the bomb blast but got taken out by Schumacher as the German fought to bring his Toyota back under control. Time for the safety car.

Fortunately, it was soon returning to the pits and Raikkonen attacked Alonso. He too was under pressure as Schumacher tried to shove his Ferrari's nose inside the silver McLaren at Abbey. Alonso weathered the storm, then eased clear as his tyres came up to temperature again and Raikkonen was

forced to heed the attacks from behind. Jenson Button lasted little longer, rotating his Honda into the gravel at Brooklands on the ninth lap after an oil leak short-changed his efforts that had taken him from 19th on the grid, after a disastrous performance in qualifying, to be 14th at the end of the opening lap before picking off Jarno Trulli then Vitantonio Liuzzi.

Ever further clear in the lead, Alonso then rubbed in his and Renault's superiority by making the first of his two planned pit stops after his two chief rivals, calling in on lap 22, some three laps after Michael and three after Raikkonen. He was faster than them, sporting a near 10s advantage, and that's with a heavier fuel load. And that was that, game over, with only Fisichella getting ahead of him for a single lap during the second round of stops before rejoining in fourth place after outrunning Massa.

Having been thwarted by coming upon Franck Montagny's Super Aguri before his first pit stop, Michael gave it his all to pass Raikkonen at the second round of pit stops and it worked, helped in no small part by a small fire in the McLaren pit that delayed the Finn. There was nothing that he could do about Alonso, who was able to back off and still win by 14s.

Raikkonen was pressed for third place as Fisichella had a crack at him, although he was unable to make Renault's straight-line speed advantage pay, and the McLaren driver took the final podium position. Juan Pablo Montoya said that his McLaren suffered all race after having one of its side-pods holed on the opening lap after contact with Jacques Villeneuve's BMW Sauber, and he was a distant sixth with Villeneuve finishing eighth behind his team-mate Nick Heidfeld. Nico Rosberg crossed the line right on Villeneuve's tail, frustrated by the Williams team's third straight non-score, but not as much as Rubens Barrichello who slipped from sixth on the grid to a lapped tenth, his Honda struggling more than most for grip as its tyres wore.

# SILVERSTONE ROUND 08

Date: **11 June 2006** Laps: **60** Distance: **191.603 miles/308.335km**
Weather: **Warm and bright**

## RACE RESULT

| Position | Driver | Team | Result | Stops | Qualifying Time | Grid |
|---|---|---|---|---|---|---|
| 1 | Fernando Alonso | Renault | 1h25m51.927s | 2 | 1m20.253s | 1 |
| 2 | Michael Schumacher | Ferrari | 1h26m05.878s | 2 | 1m20.574s | 3 |
| 3 | Kimi Raikkonen | McLaren | 1h26m10.599s | 2 | 1m20.397s | 2 |
| 4 | Giancarlo Fisichella | Renault | 1h26m11.903s | 2 | 1m20.919s | 5 |
| 5 | Felipe Massa | Ferrari | 1h26m23.486s | 2 | 1m20.764s | 4 |
| 6 | Juan Pablo Montoya | McLaren | 1h26m56.696s | 2 | 1m21.107s | 8 |
| 7 | Nick Heidfeld | BMW Sauber | 1h27m03.521s | 2 | 1m21.329s | 9 |
| 8 | Jacques Villeneuve | BMW Sauber | 1h27m10.226s | 2 | 1m21.599s | 10 |
| 9 | Nico Rosberg | Williams | 1h27m10.935s | 2 | 1m21.567s | 12 |
| 10 | Rubens Barrichello | Honda | 59 laps | 2 | 1m20.943s | 6 |
| 11 | Jarno Trulli | Toyota | 59 laps | 2 | no time | 22 |
| 12 | David Coulthard | Red Bull | 59 laps | 2 | 1m21.442s | 11 |
| 13 | Vitantonio Liuzzi | Toro Rosso | 59 laps | 1 | 1m21.699s | 13 |
| 14 | Christian Klien | Red Bull | 59 laps | 2 | 1m21.990s | 14 |
| 15 | Christijan Albers | Midland | 59 laps | 2 | 1m23.210s | 18 |
| 16 | Tiago Monteiro | Midland | 58 laps | 2 | 1m22.207s | 16 |
| 17 | Takuma Sato | Super Aguri | 57 laps | 2 | 1m26.158s | 21* |
| 18 | Franck Montagny | Super Aguri | 57 laps | 2 | 1m26.316s | 20 |
| R | Jenson Button | Honda | 8 laps/oil leak | 0 | 1m23.247s | 19 |
| R | Scott Speed | Toro Rosso | 1 lap/accident damage | 0 | 1m22.076s | 15 |
| R | Ralf Schumacher | Toyota | 0 laps/accident | 0 | 1m21.073s | 7 |
| R | Mark Webber | Williams | 0 laps/accident | 0 | 1m23.129s | 17 |

**FASTEST LAP:** ALONSO, 1M21.599S, 140.934MPH/226.801KPH ON LAP 217

* TEN-PLACE GRID PENALTY

# TALKING POINT: MONTOYA'S F1 DAYS START TO LOOK NUMBERED

**McLaren boss Ron Dennis had commented that he'd never seen a driver work as hard as Juan Pablo had over the winter. However, by early summer, it became clear that the Colombian hadn't managed to turn this into scintillating form. Team-mate Kimi Raikkonen had yet to win in 2006, but he'd been driving the MP4-21 to its maximum. Juan Pablo had been mistake-prone, and wasn't as fast. With Fernando Alonso already on the books for 2007, Juan Pablo's hopes were to find a top drive elsewhere, but none was available. Qualifying six places behind Kimi at Silverstone highlighted the malaise.**

The smile has gone, leaving Juan Pablo Montoya to consider turning his back on Formula One

# CANADIAN GP

**Eight starts, five wins and three second places was Fernando Alonso's tally after the Canadian GP. His margin over Michael Schumacher was just 2s, but the real pressure had come from Kimi Raikkonen who tripped up with two laps to go.**

If his rivals were wondering just what they and their teams could produce to stop Fernando Alonso's runaway train, they were forced to concede again after qualifying produced a Renault one-two.

Alonso finished the third and final session 0.2s up on Giancarlo Fisichella, Kimi Raikkonen lined up third on the grid, having lapped more than 0.4s down, with Alonso's chief rival, Michael Schumacher, fifth fastest behind Jarno Trulli's ever improving Toyota, and a shade over 1s slower than the faster of the flying Renaults. One hoped, for the sake of the tifosi who had ventured to Montreal, that Michael had been fuelled heavy.

The smile was wiped off the face of the Renault team, though, when Fisichella anticipated the start, lifted off and, in the process, was slower away than Kimi Raikkonen who slotted his McLaren into second place. Worse was to follow as the Italian was to be landed with a drive-through penalty for this indiscretion, which dropped him from third place to fifth.

As is now the tradition at the Circuit Gilles Villeneuve, there was contact on lap 1 with Nico Rosberg and Juan Pablo Montoya clashing at the first chicane after the German refused to give way to a move from the Colombian that required his assistance if it was to succeed. The Williams was out on the spot, but the McLaren pitted, was fitted with a new nose and pressed on until Montoya crashed at the final chicane a dozen laps later.

A few corners later on that opening lap there was internecine strife at Midland, with Tiago Monteiro failing in an attempt to pass Christijan Albers, with the contact putting his team-mate out. Ooops!

Michael realised that he was in for a hard day when he made a mess of his start, and lost places to both Rosberg and Montoya. He caught up again when the pair collided, but he'd failed to usurp Trulli and prevent Alonso and Raikkonen from making an escape.

As it was, Trulli held Michael up through the stint before the first round of pit stops. What brought Michael back into the reckoning was that he'd qualified with a heavy fuel load, and was thus able to run nine laps more than Alonso and seven more than Raikkonen before he pitted.

By the time of Michael's second pit stop, with just 13 laps remaining, he was flying, his Bridgestones clearly the tyres to have, and Raikkonen was in his sights.

The combination of tyres that had seen better days and a surface that was breaking up at the hairpin to leave a slippery covering of marbles was a major headache for all but a handful of drivers as they found their tyres degrading faster than planned, leaving them to pussyfoot around, many enduring lurid slides as they lost control and tried to get back on to the narrow racing line. Unfortunately for the Canadian fans, national hero Jacques Villeneuve suffered most dramatically. He was eighth with 11

**Two into one won't go: Nico Rosberg is about to have a nasty surprise as Juan Pablo Montoya attacks down the inside into the first chicane**

laps to go, when he slid his Sauber BMW wide while trying to lap Ralf Schumacher's Toyota and slammed into the wall, bringing out the safety car.

This bunched the field and gave Michael a great chance to have a go at Raikkonen while Alonso was protected by two lapped cars and was able to escape to victory. The win was a landmark for Michelin, as it enabled the French tyre manufacturer to beat Bridgestone to score their 100th grand prix victory.

Then, caught out by running off line, Raikkonen ceded second place to Michael with a lap to go.

When the chequered flag fell, Fisichella and Massa were the only other drivers on the lead lap, with Trulli dropping to sixth after being slowed by a misfire. Nick Heidfeld was next up, while David Coulthard hunted down his good friend Jenson Button for the final point.

At least Button finished, though, as team-mate Rubens Barrichello was one of two drivers to retire due to engine failure. The other was Franck Montagny, his Super Aguri also Honda-powered.

Takuma Sato had been giving everything to bring the lead Super Aguri home ahead of Tiago Monteiro's Midland when he pushed too hard and crashed on the very last lap.

# MONTREAL ROUND 09

Date: **25 June 2006**  Laps: **70**  Distance: **189.686 miles/305.270km**
Weather: **Hot and bright**

## RACE RESULT

| Position | Driver | Team | Result | Stops | Qualifying Time | Grid |
|---|---|---|---|---|---|---|
| 1 | **Fernando Alonso** | Renault | 1h34m37.308s | 2 | 1m14.942s | 1 |
| 2 | **Michael Schumacher** | Ferrari | 1h34m39.419s | 2 | 1m15.986s | 5 |
| 3 | **Kimi Räikkönen** | McLaren | 1h34m46.121s | 2 | 1m15.386s | 3 |
| 4 | **Giancarlo Fisichella** | Renault | 1h34m52.987s | 3 | 1m15.178s | 2 |
| 5 | **Felipe Massa** | Ferrari | 1h35m02.480s | 1 | 1m17.209s | 10 |
| 6 | **Jarno Trulli** | Toyota | 69 laps | 2 | 1m15.968s | 4 |
| 7 | **Nick Heidfeld** | BMW Sauber | 69 laps | 2 | 1m15.885s | 13 |
| 8 | **David Coulthard** | Red Bull | 69 laps | 2 | 1m16.301s | 22* |
| 9 | **Jenson Button** | Honda | 69 laps | 2 | 1m16.608s | 8 |
| 10 | **Scott Speed** | Toro Rosso | 69 laps | 2 | 1m17.016s | 17 |
| 11 | **Christian Klien** | Red Bul | 69 laps | 2 | 1m15.833s | 12 |
| 12 | **Mark Webber** | Williams | 69 laps | 2 | 1m16.985s | 16 |
| 13 | **Vitantonio Liuzzi** | Toro Rosso | 68 laps | 3 | 1m16.116s | 15 |
| 14 | **Tiago Monteiro** | Midland | 66 laps | 3 | 1m17.121s | 18 |
| 15 | **Takuma Sato** | Super Aguri | 64 laps/accident | 3 | 1m19.088s | 20 |
| R | **Jacques Villeneuve** | BMW Sauber | 58 laps/accident | 2 | 1m15.832s | 11 |
| R | **Ralf Schumacher** | Toyota | 58 laps/withdrew | 5 | 1m15.888s | 14 |
| R | **Juan Pablo Montoya** | McLaren | 13 laps/suspension | 1 | 1m16.228s | 7 |
| R | **Rubens Barrichello** | Honda | 11 laps/engine | 0 | 1m16.912s | 9 |
| R | **Franck Montagny** | Super Aguri | 2 laps/engine | 0 | 1m19.152s | 21 |
| R | **Nico Rosberg** | Williams | 1 lap/accident damage | 0 | 1m16.012s | 6 |
| R | **Christijan Albers** | Midland | 0 laps/accident | 0 | 1m17.140s | 19 |

**FASTEST LAP:** RAIKKONEN, 1M15.841S, 128.633MPH/207.005KPH, ON LAP 22

* TEN-PLACE GRID PENALTY

# TALKING POINT: HONDA RESHUFFLES ITS PACK

**Manufacturers don't race to come second, and this was made clear when Honda Racing began to shuffle its pack. In the run-up to the Canadian GP, technical director Geoff Willis had his role redefined. This is like a football manager being told the board has "every confidence" in him 24 hours before he's sacked. Willis had been made the fall-guy for the team's weak form, with Shuhei Nakamoto being promoted to the new position of senior technical director. No one could contest that changes needed to be made as the team was losing ground, falling well short of its pace-setting form in the close-season.**

Like Mike Gascoyne at Toyota, Japanese ambition led to Geoff Willis moving on from Honda

# UNITED STATES GP

**Felipe Massa put one over on Michael Schumacher from the start, but it was the Ferrari leader who was in control after a race that re-established the credibility of Formula One in the eyes of its American fans as racing replaced politics.**

Upside down you turn me: Nick Heidfeld hangs on as his BMW Sauber is propelled into flight after contact with Jenson Button's Honda on lap 1

It was hard to know who felt more down after the United States GP. BMW Sauber's Nick Heidfeld after his barrel rolls at the first corner? Or Juan Pablo Montoya after he'd clipped the back of his McLaren team-mate Kimi Raikkonen and quashed for good his slim hopes of remaining with McLaren for 2007, or indeed joining any other top team? In short, it shaped the shock decision to quit Formula One that he made before the following grand prix.

No question about who was the happiest man in town, though. That was Michael Schumacher. He'd certainly enjoyed winning at Indianapolis 12 months earlier, but that had been a six-car farce when his only opposition had been his then team-mate Rubens Barrichello. This time around, he'd

beaten everyone fair and square and, with Fernando Alonso finishing only fifth, he'd closed the gap from 25 points to 19 to keep the title race open just when it looked as though Alonso was running away with it.

Felipe Massa had delighted Ferrari by qualifying second behind Michael. Their Bridgestones were clearly way better than Michelin's tyres, the latter's choice of compounds thought to be unusually conservative after the blow-outs in 2005, and Michael's advantage was a huge 1s over the fastest of his rivals, Renault's Giancarlo Fisichella. So Massa beat Michael away from the start. Being in front was clearly the safest place to be because those left behind the red cars were inept at taking the first corner. The Renaults of Fernando Alonso and

Fisichella went through OK, but the trouble started when Mark Webber was propelled skywards by Christian Klien's Red Bull which had rotated after attempting to avoid the Williams when it braked for Turn 1. Franck Montagny got caught up in the aftermath and his Super Aguri was also out, and the Midlands collided for the second race running, but both were able to continue.

Then the midfield made a mess of its approach to Turn 2 and Juan Pablo Montoya, Jenson Button and Nick Heidfeld failed to take the left-hander three-abreast. Montoya hit the brakes last and clipped the rear of Raikkonen, then bounced into Button who spun into Heidfeld whose BMW Sauber then got airborne in spectacular style. Scott Speed, hoping to shine in his first race in front of his home fans, was left with nowhere to go. The safety car was scrambled and, of this quintet, only Button was able to continue, but he parked his Honda three laps later with a damaged radiator. No sooner had the safety car withdrawn than Takuma Sato attempted a move on Tiago Monteiro, breaking his Super Aguri and causing the Midland to quit a few laps later.

What became clear as the race settled down was that the Ferraris and their Bridgestones were superior to the Renaults and their Michelins, and there was nothing that Alonso could do to keep up. Indeed, Fisichella was faster on the day and moved up to third midway through the opening stint, a position he held to the end.

Alonso was demoted further by Jarno Trulli who thrived on a one-stop strategy that was helped by the safety car deployment. Trulli's Toyota team-mate Ralf Schumacher ought also to have been in the points, but lost fifth place when a wheel bearing failed, elevating Alonso to collect four points.

The fans had been livid in 2005 when only six cars started the race. This time only nine did, but at least it had been hard and fast and there hadn't been a predetermined withdrawal before the start. Sure, seven cars went out on lap 1, but then lovers of the Indianapolis 500 are used to that.

# INDIANAPOLIS ROUND 10
Date: **2 July 2006** Laps: **73** Distance: **190.150 miles/306.016km**
Weather: **Hot and bright**

## RACE RESULT

| Position | Driver | Team | Result | Stops | Qualifying Time | Grid |
|---|---|---|---|---|---|---|
| 1 | Michael Schumacher | Ferrari | 1h34m35.199s | 2 | 1m10.832s | 1 |
| 2 | Felipe Massa | Ferrari | 1h34m43.183s | 2 | 1m11.435s | 2 |
| 3 | Giancarlo Fisichella | Renault | 1h34m51.794s | 2 | 1m11.920s | 3 |
| 4 | Jarno Trulli | Toyota | 1h34m58.803s | 1 | 1m13.787s | 19** |
| 5 | Fernando Alonso | Renault | 1h35m03.609s | 2 | 1m12.449s | 5 |
| 6 | Rubens Barrichello | Honda | 1h35m11.715s | 2 | 1m12.109s | 4 |
| 7 | David Coulthard | Red Bull | 72 laps | 1 | 1m13.180s | 17 |
| 8 | Vitantonio Liuzzi | Toro Rosso | 72 laps | 1 | 1m14.041s | 21* |
| 9 | Nico Rosberg | Williams | 72 laps | 1 | no time | 22^ |
| R | Ralf Schumacher | Toyota | 62 laps/wheel bearing | 2 | 1m12.795s | 8 |
| R | Christijan Albers | Midland | 37 laps/gearbox | 3 | 1m12.854s | 14 |
| R | Jacques Villeneuve | BMW Sauber | 23 laps/engine | 0 | 1m12.479s | 6 |
| R | Tiago Monteiro | Midland | 9 laps/accident | 1 | 1m12.864s | 15 |
| R | Takuma Sato | Super Aguri | 6 laps/accident | 0 | 1m13.496s | 18 |
| R | Jenson Button | Honda | 3 laps/accident | 0 | 1m12.523s | 7 |
| R | Kimi Raikkonen | McLaren | 0 laps/accident | 0 | 1m13.174s | 9 |
| R | Nick Heidfeld | BMW Sauber | 0 laps/accident | 0 | 1m15.280s | 10 |
| R | Juan Pablo Montoya | McLaren | 0 laps/accident | 0 | 1m12.150s | 11 |
| R | Mark Webber | Williams | 0 laps/accident | 0 | 1m12.292s | 12 |
| R | Scott Speed | Toro Rosso | 0 laps/accident | 0 | 1m12.792s | 13 |
| R | Christian Klien | Red Bull | 0 laps/accident | 0 | 1m12.925s | 16 |
| R | Franck Montagny | Super Aguri | 0 laps/accident | 0 | 1m16.036s | 20 |

**FASTEST LAP:** MICHAEL SCHUMACHER, 1M12.719S, 128.957MPH/207.527KPH ON LAP 56

* TEN-PLACE GRID PENALTY ** STATRTED FROM PITLANE ^ SENT TO BACK OF GRID FOR MISSING WEIGH-IN

## TALKING POINT: FUTURE OF THE UNITED STATES GP IN DOUBT

**A lot was at stake when Formula One returned to the Indianapolis Motor Speedway after the 2005 débâcle when 14 cars withdrew after the formation lap and just six started, to the incredulity of everyone watching. The trust of American fans had to be regained and, just as vitally, a deal had to be done with the circuit for 2007 and beyond, with Las Vegas making noises about trying to lure the grand prix to its desert setting. However, the 11 teams and 22 drivers delivered their side of the bargain. Nick Heidfeld might have taken things a bit far with his first lap aeriel sequence, but the fans appreciated that normality had been regained.**

There were smiles in the grandstands in 2006, but Indianapolis may not keep the grand prix for ever

# FRENCH GP

**It was all about eights at Magny-Cours as Michael Schumacher scored an eighth win in the French GP and this brought his wins tally to 88. Felipe Massa did his best in support, but it was Renault's Fernando Alonso who came home second.**

Renault would have loved to win on home ground again, but Fernando Alonso couldn't match his 2005 triumph at Magny-Cours and led for just three laps out of the 70. Of the other 67 laps, fully 63 were led by Ferrari, with Michael Schumacher accounting for all but two of them, and the remaining four were led by Toyota when Jarno Trulli and then Ralf Schumacher hit the front just after the first round of pit stops because both Ferraris pitted early, being on three-stop race strategies.

No one could match Ferrari and its Bridgestones in the stifling heat. Michael claimed pole position ahead of team-mate Felipe Massa by just 0.017s, with only Alonso getting within striking distance, with the Toyotas next up, and Trulli edging out Ralf.

At the start of the race, Michael put the power down perfectly from pole and was ahead into the opening left-hander, but Alonso fancied his chances and went around the outside of Massa, only to find the Brazilian forcing him to stay wide and then have to lift slightly, which was all Massa needed to regain second place by the second corner, Estoril.

With its relatively short pit lane, Magny-Cours makes a three-stop strategy possible. And with high ambient temperatures causing increasing tyre degradation, the three-stop option looks all the more enticing, and it seemed likely that that's precisely what the front-runners would do. However, Michael flashed into such a clear lead, with Massa keeping Alonso at bay, that Renault elected to switch the Spaniard to a two-stopper. By bringing their cars in for their first pit stop at the same time that the Ferraris made theirs, Renault duped Ferrari into thinking that they were still running to a three-stop strategy, and perhaps that's why Ferrari eased off a little, only to be caught out when Alonso came in just twice during the race.

There was a horrible moment of realisation for Massa when he pitted from second on lap 34, only to see Alonso move ahead and stay there until lap 42 when he made his second stop. All the while, though, Michael was well ahead and even though he'd have to pit for a third time, victory was

**A loyal number two: Felipe Massa keeps Fernando Alonso's Renault back in third place, enabling Michael Schumacher to pull away in the lead**

clearly his. Massa was confined to third and criticised for the way that his speed dropped away. Fourth place went to Ralf as his two-stop strategy proved superior to Kimi Raikkonen's three-stopper, while team-mate Trulli, who had been running ahead of him, parked up after his second pit stop when his brake pedal went to the floor. Fisichella was a lacklustre sixth.

Pedro de la Rosa was having his first run for McLaren since his one-off in Bahrain early in the 2005 season, this time taking the place of Juan Pablo Montoya on a more permanent basis following the Colombian's shock decision to quit Formula One for NASCAR stock car racing in the USA. He finished seventh as the last unlapped driver. Mark Webber had been destined for the final point, but his car threw a tread and he spun, damaging a wheel rim. So Nick Heidfeld mopped up for BMW Sauber.

It wasn't a day of celebration for Honda, though, with Jenson Button retiring with engine failure. That he was out of the Top ten when it happened emphasised the team's mid-season malaise.

One driver who did celebrate was Scott Speed, who drove well to finish tenth for Scuderia Toro Rosso, after qualifying a commendable 14th, especially as he was still in pain from a crash in practice.

# GRAND PRIX ROUND 11
Date: **16 July 2006**  Laps: **70**  Distance: **191.746 miles/308.586km**
Weather: **Hot and bright**

## RACE RESULT

| Position | Driver | Team | Result | Stops | Qualifying Time | Grid |
|---|---|---|---|---|---|---|
| 1 | **Michael Schumacher** | Ferrari | 1h32m07.803s | 3 | 1m15.493s | 1 |
| 2 | **Fernando Alonso** | Renault | 1h32m17.934s | 2 | 1m15.785s | 3 |
| 3 | **Felipe Massa** | Ferrari | 1h32m30.349s | 3 | 1m15.510s | 2 |
| 4 | **Ralf Schumacher** | Toyota | 1h32m35.015s | 2 | 1m16.091s | 5 |
| 5 | **Kimi Raikkonen** | McLaren | 1h32m40.809s | 3 | 1m16.281s | 6 |
| 6 | **Giancarlo Fisichella** | Renault | 1h32m53.068s | 2 | 1m16.345s | 7 |
| 7 | **Pedro de la Rosa** | McLaren | 1h32m57.210s | 3 | 1m16.632s | 8 |
| 8 | **Nick Heidfeld** | BMW Sauber | 69 laps | 2 | 1m16.294s | 11 |
| 9 | **David Coulthard** | Red Bull | 69 laps | 2 | 1m18.663s | 9 |
| 10 | **Scott Speed** | Toro Rosso | 69 laps | 2 | 1m17.063s | 14 |
| 11 | **Jacques Villeneuve** | BMW Sauber | 69 laps | 3 | 1m17.304s | 16 |
| 12 | **Christian Klien** | Red Bull | 69 laps | 3 | 1m16.433s | 12 |
| 13 | **Vitantonio Liuzzi** | Toro Rosso | 69 laps | 2 | 1m17.164s | 22* |
| 14 | **Nico Rosberg** | Williams | 68 laps | 3 | 1m18.272s | 19* |
| 15 | **Christijan Albers** | Midland | 68 laps | 2 | 1m17.105s | 15 |
| 16 | **Franck Montagny** | Super Aguri | 67 laps | 3 | 1m18.637s | 20 |
| R | **Jenson Button** | Honda | 61 laps/engine | 2 | 1m17.495s | 17 |
| R | **Mark Webber** | Williams | 53 laps/wheel rim | 4 | 1m16.129s | 10 |
| R | **Jarno Trulli** | Toyota | 39 laps/brakes | 2 | 1m16.036s | 4 |
| R | **Rubens Barrichello** | Honda | 18 laps/engine | 0 | 1m17.027s | 13 |
| R | **Tiago Monteiro** | Midland | 11 laps/accident | 0 | 1m17.589s | 18 |
| R | **Takuma Sato** | Super Aguri | 0 laps/clutch | 0 | 1m18.845s | 21 |

**FASTEST LAP:** MICHAEL SCHUMACHER, 1M17.111S, 127.966MPH ON LAP 46

* TEN-PLACE GRID PENALTY

# TALKING POINT: PRODRIVE EYES MCLAREN B-TEAM DEAL FOR 2008

**With its World Championship entry in place for 2008, Prodrive made it known at the French GP that it would be interested in making its entry on to the Formula One stage with a McLaren B-team. Prodrive chief David Richards was attracted to this deal because teams would be entitled to run a contemporary chassis from another team for the first time, rather than having to run a year-old one. Richards entered into talks as McLaren's proposed Jean Alesi B-team deal with the Japanese luxury goods brand Direxiv faltered. Richards' knowledge of Formula One came from running the Benetton and, latterly, the BAR teams.**

David Richards has had two spells in Formula One and now he wants a third crack at the big time

# GERMAN GP

**Stripped of their beloved mass dampers by the sport's governing body, Renault were also-rans in Germany and the title battle swung Ferrari's way as Michael Schumacher led Felipe Massa home, and Fernando Alonso had to make do with fifth place.**

Chasing Kimi: Raikkonen is already through Turn 1 as Michael Schumacher leads the chase followed by Felipe Massa and Giancarlo Fisichella

Three wins on the trot made incredibly attractive reading for Ferrari fans. That Michael Schumacher had been backed up by his number two Felipe Massa scoring a pair of second-place finishes and a third, emphasised how Ferrari had gained the upper hand over Renault in the heat of the summer, and the gap between Michael and Fernando Alonso was now just 11 points.

Unsurprisingly, there were long faces in the Renault camp, not least because they had been told by the sport's governing body, the FIA, to race without the mass dampers that they'd pioneered towards the end of the 2005 season. (The mass damping system improves the behaviour of the chassis by optimising the contact patch of the tyres

with the track surface by restricting vertical movement after the car hits a bump.)

Ironically, Ferrari and Red Bull had been using them too, but the effect was most dramatic for Renault because they dropped from being the fastest team to the third-fastest Michelin-shod team behind McLaren and Honda.

Pat Symonds, executive director of engineering, reckoned that the system's removal was costing the team as much as 0.3 seconds per lap. Renault's loss of competitiveness was emphasised by the marked progress that Ferrari had made with its Bridgestones, and both men in red were able to control the race at ease, driving with plenty in hand.

After qualifying, it appeared that McLaren had really stirred things up because Kimi Raikkonen had lapped the fastest. But, as so often happens with this means of qualifying, no one could be sure how much fuel had been in the Finn's car, and only the timing of his first pit stop in the race would tell. Coming as early as lap 10, he'd clearly been running with a light fuel load and, since the Ferrari drivers didn't stop at their pits until 9 and 10 laps later, they had qualified with a great deal more fuel on board. In fact, Raikkonen was on a three-stop strategy, Ferrari coming in just twice.

From lap 10 on, Michael led every lap. Massa was always there or thereabouts, finishing less than one second down, but his role was to support Michael and not challenge him. He did it with aplomb. Raikkonen dropped to eighth after that first, early pit stop, but rose to fifth before his second stop, and to third before his third stop, which is where he finished after losing a place immediately after this final stop when a hydraulic problem struck while re-passing Jenson Button's Honda on the way out of the hairpin with ten laps to go.

Fifth place was the best that Alonso could do, with team-mate Giancarlo Fisichella guarding him from attack from Jarno Trulli in the closing laps. The Italian Toyota driver had raced beautifully, carving through the field after starting back in 20th place. His team-mate Ralf Schumacher started eighth, but clashed with David Coulthard on lap 1, then lost time pit stopping for a new nose, and lost more time with a drive-through penalty and ended up ninth, enabling Christian Klien to claim the final point for Red Bull Racing.

Rubens Barrichello deserved better, but retired when his Honda's engine failed, while Pedro de la Rosa also fell to mechanical failure on his second outing for McLaren. For the following race, in Hungary, Renault had successfully appealed against the FIA's decision and raced with their mass damping system.

# HOCKENHEIM ROUND 12
Date: **30 July 2006**  Laps: **67**  Distance: **190.414 miles/306.427km**
Weather: **Hot and bright**

## RACE RESULT

| Position | Driver | Team | Result | Stops | Qualifying Time | Grid |
|---|---|---|---|---|---|---|
| 1 | **Michael Schumacher** | Ferrari | 1h27m51.693s | 2 | 1m14.205s | 2 |
| 2 | **Felipe Massa** | Ferrari | 1h27m52.413s | 2 | 1m14.569s | 3 |
| 3 | **Kimi Raikkonen** | McLaren | 1h28m04.899s | 3 | 1m14.070s | 1 |
| 4 | **Jenson Button** | Honda | 1h28m10.591s | 2 | 1m14.862s | 4 |
| 5 | **Fernando Alonso** | Renault | 1h28m15.400s | 2 | 1m15.282s | 7 |
| 6 | **Giancarlo Fisichella** | Renault | 1h28m16.507s | 2 | 1m14.894s | 5 |
| 7 | **Jarno Trulli** | Toyota | 1h28m18.237s | 2 | 1m15.150s | 20* |
| 8 | **Christian Klien** | Red Bull | 1h28m39.824s | 2 | 1m15.141s | 12 |
| 9 | **Ralf Schumacher** | Toyota | 1h28m52.044s | 4 | 1m15.923s | 8 |
| 10 | **Vitantonio Liuzzi** | Toro Rosso | 66 laps | 2 | 1m16.399s | 16 |
| 11 | **David Coulthard** | Red Bull | 66 laps | 2 | 1m16.326s | 10 |
| 12 | **Scott Speed** | Toro Rosso | 66 laps | 2 | no time | 19 |
| D** | **Christijan Albers** | Midland | 66 laps | 2 | 1m17.093s | 21* |
| D** | **Tiago Monteiro** | Midland | 65 laps | 3 | 1m17.836s | 18 |
| R | **Mark Webber** | Williams | 59 laps/water leak | 2 | 1m15.094s | 11 |
| R | **Takuma Sato** | Super Aguri | 38 laps/gearbox | 1 | 1m17.185s | 17 |
| R | **Jacques Villeneuve** | BMW Sauber | 30 laps/accident | 1 | 1m15.329s | 13 |
| R | **Rubens Barrichello** | Honda | 18 laps/engine | 1 | 1m14.943s | 6 |
| R | **Nick Heidfeld** | BMW Sauber | 9 laps/brakes | 1 | 1m15.397s | 15 |
| R | **Pedro de la Rosa** | McLaren | 2 laps/fuel pump | 0 | 1m15.936s | 9 |
| R | **Sakon Yamamoto** | Super Aguri | 1 lap/driveshaft | 0 | no time | 22 |
| R | **Nico Rosberg** | Williams | 0 laps/accident | 0 | 1m15.380s | 14 |

**FASTEST LAP:** MICHAEL SCHUMACHER, 1M16.357S, 133.999MPH/215.640KPH ON LAP 17

* TEN-PLACE GRID PENALTY ** FLEXING REAR WINGS

## TALKING POINT: WHO WILL BE AT FERRARI IN 2007?

**All season, the F1 paddock had been wondering what would be happening at Ferrari in 2007. Would Michael Schumacher retire, or would he be joined by Kimi Raikkonen? The first clue that he might be retiring was the news, which broke at Hockenheim, that technical director Ross Brawn would be taking off 2007. Yes, a critical part of the Schumacher-Todt-Byrne-Brawn partnership that had claimed five titles from 2000 to 2004 would be missing. In addition, Ferrari were also thought to have taken up an option on Raikkonen. Perhaps Michael's decision would hinge on whether he became champion again.**

Everyone seemed sure that Kimi had signed for Ferrari for 2007, but not whether Michael would stay on

# HUNGARIAN GP

**Some journalists said that it would never happen, but Jenson Button claimed his first grand prix win, albeit at the 114th attempt. Doing so from 14th on the grid in a rain-hit race made it all the more dramatic for him and Honda.**

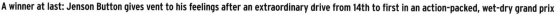
A winner at last: Jenson Button gives vent to his feelings after an extraordinary drive from 14th to first in an action-packed, wet-dry grand prix

It's hard to know where to start. Even if it hadn't produced a new winner, and a pair of drivers - Pedro de la Rosa and Nick Heidfeld - who were equally surprised to join Jenson Button on the podium, the race had enough twists and turns to fill a book. Indeed, a circuit considered the dullest visited by Formula One produced a classic. The weather was the big factor, with searingly hot, dry conditions being replaced by the cool and wet, something that caught out both tyre suppliers. They had brought tyres with too hard a compound which left the drivers short on grip.

The grid had an unusual look as both title contenders collected two-second penalties to be added to their qualifying times, leaving

Michael Schumacher 11th and Fernando Alonso 15th. The German was punished for passing under red flags, and the Spaniard for brake-testing Red Bull's third driver Robert Doornbos, and then overtaking under yellows. Button was 14th after dropping ten places for an engine change. So, it was hard to predict a winner on the Sunday morning as the rain poured down. Kimi Raikkonen was on pole for the second race running, with Felipe Massa alongside. The big question was whether the Michelins on the Finn's McLaren were better suited to the conditions than the Bridgestones on the Brazilian's Ferrari?

Raikkonen made a clean getaway, but Massa lost out big time and was seventh at

the end of the opening tour behind Rubens Barrichello, de la Rosa, Michael, Giancarlo Fisichella and Alonso. What followed over the next 17 laps was a masterclass from Alonso as he tore ahead to take the lead when Raikkonen pitted. He stayed there for nine more laps and was able to pit and resume the lead, proving the extent to which Michelin intermediates were the tyres to have. The timing of his second stop and a change to dry tyres seemed spot-on, but his Renault wriggled out of the pits, slewed through Turn 1 and crashed at Turn 2 as a wheel came off, thanks to a failed wheelnut-locking mechanism.

Raikkonen was already out, after a dramatic exit before half way. He'd realised that team-mate de la Rosa was faster, and was trying to let him through to catch Alonso. But as he looked in his mirrors as they entered the final corner, he failed to notice Tonio Liuzzi slowing to let him by and vaulted over the Toro Rosso. When Alonso crashed out, it was Button, who hadn't put a foot wrong, who hit the front.

Michael skittered around and was back in seventh in mid-race, and was now second with five laps to go. But he was still on intermediates and needed to change to dry tyres. Trying to hang on until the end, he lost out to de la Rosa but was robust in trying to stave off Heidfeld's BMW before retiring with a broken track rod from contact with his fellow German. But Michael didn't go home empty-handed because his ninth place turned into eighth behind fourth-placed Barrichello, David Coulthard, Ralf Schumacher and Massa after debutant Robert Kubica's BMW was disqualified from seventh when it was found to be 2kg underweight.

While Buttonmania was taking over the paddock, his team was equally jubilant because this was Honda's first win since 1967, and it was the first for the team that started life in 1999 as British American Racing before being taken over by the Japanese at the start of the 2006 season.

# HUNGARORING ROUND 13
Date: **6 August 2006**  Laps: **70**  Distance: **190.552 miles/306.663km**
Weather: **Wet and cool, then overcast**

## RACE RESULT

| Position | Driver | Team | Result | Stops | Qualifying Time | Grid |
|---|---|---|---|---|---|---|
| 1 | Jenson Button | Honda | 1h52m20.941s | 3 | 1m20.092s | 14* |
| 2 | Pedro de la Rosa | McLaren | 1h52m51.778s | 3 | 1m20.117s | 4 |
| 3 | Nick Heidfeld | BMW Sauber | 1h53m04.763s | 2 | 1m20.623s | 10 |
| 4 | Rubens Barrichello | Honda | 1h53m06.146s | 3 | 1m20.085s | 3 |
| 5 | David Coulthard | Red Bull | 69 laps | 2 | 1m20.890s | 12 |
| 6 | Ralf Schumacher | Toyota | 69 laps | 2 | 1m20.759s | 6 |
| D | Robert Kubica | BMW Sauber | 69 laps | 2 | 1m22.049s | 9*** |
| 7 | Felipe Massa | Ferrari | 69 laps | 3 | 1m19.886s | 2 |
| 8 | Michael Schumacher | Ferrari | 67 laps/track rod | 2 | 1m20.875s | 11** |
| 9 | Tiago Monteiro | Midland | 67 laps | 3 | 1m23.767s | 16 |
| 10 | Christijan Albers | Midland | 67 laps | 2 | 1m23.146s | 22* |
| 11 | Scott Speed | Toro Rosso | 66 laps | 4 | 1m23.006s | 20 |
| 12 | Jarno Trulli | Toyota | 65 laps/engine | 2 | 1m21.132s | 8 |
| 13 | Takuma Sato | Super Aguri | 65 laps | 2 | 1m22.967s | 19 |
| R | Fernando Alonso | Renault | 51 laps/wheel nut | 2 | 1m21.364s | 15** |
| R | Kimi Raikkonen | McLaren | 25 laps/accident | 1 | 1m19.599s | 1 |
| R | Vitantonio Liuzzi | Toro Rosso | 25 laps/accident | 0 | 1m22.068s | 17 |
| R | Nico Rosberg | Williams | 19 laps/spin | 0 | 1m22.084s | 18 |
| R | Giancarlo Fisichella | Renault | 18 laps/crash damage | 0 | 1m20.924s | 7 |
| R | Christian Klien | Red Bull | 6 laps/spin | 0 | 1m21.207s | 13 |
| R | Mark Webber | Williams | 1 lap/spin | 0 | 1m20.266s | 5 |
| R | Sakon Yamamoto | Super Aguri | 0 laps/spin | 0 | 1m24.016s | 21 |

**FASTEST LAP:** FELIPE MASSA, 1M23.516S, 117.333MPH/188.821KPH ON LAP 65
* TEN-PLACE GRID PENALTY ** TWO-SECOND PENALTY *** 2KG UNDERWEIGHT

# TALKING POINT: KUBICA ARRIVAL TRIGGERS VILLENEUVE DEPARTURE

**Polish driver Robert Kubica had been impressing all season as third driver for BMW Sauber, and some of his performances in Friday's practice had been scintillating. In fact the team were considering giving him a race outing in place of Jacques Villeneuve. The Canadian was livid. The team said they were letting him recover from the shaking he'd received when he crashed in the German GP, but this was merely a cover and the newly married Villeneuve turned his back on F1 in umbrage, opting to go off and consider his future, suggesting that he may follow fellow firebrand Juan Pablo Montoya into NASCAR stock cars in the USA.**

Robert Kubica stepped up to the mark in style on his debut. No wonder Jacques Villeneuve was worried...

# TURKISH GP

**Felipe Massa's maiden grand prix win wasn't just down to speed, but to track position when the safety car was deployed early in the race as team-mate Michael Schumacher was forced to lose ground while waiting behind him to pit.**

Michael Schumacher was caught on the hop, and there was nothing that Ferrari could do to prevent rival Fernando Alonso's Renault from demoting him as he sat queuing for 12 whole seconds behind team-mate Massa, awaiting his turn to be attended by the pit crew.

In this snap moment, on lap 14 in the Turkish GP after the safety car had been sent out while Vitantonio Liuzzi's spun and stalled Toro Rosso was cleared away to a safe position and Michael moved from shaving at least a couple of points off Alonso's meagre ten-point advantage, to adding two more to the Spaniard's tally. There were still 44 laps to run, but he had fallen from second to third, and he had to do something about

Alonso. Cynics were sure that Massa would squander his lead, which had been as much as nine seconds, and let Michael by for a ten-point maximum, as Michael's team-mates Eddie Irvine and Rubens Barrichello had done over the years.

It's worth noting that had Michael not slid wide on lap 28, he might have been able to regain second place by making his second stop four laps later than Alonso. But try as Michael might, he couldn't find a chink in Alonso's armour. Once again Alonso had proved unflappable under attack, and later admitted to tweaking his engine settings to add extra revs down the straights ahead of the key corners at Turns 8 and 9, before

turning the settings down again for the rest of the lap.

You have to ask why Michael was running behind Massa in the first place. Well, the Brazilian had outqualified him, with Michael having made a mess of the third sector of his qualifying lap when he was all set to claim the top position. With Michael unable to get ahead of Massa at the start, he was running second when the safety car was deployed, and was thus second in line at the Ferrari pit as the top six peeled off for a "free" stop which just fell into a "pit stop window". So Michael could only watch and wait as Alonso pitted and moved into second place before he could rejoin the race.

**Trouble and nice:** Felipe Massa leads away from Michael Schumacher, Fernando Alonso and Nick Heidfeld as Giancarlo Fisichella (top left) has a spin

Liuzzi's moment at Turn 1 was the second incident there, with a worse one having happened on the opening lap as Giancarlo Fisichella spun and triggered all sorts of impact and avoidance at the downhill left-hander. In the run-up to this, the Ferraris appeared to pincer Alonso as they approached the corner, and his evasive action caught out Fisichella who spun and triggered panic behind him as he caught Nick Heidfeld's BMW. Kimi Raikkonen swerved to avoid the Renault, aware that he had a locked-up Red Bull to his left. But he was hit by Scott Speed's Toro Rosso which had already hit Pedro de la Rosa's McLaren. Ralf Schumacher clipped his team-mate Jarno Trulli, while Takuma Sato collided with Speed before Monteiro thumped him. Great for TV, but not for the drivers.

Jenson Button was the best of the rest, even catching Alonso and Michael in the closing laps, with Honda's good day made even better by Rubens Barrichello – who'd been delayed on lap 1 – coming home eighth. De la Rosa, also delayed in the first corner accident, resisted a fierce push from Fisichella who drove a blinder after losing considerable time having repairs after lap 1, while both Williams ran strongly before fading, with Mark Webber dropping from fourth to tenth place.

# ISTANBUL PARK ROUND 14
Date: **27 August 2006**  Laps: **58**  Distance: **192.388 miles/309.603km**
Weather: **Hot, dry and sunny**

## RACE RESULT

| Position | Driver | Team | Result | Stops | Qualifying Time | Grid |
|---|---|---|---|---|---|---|
| 1 | **Felipe Massa** | Ferrari | 1h28m51.082s | 2 | 1m26.907s | 1 |
| 2 | **Fernando Alonso** | Renault | 1h28m56.657s | 2 | 1m27.321s | 3 |
| 3 | **Michael Schumacher** | Ferrari | 1h28m56.738s | 2 | 1m27.284s | 2 |
| 4 | **Jenson Button** | Honda | 1h29m03.416s | 2 | 1m27.790s | 6 |
| 5 | **Pedro de la Rosa** | McLaren | 1h29m36.990s | 1 | 1m27.897s | 11 |
| 6 | **Giancarlo Fisichella** | Renault | 1h29m37.676s | 2 | 1m27.564s | 4 |
| 7 | **Ralf Schumacher** | Toyota | 1h29m50.419s | 2 | 1m27.569s | 15* |
| 8 | **Rubens Barrichello** | Honda | 1h29m51.116s | 2 | 1m28.257s | 13 |
| 9 | **Jarno Trulli** | Toyota | 57 laps | 2 | 1m27.973s | 12 |
| 10 | **Mark Webber** | Williams | 57 laps | 2 | 1m29.436s | 9 |
| 11 | **Christian Klien** | Red Bull | 57 laps | 2 | 1m27.852s | 10 |
| 12 | **Robert Kubica** | BMW Sauber | 57 laps | 2 | 1m28.167s | 8 |
| 13 | **Scott Speed** | Toro Rosso | 57 laps | 3 | 1m29.158s | 17 |
| 14 | **Nick Heidfeld** | BMW Sauber | 56 laps | 3 | 1m27.785s | 5 |
| 15 | **David Coulthard** | Red Bull | 55 laps/gearbox | 2 | 1m29.136s | 16 |
| R | **Christijan Albers** | Midland | 46 laps/accident | 2 | 1m28.639s | 22* |
| NC | **Takuma Sato** | Super Aguri | 41 laps | 2 | 1m30.850s | 21 |
| R | **Nico Rosberg** | Williams | 25 laps/water pressure | 0 | 1m28.386s | 14 |
| R | **Sakon Yamamoto** | Super Aguri | 23 laps/spun off | 1 | 1m30.607s | 20 |
| R | **Vitantonio Liuzzi** | Toro Rosso | 12 laps/spun off | 0 | 1m29.250s | 18 |
| R | **Kimi Raikkonen** | McLaren | 1 laps/accident | 1 | 1m27.866s | 7 |
| R | **Tiago Monteiro** | Midland | 0 laps/accident | 0 | 1m29.901s | 19 |

**FASTEST LAP:** MICHAEL SCHUMACHER, 1M28.005S (135.869MPH) ON LAP 55

* TEN-PLACE GRID PENALTY

## TALKING POINT: WILL MICHAEL STAY OR GO?

**Would Michael Schumacher race in 2007? By the Turkish GP the question and the controversy surrounding it had reached boiling point, with all parties frustrated that Ferrari likes to keep its announcements until its home race at Monza. But any study of Michael's lack of frustration at having to queue for his first pit stop, and his inability to get past Alonso, seemed to reveal that he wasn't competing with his usual desire to dominate. Add to that Massa's confidence in his 2007 seat, the "solid" rumour that Kimi Raikkonen had a 2007 Ferrari contract, and it was hard to conclude anything other than that Michael's retirement was imminent.**

TURKISH GRAND PRIX

In previous years, Michael Schumacher would have been livid to lose out to a team-mate

# ITALIAN GP

**Neither Fernando Alonso's Renault breaking nor Michael Schumacher winning the Italian GP was the big story. But Michael Schumacher announcing his retirement from Formula One was, although it only confirmed everyone's suspicions.**

When a driver gets on the podium in only his third grand prix it's a momentous feat, but poor Robert Kubica – who raced to third place for BMW Sauber to be the first Polish driver ever to score a point – had his thunder well and truly stolen by the "Will he, won't he?" soap opera about whether Michael Schumacher would announce his retirement from Formula One.

It's not surprising that Michael hogged the limelight because not only was he in a Ferrari in Ferrari land, but he was the subject of the biggest news story in years, and one which would influence the driver market for 2007, especially what would happen to Kimi Raikkonen. All the indications, such as Heikki Kovalainen being signed to drive the second Renault rather than Raikkonen, and the Finn replacing him at Ferrari, gave credence to Michael's imminent retirement, but no one could be sure.

Michael arrived at Monza 12 points adrift of Fernando Alonso. But then came a ruling in qualifying that all but scrubbed out the Spaniard's advantage: he was docked his three fastest laps from the top-ten qualifying session for allegedly impeding Michael's team-mate Felipe Massa's final flying lap, leaving him tenth on the grid and not fifth. Renault was less than happy with the decision, and Alonso was livid.

Raikkonen led away from pole, chased by Michael, but he pitted two laps earlier than the Ferrari team leader and was second when Michael rejoined, with Giancarlo Fisichella third. But the Renault driver had yet to pit and didn't do so until lap 26, proving that he was planning to stop just the once. Fisichella returned to the track in

*Michael gave the tifosi what they really wanted – a Ferrari win on home ground – for one last time*

tenth place, but went back to fourth once his rivals had made their second stops.

Kubica had a stunning opening lap and leapt from sixth to third, helped in part by team-mate Nick Heidfeld having tried to pass Michael into the first chicane on lap 1. It didn't work and he lost three places. Once

ensconced in third, the 21-year-old Pole showed his ability by not being troubled there, easily keeping Massa's lighter Ferrari behind him.

The driver making the most progress, though, was Alonso. Still furious about his grid penalty, he'd climbed from tenth to sixth place by the first round of stops, then overtook Massa before his and Kubica's second stop, when they pitted together, before he moved up to third. Then his Renault engine blew because, he said, he'd had to stress it so hard in the race to make up lost ground.

This cemented Kubica in third, which is where he remained to the finish, comfortably clear of Fisichella and Jenson Button's Honda.

Massa should have been in the mix, but he had to make an extra pit stop to replace a tyre after he missed his braking point while blinded by the smoke from Alonso's engine explosion, dropping him out of the points. Rubens Barrichello claimed sixth place in the second Honda, having tried to make his one-stop tactic beat Button's two-stopper. Either way, it was the third consecutive race in which Honda had both drivers in the points. Jarno Trulli gave his all to finish seventh for Toyota, while Ralf Schumacher struggled in the sister car. The final point went to Heidfeld who lost all hope of a top finish when he was hit with a drive-through penalty.

The result moved Michael to within two points of Alonso, and for the first time propelled Ferrari ahead of Renault in the constructors' championship.

# MONZA ROUND 15
Date: **10 Sept 2006**  Laps: **53**  Distance: **190.787 miles/307.028km**
Weather: **Hot and bright**

## RACE RESULT

| Position | Driver | Team | Result | Stops | Qualifying Time | Grid |
|---|---|---|---|---|---|---|
| 1 | Michael Schumacher | Ferrari | 1h14m51.975s | 2 | 1m21.486s | 2 |
| 2 | Kimi Raikkonen | McLaren | 1h15m00.021s | 2 | 1m21.484s | 1 |
| 3 | Robert Kubica | BMW Sauber | 1h15m18.389s | 2 | 1m22.258s | 6 |
| 4 | Giancarlo Fisichella | Renault | 1h15m24.020s | 1 | 1m23.175s | 9 |
| 5 | Jenson Button | Honda | 1h15m24.660s | 2 | 1m22.011s | 5 |
| 6 | Rubens Barrichello | Honda | 1h15m34.384s | 1 | 1m22.787s | 8 |
| 7 | Jarno Trulli | Toyota | 1h15m36.637s | 1 | 1m21.924s | 11 |
| 8 | Nick Heidfeld | BMW Sauber | 1h15m37.284s | 3 | 1m21.653s | 3 |
| 9 | Felipe Massa | Ferrari | 1h15m37.930s | 3 | 1m21.704s | 4 |
| 10 | Mark Webber | Williams | 1h16m04.577s | 1 | 1m23.341s | 19 |
| 11 | Christian Klien | Red Bull | 52 laps | 1 | no time | 16 |
| 12 | David Coulthard | Red Bull | 52 laps | 1 | 1m22.589s | 14 |
| 13 | Scott Speed | Toro Rosso | 52 laps | 1 | 1m23.165s | 15 |
| 14 | Vitantonio Liuzzi | Toro Rosso | 52 laps | 1 | 1m23.043s | 17 |
| 15 | Ralf Schumacher | Toyota | 52 laps | 1 | 1m22.280s | 13 |
| 16 | Takuma Sato | Super Aguri | 51 laps | 1 | 1m24.289s | 21 |
| 17 | Christijan Albers | Midland | 51 laps | 1 | 1m23.116s | 18 |
| R | Tiago Monteiro | Midland | 44 laps/brakes | 3 | 1m23.920s | 20 |
| R | Fernando Alonso | Renault | 43 laps/engine | 2 | 1m25.688s | 10* |
| R | Pedro de la Rosa | McLaren | 20 laps/engine | 1 | 1m22.280s | 7 |
| R | Sakon Yamamoto | Super Aguri | 18 laps/hydraulics | 0 | 1m26.001s | 22 |
| R | Nico Rosberg | Williams | 9 laps/driveshaft | 0 | 1m22.203s | 12 |

**FASTEST LAP:** RAIKKONEN, 1M22.559S, 156.968MPH/252.604KPH ON LAP 13

* BEST THREE LAPS ANNULLED

# TALKING POINT: DRIVERS SEEK CHANGES TO MONZA CIRCUIT

**The Grand Prix Drivers Association met at Monza and came away seeking changes to the oldest circuit in the World Championship. Their concern was the second chicane. They wanted tarmac run-off areas – rather than gravel ones – to slow cars which had left the track and reduce the possibility of their flipping, and also the kerbs changed. Having asked for these changes for several years and been told that they couldn't be made on the grounds of cost, David Coulthard, Michael Schumacher and Jarno Trulli were dismayed that the track had been resurfaced instead, and that a circuit representative cancelled a meeting with them.**

The drivers were pushing for revised kerbs and tarmac run-off areas at the Varianate della Roggia

# CHINESE GP

This race at the Shanghai International Circuit made it clear to Formula One fans that the sport will have lost a key ingredient with the loss of a tyre war for 2007, because it is what made this grand prix so special and won it for Michael Schumacher and Ferrari.

Advantage Renault: Fernando Alonso and Giancarlo Fisichella lead away from the Hondas and McLarens, but Michael Schumacher's Ferrari won the day

Changing weather conditions always spice up a race, and this was clearly the case at the Shanghai International Circuit; not that the finely balanced title battle needed anything extra to become a cliff-hanger. The reigning champion Fernando Alonso arrived in China with a scant two-point lead over Michael Schumacher, while his Renault team trailed Ferrari by three.

After qualifying, it appeared to be advantage Renault because they had blocked out the front row, with Alonso on pole and Giancarlo Fisichella alongside. Michael was back in sixth, with team-mate Felipe Massa offering no support because he was starting in 20th place after his car had an engine change.

Rain meant that intermediate tyres were the most popular, with Michelin's proving the ones to have in qualifying, with both Hondas and Kimi Raikkonen's McLaren lapping faster than Michael's Ferrari. In fact, Michael was the only driver on the harder compound Bridgestones to make it into the top-ten shoot-out. Whenever track conditions were wet rather than damp, Bridgestone's full wets were superior, so Ferrari must have been disappointed when rain on race morning stopped 90 minutes before the start.

All 22 cars started on intermediates and Alonso streaked away. But, eight laps in, the track had dried to a point at which the Bridgestone intermediates came good.

Michael passed Rubens Barrichello and, five laps later, Jenson Button's Honda. Michael advanced to third when Raikkonen pitted, and his place was made safer a few laps later when the Finn's McLaren retired with a throttle problem. At this point, Alonso was some 20s ahead of Michael.

Michael soon caught Fisichella but elected to make his pit stop rather than try to pass him, and kept the same set of tyres. When Alonso pitted a lap later, the team opted to fit new front intermediates. Almost instantly, Alonso wished they'd fitted new rears as well because he fell 3s off the pace with Fisichella and Michael closing on to his tail on lap 28. Two laps later Alonso had to let Fisichella by but could only briefy contain Michael, his graining tyres offering him no hope. Now, like others, he waited for the track to dry so he could have dry tyres fitted.

Having seen the pace of fellow Michelin users who had fitted dry tyres, Alonso pitted on lap 35 when he was trailing Michael by 6s. Then disaster struck as the right rear wheel nut was dropped, costing close on 9s. Michael waited until lap 40 to change to dries, with Fisichella staying out one lap longer before pitting. The Italian emerged in the lead, just, but slid wide at the first corner and Michael went past him.

The man on the move was Alonso, and Fisichella slowed to accommodate him, the Spaniard relieving him of second place with nine laps to run and haring off after Michael, throwing caution to the wind. Although he raced ever closer, a flurry of rain with two laps to go thwarted his attack and he ended up 3s behind an ecstatic Michael. This famous and fabulous victory brought Michael level on points with Alonso and, not surprisingly, he ranked this as one of the very best of his 90-plus wins. With Massa not scoring, at least Renault worked their way back in front of Ferrari by a solitary point in the battle for constructors' honours thanks to Fisichella finishing third.

# SHANGHAI ROUND 16

Date: **1 October 2006**  Laps: **56**  Distance: **189.68 miles/305.25km**
Weather: **Warm and wet**

## RACE RESULT

| Position | Driver | Team | Result | Stops | Qualifying Time | Grid |
|---|---|---|---|---|---|---|
| 1 | Michael Schumacher | Ferrari | 1h37m32.747s | 2 | 1m45.775s | 6 |
| 2 | Felipe Alonso | Renault | 1h37m35.868s | 2 | 1m44.360s | 1 |
| 3 | Giancarlo Fisichella | Renault | 1h38m16.944s | 2 | 1m44.992s | 2 |
| 4 | Jenson Button | Honda | 1h38m44.803s | 2 | 1m45.503s | 4 |
| 5 | Pedro de la Rosa | McLaren | 1h38m49.884s | 2 | 1m45.877s | 7 |
| 6 | Rubens Barrichello | Honda | 1h38m51.878s | 2 | 1m45.503s | 3 |
| 7 | Nick Heidfeld | BMW Sauber | 1h39m04.726s | 2 | 1m46.053s | 8 |
| 8 | Mark Webber | Williams | 1h39m16.335s | 2 | 1m46.413s | 14 |
| 9 | David Coulthard | Red Bull | 1h39m16.543s | 2 | 1m45.968s | 12 |
| 10 | Vitantonio Liuzzi | Toro Rosso | 55 laps | 1 | 1m46.172s | 13 |
| 11 | Nico Rosberg | Williams | 55 laps | 2 | 1m47.419s | 15 |
| 12 | Robert Doornbos | Red Bull | 55 laps | 3 | 1m48.021s | 10 |
| 13 | Robert Kubica | BMW Sauber | 55 laps | 3 | 1m46.632s | 9 |
| 14 | Takuma Sato | Super Aguri | 55 laps | 2 | 1m50.326s | 21* |
| 15 | Scott Speed | Toro Rosso | 55 laps | 2 | 1m45.851s | 11 |
| 16 | Christijan Albers | Midland | 53 laps | 3 | 1m49.542s | 22* |
| 17 | Sakon Yamamoto | Super Aguri | 52 laps | 4 | 1m55.560s | 19 |
| R | Ralf Schumacher | Toyota | 49 laps/engine | 1 | 1m48.894s | 16 |
| R | Felipe Massa | Ferrari | 44 laps/crash damage | 2 | 1m45.970s | 20* |
| R | Jarno Trulli | Toyota | 38 laps/engine | 1 | 1m49.098s | 17 |
| R | Tiago Monteiro | Midland | 37 laps/spun off | 2 | 1m49.903s | 18 |
| R | Kimi Raikkonen | McLaren | 18 laps/throttle | 1 | 1m45.754s | 5 |

FASTEST LAP: ALONSO, 1M37.586S, 124.957MPH ON LAP 49

* TEN-PLACE GRID PENALTY

# TALKING POINT: CHASSIS-SHARING PLANS ARE BLOCKED

**All Formula One teams have an eye on the future, trying to protect and improve their position. So it came as no surprise that Williams and Spyker MF1 voted to block chassis-sharing proposals being brought forward a year from 2008 to 2007. They did this to prevent Red Bull Racing and Scuderia Toro Rosso from running identical, Adrian Newey-designed cars next year, perhaps fearing that Formula One's leading designer might produce a chassis that would put them in the shade. Honda was also keen for the proposal to be ratified so that Super Aguri Racing could run an updated version of its 2006 car.**

Teams feared Scuderia Toro Rosso and Red Bull Racing might be together even more in 2007

# JAPANESE GP

Engine failures and Ferrari are not often associated, but the wisp of smoke from Michael Schumacher's exhaust heralded an almost unimaginable retirement. He'd been leading, too, and title rival Fernando Alonso took the ten points.

Fernando Alonso and his Renault crew celebrate a victory that was worth effectively rather more than just ten points as Michael Schumacher scored

Michael Schumacher had the Japanese GP in the bag. He wasn't quite home when it all went wrong for his Ferrari engine with a third of the race to go, but he was on the way to ten points. This would have seen him gain a two-point advantage over title rival Fernando Alonso, who was heading for second, but the consequences of his retirement were awful. Alonso was given a ten-point advantage with just ten points to play for at the final round in Brazil.

Just a week after the tyre wars of China, the Japanese GP offered more of the same except the Bridgestone teams gained the upper hand. Ferrari filled the front row, with Fernando Alonso back in fifth and Giancarlo Fisichella sixth. Between them lay the Toyotas, also on Bridgestones.

Pole didn't go to Michael but his team-mate Felipe Massa. Michael had carried a heavier fuel load in qualifying and knew that he would assume the advantage when Massa pitted before him. In fact he didn't have to wait that long, taking the lead when Massa backed off on the straight after a few laps. Alonso was back in fourth, having passed Trulli at the start, but got stuck behind Jarno's Toyota team-mate Ralf.

Michael made a late pit stop that all but ensured he'd emerge in the lead. He did, and stayed there up to his second stop on lap 36 when he slotted back into the lead, ahead of Alonso who'd jumped Ralf at Turn 1 on lap 14 and then the early-pitting Massa in the first round of stops. Gathering clouds and falling temperatures meant that Michelins had now become the tyres to have. Post-race, it turned out that Massa had been due to stay out for a further two laps, which might have kept the Ferrari driver ahead, but a slow puncture had brought him in early.

Roughly half way around the lap, as Michael accelerated towards the first of the Degner curves, he realised that he no longer had power, and that his shot at the championship had all but missed the target. Lest people blame Ferrari, it's worth pointing out that that was Michael's first engine failure in a race for six years. With Massa no match for Alonso, the reigning champion simply rattled off the remaining laps.

Massa was untroubled in second and, once the late-pitting Nick Heidfeld had brought his BMW Sauber in for a second time on lap 41, Fisichella slotted into third position. This was extremely important to Renault's push for the constructors' championship and Jenson Button's Honda as it reeled off yet another good points score.

Like Alonso, Fisichella had to work his way past the Toyotas, but they became involved in a fratricidal battle of their own, with Trulli three times refusing to let a clearly quicker Ralf through. It seems there were the same arguments over BMW Sauber's radio waves as Kubica hovered on Heidfeld's tail in the middle section of the race, then spun in a failed attempt to pass. He ended up just behind Heidfeld and out of the points in ninth, although his pace might have helped him take on and pass the Toyotas had he been allowed through.

As if Michael's engine failure wasn't dramatic enough, the Japanese GP had some spectacular accidents. The first involved a leaking exhaust on Christijan Albers' Spyker MF1 which caused its rear suspension to overheat and collapse under braking for the chicane, scattering debris right across the track. This might have brought out the safety car and reduced Michael's lead, but it wasn't needed.

# SUZUKA ROUND 17
Date: **8 October 2006** Laps: **53** Distance: **191.248 miles/307.770km**
Weather: **Warm and bright**

## RACE RESULT

| Position | Driver | Team | Result | Stops | Qualifying Time | Grid |
|---|---|---|---|---|---|---|
| 1 | Fernando Alonso | Renault | 1h23m53.413s | 2 | 1m30.371s | 5 |
| 2 | Felipe Massa | Ferrari | 1h24m09.564s | 2 | 1m29.599s | 1 |
| 3 | Giancarlo Fisichella | Renault | 1h24m17.366s | 2 | 1m30.599s | 6 |
| 4 | Jenson Button | Honda | 1h24m27.514s | 2 | 1m30.992s | 7 |
| 5 | Kimi Raikkonen | McLaren | 1h24m37.009s | 2 | 1m30.827s | 11 |
| 6 | Jarno Trulli | Toyota | 1h24m40.130s | 2 | 1m30.039s | 4 |
| 7 | Ralf Schumacher | Toyota | 1h24m42.282s | 2 | 1m29.989s | 3 |
| 8 | Nick Heidfeld | BMW Sauber | 1h25m09.508s | 2 | 1m31.513s | 9 |
| 9 | Robert Kubica | BMW Sauber | 1h25m10.345s | 2 | 1m31.094s | 12 |
| 10 | Nico Rosberg | Williams | 52 laps | 2 | 1m31.856s | 10 |
| 11 | Pedro de la Rosa | McLaren | 52 laps | 2 | 1m31.254s | 13 |
| 12 | Rubens Barrichello | Honda | 52 laps | 3 | 1m31.478s | 8 |
| 13 | Robert Doornbos | Red Bull | 52 laps | 2 | 1m32.402s | 18 |
| 14 | Vitantonio Liuzzi | Toro Rosso | 52 laps | 2 | 1m31.943s | 15 |
| 15 | Takuma Sato | Super Aguri | 52 laps | 2 | 1m33.666s | 20 |
| 16 | Tiago Monteiro | Midland | 51 laps | 2 | 1m33.709s | 21 |
| 17 | Sakon Yamamoto | Super Aguri | 50 laps | 3 | no time | 22 |
| 18 | Scott Speed | Toro Rosso | 48 laps/power steering | 2 | 1m32.867s | 19 |
| R | Mark Webber | Williams | 39 laps/accident | 2 | 1m31.276s | 14 |
| R | Michael Schumacher | Ferrari | 36 laps/engine | 2 | 1m29.711s | 2 |
| R | David Coulthard | Red Bull | 35 laps/gearbox | 1 | 1m32.252s | 17 |
| R | Christijan Albers | Midland | 20 laps/suspension | 0 | 1m33.750s | 16 |

**FASTEST LAP:** ALONSO, 1M32.676S, 140.170MPH ON LAP 14

# TALKING POINT: WHY SUZUKA WANTS TO STAY ON THE CALENDAR

**The Japanese GP will be moving to Fuji Speedway for 2007, but pressure was mounting at last October's Japanese GP for Suzuka to be retained. The pits and the paddock are outdated, but almost all the main players reckon that Suzuka – home of the race for 20 years – is too good to be ousted. The drivers love the challenge, which Fuji doesn't offer, but their desires are seldom considered. Conversely, McLaren boss Ron Dennis supported the move to Fuji by saying that the hotel rooms near Suzuka smelt bad. So, no Suzuka in 2007, but perhaps it'll be reinstated in the World Championship schedule under the convenience title of the Asian GP or something similar in 2008.**

The drivers all praise Suzuka for the challenge that it offers and will miss their annual visit

# BRAZILIAN GP

**Was this the end of an era, or the start of another? Felipe Massa was peerless as he raced to victory, albeit in a dominant car, but Michael Schumacher remained the star in his final race. And Fernando Alonso became world champion, again.**

This was it: Michael Schumacher's final grand prix. The media couldn't get enough of the seven-time world champion, tracking his every move as he packed his final grand prix with incredible action. It was great viewing, but his team-mate Felipe Massa was in pole position and looking to become the first Brazilian to win on home ground since Ayrton Senna did in 1993, while Renault's Fernando Alonso still had a big job to secure his second world title in succession. He only needed a point, but the Ferraris were in top form.

Tyres had a big part to play in Brazil and the advantage swung increasingly Bridgestone's way as temperatures rose from Friday to Sunday. Come the race, Ferrari were untouchable and even Super Aguri showed unprecedented speed on their rubber, which emphasises how disastrous it was for midfield Bridgestone teams – Toyota and Williams – to have both their cars out early in the race.

As it was, Massa led from Kimi Raikkonen's McLaren, Jarno Trulli's Toyota and Alonso. Michael, starting tenth after mechanical trouble struck for the second race running, was up to seventh before the opening lap was out, bypassing both BMW Saubers and his brother Ralf. He had to win, with Alonso not getting a point, to be world champion.

And how he tried, passing Rubens Barrichello's Honda on lap 2. But first of all there was a safety car period triggered when

Nico Rosberg ran his Williams into the tyre wall coming on to the pit straight on lap 1, clearly the result of something breaking following contact with team-mate Mark Webber earlier in the lap. To add to Williams' woe, the damage to Webber's car put him out of the race, too.

While Massa stretched away in the lead on the restart on lap 5, delighting his home crowd as he controlled the race, Michael chased after Giancarlo Fisichella. He caught him but getting past was another matter, even with Ferrari's straight-line advantage. He made his move diving into the Senna S at the start of lap 9 and got through, just. But the red Ferrari slewed sideways at the bottom of the dip and Fisichella went back

Pure pleasure: Felipe Massa, sporting patriotically coloured overalls for the occasion of his home race, celebrates his dominant victory

past. There had been the slightest of contact and Michael's left rear sidewall was ripped.

With a lengthy, slow tour back to the pits this ought to have confirmed Alonso as world champion, but Michael wasn't finished yet and produced one of his most remarkable drives in his 16 seasons. He pitted, refuelled and rejoined 20th, 1m 10s behind Massa, and it was stunning how this gap tumbled with every subsequent lap. He should have been out, but still came within a whisker of finishing on the podium.

Up front, Massa remained untroubled but Trulli was out of the equation by lap 10 when his rear suspension failed, as had Ralf's a lap earlier. By running five laps longer than Raikkonen, Alonso was up to second, or he was when Pedro de la Rosa pulled in for his only pit stop on lap 35. By this stage Michael was up to eighth and good for a point, but not the ten that he needed. But he pressed on and it was the driver who had just advanced to third, Honda's Jenson Button, who had shot forward from 14th, and who became the final driver in his sights. Button held on to show how solid Honda's progress had been over the final rounds. His had been a hero's drive, but in many ways it would have been wrong for him to take the spotlight away from Brazil's new hero Massa, and the new two-time champion, Alonso.

# INTERLAGOS ROUND 18

Date: **22 October 2006** Laps: **71** Distance: **189.357 miles/304.762km**
Weather: **Warm and bright**

## RACE RESULT

| Position | Driver | Team | Result | Stops | Qualifying Time | Grid |
|---|---|---|---|---|---|---|
| 1 | Felipe Massa | Ferrari | 1h31m53.751s | 2 | 1m10.680s | 1 |
| 2 | Fernando Alonso | Renault | 1h32m12.409s | 2 | 1m11.567s | 4 |
| 3 | Jenson Button | Honda | 1h32m13.145s | 2 | 1m11.742s | 14 |
| 4 | Michael Schumacher | Ferrari | 1h32m17.845s | 2 | no time | 10 |
| 5 | Kimi Raikkonen | McLaren | 1h32m22.254s | 2 | 1m11.299s | 2 |
| 6 | Giancarlo Fisichella | Renault | 1h32m24.038s | 2 | 1m11.629s | 6 |
| 7 | Rubens Barrichello | Honda | 1h32m34.045s | 2 | 1m11.619s | 5 |
| 8 | Pedro de la Rosa | McLaren | 1h32m45.819s | 1 | 1m11.658s | 12 |
| 9 | Robert Kubica | BMW Sauber | 1h33m01.393s | 2 | 1m12.131s | 9 |
| 10 | Takuma Sato | Super Aguri | 70 laps | 2 | 1m13.269s | 19 |
| 11 | Scott Speed | Toro Rosso | 70 laps | 2 | 1m12.856s | 16 |
| 12 | Robert Doornbos | Red Bull | 70 laps | 2 | 1m12.591s | 22* |
| 13 | Vitantonio Liuzzi | Toro Rosso | 70 laps | 2 | 1m12.861s | 15 |
| 14 | Christijan Albers | Spyker MF1 | 70 laps | 2 | 1m13.138s | 17 |
| 15 | Tiago Monteiro | Spyker MF1 | 69 laps | 1 | no time | 21 |
| 16 | Sakon Yamamoto | Super Aguri | 69 laps | 3 | 1m13.357s | 20 |
| 17 | Nick Heidfeld | BMW Sauber | 63 laps/accident | 2 | 1m11.882s | 8 |
| R | David Coulthard | Red Bull | 14 laps/gearbox | 0 | 1m13.249s | 18 |
| R | Jarno Trulli | Toyota | 10 laps/suspension | 0 | 1m11.328s | 3 |
| R | Ralf Schumacher | Toyota | 9 laps/suspension | 0 | 1m11.695s | 7 |
| R | Mark Webber | Williams | 1 laps/crash damage | 0 | 1m11.650s | 11 |
| R | Nico Rosberg | Williams | 0 laps/accident | 0 | 1m11.679s | 13 |

FASTEST LAP: MICHAEL SCHUMACHER, 1M12.162S, 133.580MPH/214.966KPH ON LAP 70

* 10-PLACE GRID PENALTY

# TALKING POINT: SUPER AGURI FINISHES IN STYLE

**It was all too easy to focus on what was happening at the front and Michael Schumacher's charge back up the order. But one of the most remarkable stories in years was unfolding in midfield where Takuma Sato was mixing it for Super Aguri Racing, the team that didn't exist even 12 months earlier. To many, their greatest success was getting two cars ready for the opening race, which was little short of a miracle. However, finishing tenth, and easily outpacing both the Toro Rossos showed what progress had been made. Their Bridgestone tyres were superior, but Spyker used those too and were some way adrift. Hats off to Aguri Suzuki and his gang.**

Takuma Sato's Interlagos charge was the culmination of a season's steady progress

# FINAL RESULTS 2006

| | DRIVER | NAT. | ENGINE | R1 | R2 | R3 | R4 |
|---|---|---|---|---|---|---|---|
| 1. | FERNANDO ALONSO | SPA | RENAULT R26 | 1 | 2F | 1 | 2F |
| 2. | MICHAEL SCHUMACHER | GER | FERRARI 248 | 2P | 6 | R | 1P |
| 3. | FELIPE MASSA | BRA | FERRARI 248 | 9 | 5 | R | 4 |
| 4. | GIANCARLO FISICHELLA | ITA | RENAULT R26 | R | 1P | 5 | 8 |
| 5. | KIMI RAIKKONEN | FIN | McLAREN-MERCEDES MP4-21 | 3 | R | 2F | 5 |
| 6. | JENSON BUTTON | GBR | HONDA RA106 | 4 | 3 | 9P | 7 |
| 7. | RUBENS BARRICHELLO | BRA | HONDA RA106 | 15 | 10 | 7 | 10 |
| 8. | JUAN PABLO MONTOYA | COL | McLAREN-MERCEDES MP4-21 | 5 | 4 | R | 3 |
| 9. | NICK HEIDFELD | GER | BMW SAUBER F1.06 | 12 | R | 4 | 13 |
| 10. | RALF SCHUMACHER | GER | TOYOTA TF106 | 14 | 8 | 3 | 9 |
| | | | TOYOTA TF106B | - | - | - | - |
| 11. | PEDRO DE LA ROSA | SPA | McLAREN-MERCEDES MP4-21 | - | - | - | - |
| 12. | JARNO TRULLI | ITA | TOYOTA TF106 | 16 | 9 | R | R |
| | | | TOYOTA TF106B | - | - | - | - |
| 13. | DAVID COULTHARD | GBR | RED BULL-FERRARI RB2 | 10 | R | 8 | R |
| 14. | MARK WEBBER | AUS | WILLIAMS-COSWORTH FW28 | 6 | R | R | 6 |
| 15. | JACQUES VILLENEUVE | CDN | BMW SAUBER F1.06 | R | 7 | 6 | 12 |
| 16. | ROBERT KUBICA | POL | BMW SAUBER F1.06 | - | - | - | - |
| 17. | NICO ROSBERG | GER | WILLIAMS-COSWORTH FW28 | 7F | R | R | 11 |
| 18. | CHRISTIAN KLIEN | AUT | RED BULL-FERRARI RB2 | 8 | R | R | R |
| 19. | VITANTONIO LIUZZI | ITA | TORO ROSSO-COSWORTH STR01 | 11 | 11 | R | 14 |
| | SCOTT SPEED | USA | TORO ROSSO-COSWORTH STR01 | 13 | R | 11 | 15 |
| | TIAGO MONTEIRO | POR | MIDLAND-TOYOTA M16 | 17 | 13 | R | 16 |
| | CHRISTIJAN ALBERS | NED | MIDLAND-TOYOTA M16 | R | 12 | 10 | R |
| | TAKUMA SATO | JAP | SUPER AGURI-HONDA SA05 | 18 | 14 | 12 | R |
| | | | SUPER AGURI-HONDA SA06 | - | - | - | - |
| | ROBERT DOORNBOS | NED | RED BULL-FERRARI RB2 | - | - | - | - |
| | YUJI IDE | JAP | SUPER AGURI-HONDA SA05 | R | R | 13 | R |
| | FRANCK MONTAGNY | FRA | SUPER AGURI-HONDA SA05 | - | - | - | - |
| | SAKON YAMAMOTO | JAP | SUPER AGURI-HONDA SA06 | - | - | - | - |

## SCORING

| | |
|---|---|
| 1st | 10 points |
| 2nd | 8 points |
| 3rd | 6 points |
| 4th | 5 points |
| 5th | 4 points |
| 6th | 3 points |
| 7th | 2 points |
| 8th | 1 point |

(RACE RESULTS FOR BOTH DRIVERS, i.e. FIRST AND SECOND LISTED AS 1/2, WITH THE TEAM'S BETTER RESULT LISTED FIRST)

| | | R1 | R2 | R3 | R4 |
|---|---|---|---|---|---|
| 1. | RENAULT | 1/R | 1P/2 | 1/5 | 2/8 |
| 2. | FERRARI | 2/9 | 5/6 | R/R | 1/4 |
| 3. | McLAREN-MERCEDES | 3/5 | 4/R | 2/R | 3/5 |
| 4. | HONDA | 4/15 | 3/10 | 7/9 | 7/10 |
| 5. | BMW SAUBER | 12/R | 7/R | 4/6 | 12/13 |
| 6. | TOYOTA | 14/16 | 8/9 | 3/R | 9/R |
| 7. | RED BULL-FERRARI | 8/10 | R/R | 8/R | R/R |
| 8. | WILLIAMS-COSWORTH | 6/7 | R/R | R/R | 6/11 |
| 9. | TORO ROSSO-COSWORTH | 11/13 | 11/R | 11/R | 14/15 |
| 10. | SPYKER MF1-TOYOTA | 17/R | 12/13 | 10/R | 16/R |
| 11. | SUPER AGURI-HONDA | 18/R | 14/R | 12/13 | R/R |

# SYMBOLS AND GRAND PRIX KEY

**D** DISQUALIFIED  **F** FASTEST LAP  **NC** NOT CLASSIFIED  **NS** NON-STARTER  **P** POLE POSITION  **R** RETIRED  **W** WITHDREW

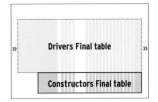

Drivers Final table

Constructors Final table

| R5 | R6 | R7 | R8 | R9 | R10 | R11 | R12 | R13 | R14 | R15 | R16 | R17 | R18 | TOTAL POINTS |
|---|---|---|---|---|---|---|---|---|---|---|---|---|---|---|
| 2P | 1P | 1 | 1PF | 1P | 5 | 2 | 5 | R | 2 | R | 2PF | 1F | 2 | 134 |
| 1F | 2 | 5F | 2 | 2 | 1PF | 1PF | 1F | 8 | 3F | 1 | 1 | R | 4F | 121 |
| 3 | 4F | 9 | 5 | 5 | 2 | 3 | 2 | 7F | 1P | 9 | R | 2P | 1P | 80 |
| 6 | 3 | 6 | 4 | 4 | 3 | 6 | 6 | R | 6 | 4 | 3 | 3 | 6 | 72 |
| 4 | 5 | R | 3 | 3F | R | 5 | 3P | RP | R | 2PF | R | 5 | 5 | 65 |
| R | 6 | 11 | R | 9 | R | R | 4 | 1 | 4 | 5 | 4 | 4 | 3 | 56 |
| 5 | 7 | 4 | 10 | R | 6 | R | R | 4 | 8 | 6 | 6 | 12 | 7 | 30 |
| R | R | 2 | 6 | R | R | - | - | - | - | - | - | - | - | 26 |
| 10 | 8 | 7 | 7 | 7 | R | 8 | R | 3 | 14 | 8 | 7 | 8 | 17 | 23 |
| R | R | - | - | - | - | - | - | - | - | - | - | - | - | |
| - | - | 8 | R | R | R | 4 | 9 | 6 | 7 | 15 | R | 7 | R | 20 |
| - | - | - | - | - | - | 7 | R | 2 | 5 | R | 5 | 11 | 8 | 19 |
| 9 | 10 | - | - | - | - | - | - | - | - | - | - | - | - | |
| - | - | 17 | 11 | 6 | 4 | R | 7 | 12 | 9 | 7 | R | 6 | R | 15 |
| R | 14 | 3 | 12 | 8 | 7 | 9 | 11 | 5 | 15 | 12 | 9 | R | R | 14 |
| R | 9 | R | R | 12 | R | R | R | R | 10 | 10 | 8 | R | R | 7 |
| 8 | 12 | 14 | 8 | R | R | 11 | R | - | - | - | - | - | - | 7 |
| - | - | - | - | - | - | - | - | D | 12 | 3 | 13 | 9 | 9 | 6 |
| 7 | 11 | R | 9 | R | 9 | 14 | R | R | R | R | 11 | 10 | R | 4 |
| R | 13 | R | 14 | 11 | R | 12 | 8 | R | 11 | 11 | - | - | - | 2 |
| R | 15 | 10 | 13 | 13 | 8 | 13 | 10 | R | R | 14 | 10 | 14 | 13 | 1 |
| 11 | R | 13 | R | 10 | R | 10 | 12 | 11 | 13 | 13 | 15 | 18 | 11 | |
| 12 | 16 | 15 | 16 | 14 | R | R | D | 9 | R | R | R | 16 | 15 | |
| 13 | R | 12 | 15 | R | 15 | D | 10 | R | 17 | 16 | R | 14 | | |
| R | 17 | R | 17 | 15 | R | R | - | - | - | - | - | - | - | |
| - | - | - | - | - | - | R | 13 | NC | 16 | 14 | 15 | 10 | | |
| - | - | - | - | - | - | - | - | - | - | 12 | 13 | 12 | | |
| - | - | - | - | - | - | - | - | - | - | - | - | - | | |
| R | R | 16 | 18 | R | R | 16 | - | - | - | - | - | - | - | |
| - | - | - | - | - | - | R | R | R | R | 17 | 17 | 16 | | |
| 2/6 | 1/3 | 1/6 | 1/4 | 1/4 | 3/5 | 2/6 | 5/6 | R/R | 2/6 | 4/R | 2/3 | 1/3 | 2/6 | 206 |
| 1/3 | 2/4 | 5/9 | 2/5 | 2/5 | 1/2 | 1/3 | 1/2 | 7/8 | 1/3 | 1/9 | 1/R | 2/R | 1/4 | 201 |
| 4/R | 5/R | 2/R | 3/6 | 3/R | R/R | 5/7 | 3/R | 2/R | 5/R | 2/R | 5/R | 5/11 | 5/8 | 110 |
| 5/R | 6/7 | 4/11 | 10/R | 9/R | 6/R | R/R | 4/R | 1/4 | 4/8 | 5/6 | 4/6 | 4/12 | 3/7 | 86 |
| 8/10 | 8/12 | 7/14 | 7/8 | 7/R | R/R | 8/11 | R/R | 3/D | 12/14 | 3/8 | 7/13 | 8/9 | 9/17 | 36 |
| 9/R | 10/R | 8/17 | 11/R | 6/R | 4/R | 4/R | 7/9 | 6/12 | 7/9 | 7/15 | R/R | 6/7 | R/R | 35 |
| R/R | 13/14 | 3/R | 12/14 | 8/11 | 7/R | 9/12 | 8/11 | 5/R | 11/15 | 11/12 | 9/12 | 13/R | 12/R | 16 |
| 7/R | 9/11 | R/R | 9/R | 12/R | 9/R | R/14 | R/R | R/R | 10/R | 10/R | 8/11 | 10/R | R/R | 11 |
| 11/R | 15/R | 10/13 | 13/R | 10/13 | 8/R | 10/13 | 10/12 | 11/R | 13/R | 13/14 | 10/15 | 14/18 | 11/13 | 1 |
| 12/13 | 16/R | 12/15 | 15/16 | 14/R | R/R | 15/R | D/D | 9/10 | R/R | 17/R | 16/R | 16/R | 14/15 | |
| R/R | 17/R | 16/R | 17/18 | 15/R | R/R | 16/R | R/R | 13/R | NC/R | 16/R | 14/17 | 15/17 | 10/16 | |

# THRILLS AND SPILLS OF 2006

One inherent rule of racing that can never be escaped is that anything can happen at any time. This is seldom more true than in Formula One, as the drivers are always giving their all in their quest for points and glory. The thrills and spills these incidents provide can be driver-induced, but mechanical failures can be just as spectacular.

Three, two, one, action ... (clockwise from top left): the normally careful Nick Heidfeld was pitched into a roll at Indianapolis; Michael Schumacher feels the heat in practice at Magny-Cours; Christian Klien's Red Bull smashes its way along a wall at the Australian GP; third race, last corner and Jenson Button's Honda engine lets go in Melbourne; collapsed suspension led to Kimi Raikkonen going on a bucking bronco ride in Bahrain.

# THE FACES OF F1

To some, the cars are the stars, but to many, it's the drivers, the bosses, the VIPs and the girls who are the main attraction and Formula One offers something for everyone on this count. Colour, glamour and frivolity may appear to be the message, but even dressing the drivers in capes, as Red Bull Racing did at Monaco last year, fails to mask how serious the business is, with the passion to succeed present in us all.

All things bright and beautiful (clockwise from top left): a taste of glamour in the Melbourne paddock; complete focus from World Champion Fernando Alonso; Jenson Button addresses his fans at the British GP; is this Honda engineer ready to die for the cause? Red Bull Racing's Doornbos, Klien and Coulthard are dressed to impress at Monaco ... where Flavio Briatore meets tennis ace Boris Becker on the grid.

# THE KING HAS RETIRED

Formula One won't feel the same in 2007 without Michael Schumacher, who retired last October. He smashed all records and left at the top of his game. This is a celebration of the pick of his 91 wins, and one of his occasional less celebrated moments in a rich but controversial career.

The ultimate winner (clockwise from right): Michael prepares for his first F1 outing with Jordan at Spa in 1991; Michael's first win at Spa in 1992; celebrating with Eddie Irvine and Jean Todt at Silverstone in 1998; his first Ferrari win at Barcelona in 1996; driving into Jacques Villeneuve at the 1997 finale at Jerez; win number 91 at Shanghai in 2006

# FORMULA 1 RECORDS

## MOST GRANDS PRIX STARTS

### DRIVERS

| | | | | | | | | |
|---|---|---|---|---|---|---|---|
| 256 | Riccardo Patrese | (ITA) | 165 | Jacques Villeneuve | (CDN) | 132 | Eddie Cheever | (USA) |
| 250 | Michael Schumacher | (GER) | 163 | Thierry Boutsen | (BEL) | | Clay Regazzoni | (SUI) |
| 235 | Rubens Barrichello | (BRA) | | Ralf Schumacher | (GER) | 128 | Mario Andretti | (USA) |
| 212 | David Coulthard | (GBR) | 162 | Mika Hakkinen | (FIN) | 126 | Jack Brabham | (AUS) |
| 210 | Gerhard Berger | (AUT) | | Johnny Herbert | (GBR) | 123 | Ronnie Peterson | (SWE) |
| 208 | Andrea de Cesaris | (ITA) | 161 | Ayrton Senna | (BRA) | 119 | Jenson Button | (GBR) |
| 204 | Nelson Piquet | (BRA) | 159 | Heinz-Harald Frentzen | (GER) | | Pierluigi Martini | (ITA) |
| 201 | Jean Alesi | FRA) | 158 | Martin Brundle | (GBR) | 117 | Nick Heidfeld | (GER) |
| 199 | Alain Prost | (FRA) | | Olivier Panis | (FRA) | 116 | Damon Hill | (GBR) |
| 194 | Michele Alboreto | (ITA) | 152 | John Watson | (GBR) | | Jacky Ickx | (BEL) |
| 187 | Nigel Mansell | (GBR) | 149 | Rene Arnoux | (FRA) | | Alan Jones | (AUS) |
| 179 | Giancarlo Fisichella | (ITA) | 147 | Eddie Irvine | (GBR) | 114 | Keke Rosberg | (FIN) |
| 176 | Graham Hill | (GBR) | | Derek Warwick | (GBR) | | Patrick Tambay | (FRA) |
| 175 | Jacques Laffite | (FRA) | 146 | Carlos Reutemann | (ARG) | 112 | Denny Hulme | (NZL) |
| 171 | Niki Lauda | (AUT) | 144 | Emerson Fittipaldi | (BRA) | | Jody Scheckter | (RSA) |
| 167 | Jarno Trulli | (ITA) | 135 | Jean-Pierre Jarier | (FRA) | | | |

### CONSTRUCTORS

| | | | | | | |
|---|---|---|---|---|---|
| 741 | Ferrari | 383 | Arrows | 197 | BRM |
| 614 | McLaren | 359 | Toro Rosso (né Minardi) | 171 | Red Bull (né Stewart then Jaguar Racing) |
| 533 | Williams | 317 | Benetton | | |
| 490 | Lotus | 268 | Spyker MF1 (né Jordan) | 136 | Honda Racing (né BAR) |
| 418 | Tyrrell | 235 | BMW Sauber | 132 | Osella |
| 409 | Prost | 230 | March | | |
| 394 | Brabham | 211 | Renault | | |

Above: Riccardo Patrese in 1993, his last season with Benetton, remains the driver with the most grands prix starts. Opposite: Jack Brabham leads third-placed Maurice Trintingnant across the line at Monaco in 1959 to become the first driver to win a world title with the engine behind him

# MOST GRANDS PRIX WINS

## DRIVERS

| | | | | | | | | | |
|---|---|---|---|---|---|---|---|---|---|
| 91 | Michael Schumacher | (GER) | 14 | Jack Brabham | (AUS) | 9 | Rubens Barrichello | (BRA) |
| 51 | Alain Prost | (FRA) | | Emerson Fittipaldi | (BRA) | | Kimi Raikkonen | (FIN) |
| 41 | Ayrton Senna | (BRA) | | Graham Hill | (GBR) | 8 | Denny Hulme | (NZL) |
| 31 | Nigel Mansell | (GBR) | 13 | Alberto Ascari | (ITA) | | Jacky Ickx | (BEL) |
| 27 | Jackie Stewart | (GBR) | | David Coulthard | (GBR) | 7 | Rene Arnoux | (FRA) |
| 25 | Jim Clark | (GBR) | 12 | Mario Andretti | (USA) | | Juan Pablo Montoya | (COL) |
| | Niki Lauda | (AUT) | | Alan Jones | (AUS) | 6 | Tony Brooks | (GBR) |
| 24 | Juan Manuel Fangio | (ARG) | | Carlos Reutemann | (ARG) | | Jacques Laffite | (FRA) |
| 23 | Nelson Piquet | (BRA) | 11 | Jacques Villeneuve | (CDN) | | Riccardo Patrese | (FRA) |
| 22 | Damon Hill | (GBR) | 10 | Gerhard Berger | (AUT) | | Jochen Rindt | (AUT) |
| 20 | Mika Hakkinen | (FIN) | | James Hunt | (GBR) | | Ralf Schumacher | (GER) |
| 16 | Stirling Moss | (GBR) | | Ronnie Peterson | (SWE) | | John Surtees | (GBR) |
| 15 | Fernando Alonso | (SPA) | | Jody Scheckter | (RSA) | | Gilles Villeneuve | (CDN) |

## CONSTRUCTORS

| | | | | | |
|---|---|---|---|---|---|
| 192 | Ferrari | 10 | Alfa Romeo | 1 | Eagle |
| 148 | McLaren | 9 | Ligier | | Hesketh |
| 113 | Williams | | Maserati | | Honda Racing (né BAR) |
| 79 | Lotus | | Matra | | Penske |
| 35 | Brabham | | Mercedes | | Porsche |
| 33 | Renault | | Vanwall | | Shadow |
| 27 | Benetton | 4 | Spyker MF1 (né Jordan) | | Red Bull (né Stewart then |
| 23 | Tyrrell | 3 | March | | Jaguar Racing) |
| 17 | BRM | | Wolf | | |
| 16 | Cooper | 2 | Honda | | |

Left: Four-time World Champion Alain Prost began his Formula One career with McLaren in Argentina in 1980. Opposite top: Victory at Monaco in 1994 put Michael Schumacher on the way to his first world title. Opposite right: Alberto Ascari completes his record run of nine wins at Spa in 1953

## MOST GRANDS PRIX WINS IN ONE SEASON

### DRIVERS

| | | | | | | | | | | | |
|---|---|---|---|---|---|---|---|---|---|---|---|
| 13 | Michael Schumacher | (GER) | 2004 | | Fernando Alonso | (SPA) | 2006 | | Juan Manuel Fangio | (ARG) | 1954 |
| 11 | Michael Schumacher | (GER) | 2002 | | Jim Clark | (GBR) | 1963 | | Damon Hill | (GBR) | 1994 |
| 9 | Nigel Mansell | (GBR) | 1992 | | Alain Prost | (FRA) | 1984 | | James Hunt | (GBR) | 1976 |
| | Michael Schumacher | (GER) | 1995 | | Alain Prost | (FRA) | 1988 | | Nigel Mansell | (GBR) | 1987 |
| | Michael Schumacher | (GER) | 2000 | | Alain Prost | (FRA) | 1993 | | Michael Schumacher | (GER) | 1998 |
| | Michael Schumacher | (GER) | 2001 | | Kimi Raikkonen | (FIN) | 2005 | | Michael Schumacher | (GER) | 2003 |
| 8 | Mika Hakkinen | (FIN) | 1998 | | Ayrton Senna | (BRA) | 1991 | | Michael Schumacher | (GER) | 2006 |
| | Damon Hill | (GBR) | 1996 | | Jacques Villeneuve | (CDN) | 1997 | | Ayrton Senna | (BRA) | 1989 |
| | Michael Schumacher | (GER) | 1994 | 6 | Mario Andretti | (USA) | 1978 | | Ayrton Senna | (BRA) | 1990 |
| | Ayrton Senna | (BRA) | 1988 | | Alberto Ascari | (ITA) | 1952 | | | | |
| 7 | Fernando Alonso | (SPA) | 2005 | | Jim Clark | (GBR) | 1965 | | | | |

### CONSTRUCTORS

| | | | | | | | | | | | | |
|---|---|---|---|---|---|---|---|---|---|---|---|---|
| 15 | Ferrari | 2004 | | McLaren | 1998 | | Lotus | 1973 | | Ferrari | 1996 |
| | Ferrari | 2002 | | Williams | 1986 | | McLaren | 1999 | | Ferrari | 1998 |
| | McLaren | 1988 | | Williams | 1987 | | McLaren | 2000 | | Ferrari | 1999 |
| 12 | McLaren | 1984 | 8 | Benetton | 1994 | | Tyrrell | 1971 | | Lotus | 1965 |
| | Williams | 1996 | | Ferrari | 2003 | | Williams | 1991 | | Lotus | 1970 |
| 11 | Benetton | 1995 | | Lotus | 1978 | | Williams | 1994 | | Matra | 1969 |
| 10 | Ferrari | 2000 | | McLaren | 1991 | 6 | Alfa Romeo | 1950 | | McLaren | 1976 |
| | McLaren | 2005 | | Renault | 2005 | | Alfa Romeo | 1951 | | McLaren | 1985 |
| | McLaren | 1989 | | Renault | 2006 | | Cooper | 1960 | | McLaren | 1990 |
| | Williams | 1992 | | Williams | 1997 | | Ferrari | 1975 | | Vanwall | 1958 |
| | Williams | 1993 | 7 | Ferrari | 1952 | | Ferrari | 1976 | | Williams | 1980 |
| 9 | Ferrari | 2001 | | Ferrari | 1953 | | Ferrari | 1979 | | | |
| | Ferrari | 2006 | | Lotus | 1963 | | Ferrari | 1990 | | | |

## MOST CONSECUTIVE WINS

| 9 | Alberto Ascari | (ITA) | 1952/53 |
|---|---|---|---|
| 7 | Michael Schumacher | (GER) | 2004 |
| 6 | Michael Schumacher | (GER) | 2000/01 |
| 5 | Jack Brabham | (AUS) | 1960 |
| | Jim Clark | (GBR) | 1965 |
| | Nigel Mansell | (GBR) | 1992 |
| | Michael Schumacher | (GER) | 2004 |
| 4 | Fernando Alonso | (SPA) | 2006 |
| | Jack Brabham | (AUS) | 1966 |
| | Jim Clark | (GBR) | 1963 |
| | Juan Manuel Fangio | (ARG) | 1953/54 |
| | Damon Hill | (GBR) | 1995/96 |
| | Alain Prost | (FRA) | 1993 |
| | Jochen Rindt | (AUT) | 1970 |
| | Michael Schumacher | (GER) | 1994 |
| | Michael Schumacher | (GER) | 2002 |
| | Ayrton Senna | (BRA) | 1988 |
| | Ayrton Senna | (BRA) | 1991 |

## GRANDS PRIX STARTS WITHOUT A WIN

| 208 | Andrea de Cesaris | (ITA) |
|---|---|---|
| 158 | Martin Brundle | (GBR) |
| 147 | Derek Warwick | (GBR) |
| 135 | Jean-Pierre Jarier | (FRA) |
| 132 | Eddie Cheever | (USA) |
| 119 | Pierluigi Martini | (ITA) |
| 117 | Nick Heidfeld | (GER) |
| 111 | Mika Salo | (FIN) |
| 109 | Philippe Alliot | (FRA) |
| 107 | Jos Verstappen | (NED) |
| 99 | Pedro Diniz | (BRA) |
| 97 | Chris Amon | (NZL) |
| 95 | Ukyo Katayama | (JAP) |
| 93 | Ivan Capelli | (ITA) |
| 87 | Mark Webber | (AUS) |
| 84 | Jonathan Palmer | (GBR) |
| 82 | Marc Surer | (SUI) |
| 79 | Stefan Johansson | (SWE) |

# MOST POLE POSITIONS

## DRIVERS

| | | | | | | |
|---|---|---|---|---|---|---|
| 68 | Michael Schumacher | (GER) | | Alberto Ascari | (ITA) |
| 65 | Ayrton Senna | (BRA) | | James Hunt | (GBR) |
| 33 | Jim Clark | (GBR) | | Ronnie Peterson | (SWE) |
| | Alain Prost | (FRA) | 13 | Rubens Barrichello | (BRA) |
| 32 | Nigel Mansell | (GBR) | | Jack Brabham | (AUS) |
| 29 | Juan Manuel Fangio | (ARG) | | Graham Hill | (GBR) |
| 26 | Mika Hakkinen | (FIN) | | Jacky Ickx | (BEL) |
| 24 | Niki Lauda | (AUT) | | Juan Pablo Montoya | (COL) |
| | Nelson Piquet | (BRA) | | Jacques Villeneuve | (CDN) |
| 20 | Damon Hill | (GBR) | 12 | Gerhard Berger | (AUT) |
| 18 | Mario Andretti | (USA) | | David Coulthard | (GBR) |
| | Rene Arnoux | (FRA) | 11 | Kimi Raikkonen | (FIN) |
| 17 | Jackie Stewart | (GBR) | 10 | Jochen Rindt | (AUT) |
| 16 | Stirling Moss | (GBR) | 8 | Riccardo Patrese | (ITA) |
| 14 | Fernando Alonso | (SPA) | | John Surtees | (GBR) |

## CONSTRUCTORS

| | |
|---|---|
| 186 | Ferrari |
| 125 | McLaren |
| | Williams |
| 107 | Lotus |
| 50 | Renault |
| 39 | Brabham |
| 16 | Benetton |
| 14 | Tyrrell |
| 12 | Alfa Romeo |
| 11 | BRM |
| | Cooper |
| 10 | Maserati |
| 9 | Prost |
| 8 | Mercedes |
| 7 | Vanwall |
| 5 | March |
| 4 | Matra |
| 3 | Honda Racing *(né BAR)* |
| | Shadow |
| 2 | Spyker MF1 *(né Jordan)* |
| | Lancia |
| | Toyota |
| 1 | Jaguar |

**Double World Champion Jim Clark was always the centre of attention, such as at Zandvoort after winning the 1965 Dutch Grand Prix for Lotus**

# MOST POLE POSITIONS IN ONE SEASON

## DRIVERS

| | | | | | | | | | | | | |
|---|---|---|---|---|---|---|---|---|---|---|---|---|
| **14** | Nigel Mansell | (GBR) | 1992 | | Damon Hill | (GBR) | 1996 | | Michael Schumacher | (GER) | 2004 |
| **13** | Alain Prost | (FRA) | 1993 | | Niki Lauda | (AUT) | 1974 | | Ayrton Senna | (BRA) | 1986 |
| | Ayrton Senna | (BRA) | 1988 | | Niki Lauda | (AUT) | 1975 | | Ayrton Senna | (BRA) | 1991 |
| | Ayrton Senna | (BRA) | 1989 | | Ronnie Peterson | (SWE) | 1973 | **7** | Mario Andretti | (USA) | 1977 |
| **11** | Mika Hakkinen | (FIN) | 1999 | | Nelson Piquet | (BRA) | 1984 | | Jim Clark | (GBR) | 1963 |
| | Michael Schumacher | (GER) | 2001 | | Michael Schumacher | (GER) | 2000 | | Damon Hill | (GBR) | 1995 |
| **10** | Ayrton Senna | (BRA) | 1990 | **8** | Mario Andretti | (USA) | 1978 | | Juan Pablo Montoya | (COL) | 2002 |
| | Jacques Villeneuve | (CDN) | 1997 | | James Hunt | (GBR) | 1976 | | Michael Schumacher | (GER) | 2002 |
| **9** | Mika Hakkinen | (FIN) | 1998 | | Nigel Mansell | (GBR) | 1987 | | Ayrton Senna | (BRA) | 1985 |

## CONSTRUCTORS

| | | | | | | |
|---|---|---|---|---|---|---|
| **15** | McLaren | 1988 | **11** | Ferrari | 2001 |
| | McLaren | 1989 | | McLaren | 1999 |
| | Williams | 1992 | | Williams | 1997 |
| | Williams | 1993 | **10** | Ferrari | 1974 |
| **12** | Ferrari | 2004 | | Ferrari | 2000 |
| | Lotus | 1978 | | Ferrari | 2002 |
| | McLaren | 1990 | | Lotus | 1973 |
| | McLaren | 1998 | | McLaren | 1991 |
| | Williams | 1987 | | Renault | 1982 |
| | Williams | 1995 | **9** | Brabham | 1984 |
| | Williams | 1996 | | Ferrari | 1975 |

**Nigel Mansell had been crowned World Champion long before he reached the final round at Adelaide in 1992, but he still powered his Williams to a record-breaking 14th pole position in a single season**

# MOST FASTEST LAPS

## DRIVERS

| | | | | | | | | |
|---|---|---|---|---|---|---|---|---|
| 75 | Michael Schumacher | (GER) | 19 | Damon Hill | (GBR) | 13 | Alberto Ascari | (ITA) |
| 41 | Alain Prost | (FRA) | | Stirling Moss | (GBR) | | Alan Jones | (AUS) |
| 30 | Nigel Mansell | (GBR) | | Kimi Raikkonen | (FIN) | | Riccardo Patrese | (ITA) |
| 28 | Jim Clark | (GBR) | | Ayrton Senna | (BRA) | 12 | Rene Arnoux | (FRA) |
| 25 | Mika Hakkinen | (FIN) | 18 | David Coulthard | (GBR) | | Jack Brabham | (AUS) |
| 24 | Niki Lauda | (AUT) | 15 | Rubens Barrichello | (BRA) | | Juan Pablo Montoya | (COL) |
| 23 | Juan Manuel Fangio | (ARG) | | Clay Regazzoni | (SUI) | 11 | John Surtees | (GBR) |
| | Nelson Piquet | (BRA) | | Jackie Stewart | (GBR) | | | |
| 21 | Gerhard Berger | (AUT) | 14 | Jacky Ickx | (BEL) | | | |

## CONSTRUCTORS

| | | | | | | | |
|---|---|---|---|---|---|---|---|
| 192 | Ferrari | 27 | Renault | 12 | Matra | | |
| 129 | McLaren | 20 | Tyrrell | 11 | Prost | | |
| | Williams | 15 | BRM | 9 | Mercedes | | |
| 71 | Lotus | | Maserati | 7 | March | | |
| 40 | Brabham | 14 | Alfa Romeo | 6 | Vanwall | | |
| 35 | Benetton | 13 | Cooper | | | | |

**Michael Schumacher set the last of his 75 fastest laps in his final race, the 2006 Brazilian Grand Prix**

# MOST POINTS (THIS FIGURE IS GROSS TALLY, I.E. INCLUDING SCORES THAT WERE LATER DROPPED)

## DRIVERS

| | | | | | | | | |
|---|---|---|---|---|---|---|---|---|
| 1369 | Michael Schumacher | (GER) | 385 | Gerhard Berger | (AUT) | 281 | Emerson Fittipaldi | (BRA) |
| 798.5 | Alain Prost | (FRA) | 371 | Fernando Alonso | (SPA) | | Riccardo Patrese | (ITA) |
| 614 | Ayrton Senna | (BRA) | 360 | Damon Hill | (GBR) | 277.5 | Juan Manuel Fangio | (ARG) |
| 519 | Rubens Barrichello | (BRA) | | Jackie Stewart | (GBR) | 274 | Jim Clark | (GBR) |
| 513 | David Coulthard | (GBR) | 346 | Kimi Raikkonen | (FIN) | 261 | Jack Brabham | (AUS) |
| 485.5 | Nelson Piquet | (BRA) | 324 | Ralf Schumacher | (GER) | 255 | Jody Scheckter | (RSA) |
| 482 | Nigel Mansell | (GBR) | 310 | Carlos Reutemann | (ARG) | 248 | Denny Hulme | (NZL) |
| 420.5 | Niki Lauda | (AUT) | 307 | Juan Pablo Montoya | (COL) | 246 | Giancarlo Fisichella | (ITA) |
| 420 | Mika Hakkinen | (FIN) | 289 | Graham Hill | (GBR) | 242 | Jean Alesi | (FRA) |

## CONSTRUCTORS

| | | | | | | |
|---|---|---|---|---|---|---|
| 3645.5 | Ferrari | 439 | BRM | 155 | Matra | |
| 3150.5 | McLaren | 424 | Prost | 150 | Toyota | |
| 2512.5 | Williams | 333 | Cooper | 138 | Red Bull (né Stewart then Jaguar Racing) | |
| 1352 | Lotus | 306 | Honda Racing (né BAR) | | | |
| 925 | Renault | 287 | Spyker MF1 (né Jordan) | 79 | Wolf | |
| 877.5 | Benetton | 232 | BMW Sauber | 67.5 | Shadow | |
| 854 | Brabham | 171.5 | March | 57 | Vanwall | |
| 617 | Tyrrell | 167 | Arrows | 54 | Surtees | |

## MOST DRIVERS' TITLES

| | | | | | | | | |
|---|---|---|---|---|---|---|---|---|
| 7 | Michael Schumacher | (GER) | | Jim Clark | (GBR) | Denis Hulme | (NZL) |
| 5 | Juan Manuel Fangio | (ARG) | | Emerson Fittipaldi | (BRA) | James Hunt | (GBR) |
| 4 | Alain Prost | (FRA) | | Mika Hakkinen | (FIN) | Alan Jones | (AUS) |
| 3 | Jack Brabham | (AUS) | | Graham Hill | (GBR) | Nigel Mansell | (GBR) |
| | Niki Lauda | (AUT) | 1 | Fernando Alonso | (SPA) | Jochen Rindt | (AUT) |
| | Nelson Piquet | (BRA) | | Mario Andretti | (USA) | Keke Rosberg | (FIN) |
| | Ayrton Senna | (BRA) | | Giuseppe Farina | (ITA) | Jody Scheckter | (ZA) |
| | Jackie Stewart | (GBR) | | Mike Hawthorn | (GBR) | John Surtees | (GBR) |
| 2 | Fernando Alonso | (SPA) | | Damon Hill | (GBR) | Jacques Villeneuve | (CDN) |
| | Alberto Ascari | (ITA) | | Phil Hill | (USA) | | |

## MOST CONSTRUCTORS' TITLES

| | | | | |
|---|---|---|---|---|
| 14 | Ferrari | | | Renault |
| 9 | Williams | 1 | | Benetton |
| 8 | McLaren | | | BRM |
| 7 | Lotus | | | Matra |
| 2 | Brabham | | | Tyrrell |
| | Cooper | | | Vanwall |

Second place in the 1957 Italian Grand Prix was enough for Juan Manuel Fangio to claim his fifth and final world title. His Maserati leads Stuart Lewis-Evans's Vanwall at Monza

# 2007 FILL-IN CHART

| DRIVER | TEAM | Round 1 18 March AUSTRALIAN GP | Round 2 8 April MALAYSIAN GP | Round 3 15 April BAHRAIN GP | Round 4 13 May SPANISH GP | Round 5 27 May MONACO GP |
|---|---|---|---|---|---|---|
| 1. FERNANDO ALONSO | McLAREN | | | | | |
| 2. LEWIS HAMILTON | McLAREN | | | | | |
| 3. GIANCARLO FISICHELLA | RENAULT | | | | | |
| 4. HEIKKI KOVALAINEN | RENAULT | | | | | |
| 5. FELIPE MASSA | FERRARI | | | | | |
| 6. KIMI RAIKKONEN | FERRARI | | | | | |
| 7. JENSON BUTTON | HONDA | | | | | |
| 8. RUBENS BARRICHELLO | HONDA | | | | | |
| 9. NICK HEIDFELD | BMW SAUBER | | | | | |
| 10. ROBERT KUBICA | BMW SAUBER | | | | | |
| 11. RALF SCHUMACHER | TOYOTA | | | | | |
| 12. JARNO TRULLI | TOYOTA | | | | | |
| 14. DAVID COULTHARD | RED BULL | | | | | |
| 15. MARK WEBBER | RED BULL | | | | | |
| 16. NICO ROSBERG | WILLIAMS | | | | | |
| 17. ALEXANDER WURZ | WILLIAMS | | | | | |
| 18. VITANTONIO LIUZZI *(to be confirmed)* | TORO ROSSO | | | | | |
| 19. SCOTT SPEED *(to be confirmed)* | TORO ROSSO | | | | | |
| 20. CHRISTIJAN ALBERS | SPYKER | | | | | |
| 21. ADRIAN SUTIL | SPYKER | | | | | |
| 22. TAKUMA SATO | SUPER AGURI | | | | | |
| 23. ANTHONY DAVIDSON | SUPER AGURI | | | | | |

| **Round 6** 10 June CANADIAN GP | **Round 7** 17 June US GP | **Round 8** 1 July FRENCH GP | **Round 9** 8 July BRITISH GP | **Round 10** 22 July GERMAN GP | **Round 11** 5 August HUNGARIAN GP | **Round 12** 26 August TURKISH GP | **Round 13** 9 September ITALIAN GP | **Round 14** 16 September BELGIAN GP | **Round 15** 30 September JAPANESE GP | **Round 16** 7 October CHINESE GP | **Round 17** 21 October BRAZILIAN GP | **POINTS TOTAL** |
|---|---|---|---|---|---|---|---|---|---|---|---|---|
|  |  |  |  |  |  |  |  |  |  |  |  |  |
|  |  |  |  |  |  |  |  |  |  |  |  |  |
|  |  |  |  |  |  |  |  |  |  |  |  |  |
|  |  |  |  |  |  |  |  |  |  |  |  |  |
|  |  |  |  |  |  |  |  |  |  |  |  |  |
|  |  |  |  |  |  |  |  |  |  |  |  |  |
|  |  |  |  |  |  |  |  |  |  |  |  |  |
|  |  |  |  |  |  |  |  |  |  |  |  |  |
|  |  |  |  |  |  |  |  |  |  |  |  |  |
|  |  |  |  |  |  |  |  |  |  |  |  |  |
|  |  |  |  |  |  |  |  |  |  |  |  |  |
|  |  |  |  |  |  |  |  |  |  |  |  |  |
|  |  |  |  |  |  |  |  |  |  |  |  |  |
|  |  |  |  |  |  |  |  |  |  |  |  |  |
|  |  |  |  |  |  |  |  |  |  |  |  |  |
|  |  |  |  |  |  |  |  |  |  |  |  |  |
|  |  |  |  |  |  |  |  |  |  |  |  |  |
|  |  |  |  |  |  |  |  |  |  |  |  |  |
|  |  |  |  |  |  |  |  |  |  |  |  |  |
|  |  |  |  |  |  |  |  |  |  |  |  |  |

# PICTURE CREDITS

The King is gone: who will fill Michael Schumacher's boots in 2007?

The publishers would like to thank the following sources for their kind permission to reproduce the pictures in this book.